CRITICAL SURVEY
OF
LONG FICTION

Native American Novelists

Editor

Carl Rollyson
Baruch College, City University of New York

SALEM PRESS
Ipswich, Massachusetts • Hackensack, New Jersey

Cover photo:
Louise Erdrich (© David Ash/Corbis)

ISBN: 978-1-4298-3696-8

CONTENTS

CONTRIBUTORS

Terry L. Andrews
Original Contributor

Karen L. Arnold
Columbia, Maryland

Edwin T. Arnold III
Original Contributor

Jane L. Ball
Yellow Springs, Ohio

Carl L. Bankston III
Tulane University

Harold Branam
Savannah, Georgia

Robin Payne Cohen
*Texas State University-
San Marcos*

Virginia A. Duck
Original Contributor

Bruce L. Edwards, Jr.
Original Contributor

Craig Gilbert
Portland State University

Terry L. Hansen
Original Contributor

Terry Heller
University of Iowa

Rebecca Kuzins
Pasadena, California

Brooks Landon
Original Contributor

William Laskowski
Jamestown College

Tim Lyons
Original Contributor

Joanne McCarthy
Tacoma, Washington

Ron McFarland
University of Idaho

Laurence W. Mazzeno
Alvernia College

C. Lynn Munro
Original Contributor

David Peck
Laguna Beach, California

Troy Place
Western Michigan University

Martha E. Rhynes
Stonewall, Oklahoma

Katherine Snipes
Original Contributor

Scott D. Yarbrough
*Charleston Southern
University*

NATIVE AMERICAN LONG FICTION

Although Native Americans, or American Indians, are an ancient people, most of their written literature is fairly recent. It was only in the twentieth century that Native American authors began to produce long fiction and that Native American ethnicity became a central theme in novels and other forms of writing. Nevertheless, the literature of America's oldest ethnic group does have deep cultural roots.

Long before the arrival of Europeans in the Americas, indigenous tribes and nations passed stories from generation to generation. These stories were intended to educate the young and to perpetuate cultural traditions, as well as to entertain. They told of the origins of the earth and of the human race, of the order of the universe and of the human place in it, and of bawdy tricksters who are mischievous but creative. Modern Native American fiction writers have frequently woven traditional narratives into their works.

Many of the earliest works of Native American written literature were autobiographies, intended for communication with the written culture of the invading Euro-Americans. In 1829, William Apes of the Pequot tribe published *A Son of the Forest: The Experience of William Apes, A Native of the Forest* to tell the story of the defeated and beleaguered Pequot people. Black Hawk, a Sauk, published *Black Hawk: An Autobiography* in 1833, after being defeated by Euro-American forces. The most famous of all Native American autobiographies is *Black Elk Speaks* (1932), the memoirs of the Oglala Sioux medicine man Black Elk, as told to poet John G. Neihardt. Although these autobiographies were generally intended for Euro-American audiences, they also influenced Native American writers. Much of contemporary Native American literature is heavily autobiographical.

The oral narratives and even the early autobiographies were works of people who saw themselves as parts of small communities, such as Pequot, Sauk, or Oglala. Over the course of the late nineteenth and early twentieth centuries, as anthropologist Peter Nabokov pointed out, Native Americans developed a sense of belonging to a wider group. By the mid-twentieth century, when Native American written fiction began to flourish, writers such as N. Scott Momaday and James Welch were writing self-consciously as people with an ethnic or racial identity and as members of specific tribes or nations. The sense of belonging to a single group, the autobiographical written tradition, and oral narratives may be identified as the primary cultural roots of modern Native American fiction.

EARLY NATIVE AMERICAN FICTION

The early twentieth century saw the first written works of fiction by Native American authors. In 1927, Mourning Dove published the romance *Cogewea, the Half-Blood*. During the same decade, the Oklahoma Cherokee John Milton Oskison became widely known as a short-story writer and novelist. His novels, which deal with life in and around the Indian Territory—which became Oklahoma—include *Wild Harvest* (1925), *Black Jack Davey* (1926), and *Brothers Three* (1935). Both Mourning Dove and Oskison are frequently criticized for their stock characters and their adherence to the conventions of popular fiction.

Literary critics generally regard the mixed-race Osage Indian John Joseph Matthews as a more sophisticated author than Mourning Dove or Oskison. Matthews wrote mainly history and autobiography, but he did publish one highly regarded novel, *Sundown* (1934). He set the story in the Osage country of Oklahoma, where the Osage are divided into the "full-bloods" and the "mixed-bloods" and into those who have money from oil leases and those who do not. The novel's hero goes away to college and then returns to struggle with his emotions about tribal life. Many of the themes, such as the tensions between tribal life and the modern economy and the struggle between assimilation and cultural traditionalism, became dominant in later Native American fiction.

D'Arcy McNickle (1904-1977), a member of the Confederation of Salish and Kutenai tribes of Montana, is often regarded as one of the best of the early Native American authors. Educated at the University of Montana and Oxford University, McNickle went to work for the U.S. Bureau of Indian Affairs in 1936, where he served as assistant to commissioner John Collier. McNickle dedicated himself to Collier's attempts to reverse the efforts of the U.S. government to force Native Americans to give up their cultural and political identities. McNickle gives passionate expression to the struggles of Native Americans in his novel *The Surrounded* (1936), which tells the story of a young man who returns from a government Indian school to his reservation.

THE NATIVE AMERICAN RENAISSANCE

By the 1960's and 1970's, a new generation of university-educated Native Americans, many of whom were influenced by the Civil Rights movement, began to produce novels that met with wide popular acceptance. N. Scott Momaday (born 1934) was one of the first of this generation to be recognized as a major American author. A professor of literature, Momaday has explored his Kiowa heritage in both poetry and prose. In 1968, he published the novel *House Made of Dawn*, which won the Pulitzer Prize in fiction in 1969. The protagonist of Momaday's novel, Abel, returns to his reservation after serving in the military in World War II. He kills an albino, whom he believes to have been an evil sorcerer, and serves a prison term. After his release, Abel settles in Los Angeles, where he meets with hardship and brutality from white society and the corruption of traditional ways by other Native Americans. At the end, he returns to the reservation and runs a ritual race against death and evil at dawn.

Gerald Vizenor (born 1934), whose father was Ojibwa, also became both a professor and a writer. A prolific author, Vizenor has written poetry, history, ethnography, and literary criticism, in addition to novels. His first novel, *Darkness in Saint Louis Bearheart* (1978; revised as *Bearheart: The Heirship Chronicles*, 1990), is an autobiographical work that examines his own experience as a Native American. Another of Vizenor's novels, *Dead Voices: Natural Agonies in the New World* (1992), draws on Native American traditions of oral narrative. This difficult, experimental novel looks at the trickster figure of Native American myth in the context of contemporary society.

Poet and novelist James Welch, part Blackfoot and part Gros Ventre Indian, looked at the Native American experience in works set in both contemporary and historical settings. Welch's first novel, *Winter in the Blood* (1974), is a story with some autobiographical basis, about a young Indian on a Montana reservation. The reservation and its social problems are also at the center of Welch's second work of long fiction, *The Death of Jim Loney* (1979), which deals with alcoholism and the confusion of a man of mixed race. *Fools Crow* (1986) tells of a band of Blackfoot Indians in Montana in the 1870's. A fourth novel, *The Indian Lawyer* (1990), returns to the modern reservation in a tale of a successful Native American's struggles with the temptations of political corruption. *The Heartsong of Charging Elk* (2000) follows its Native American protagonist from the Little Big Horn to France with Buffalo Bill's Wild West Show. He is abandoned in France and must struggle with late nineteenth century French culture on his own.

Leslie Marmon Silko (born 1948) achieved critical acclaim with her first novel, *Ceremony* (1977), which deals with a mixed-race Navajo veteran's struggles against insanity after returning from World War II. Under the guidance of a wise, elderly, mixed-race man, the protagonist finds peace and cosmic order through participation in traditional ceremony. Marmon's second novel, *Almanac of the Dead* (1991), is an epic that took the author ten years to complete. It covers five hundred years of the struggle between Native Americans and settlers from Europe.

THE NEW GENERATION

By the 1980's, the Native American novel was well established, and works of fiction on Native American themes were popular with a large readership. Louise Erdrich (born 1954), daughter of a Chippewa mother and a German American father, was one of the most successful Native American authors of the decade. In 1984, after having published a volume of poetry, Erdrich published her first novel, *Love Medicine* (revised and expanded, 1993). She followed this with a series of related novels: *The Beet Queen* (1986), *Tracks* (1988), *The Bingo Palace* (1994), and *Tales of Burning Love* (1996). The novels in this series tell the stories of three related Native American families living in North Dakota from 1912 through the 1980's. Sometimes compared to William Faulkner, Erdrich is concerned with universal patterns of family life, as well as with contemporary Native American issues. She collaborated with her late husband, Michael Dorris, on both fiction and nonfiction works. Her later novels mine the same areas and themes, at the same time as they explore new territory. *The Antelope Wife* (1998) is set in Minnesota, *The Last Report on the Miracles at Little No Horse* (2001) returns to North Dakota, *The Master Butchers Singing Club* (2003) explores Erdrich's German American family legacy, and *The Painted Drum* (2005) starts out in New Hampshire before returning with the sacred drum of the title to North Dakota.

New Native American novelists emerged during the last decade of the twentieth century. Ray A. Young Bear's *Black Eagle Child: The Facepaint Narratives* (1992) is an autobiographical novel in the form of a long blank-verse poem. It tells the story of Edgar Bearchild, a member of the Black Eagle Child settlement of the Mesquakie tribe. A dominant theme of the novel, one found in many Native American works, is the perplexing relationship between an individual who is part of modern American culture and the individual's ancient tribal heritage.

Sherman Alexie (born 1966) was the most widely praised new Native American author of the 1990's. A Spokane/Coeur d'Alene Indian, Alexie grew up on the Wellpinit Indian reservation and continued to live on the reservation after achieving literary renown. Most of Alexie's poetry and fiction focuses on contemporary reservation life, mixing portrayals of alcoholism and poverty with bitter but sympathetic humor and flashes of fantasy. *Reservation Blues* (1995) is set on a Spokane reservation. Its main characters are young Native Americans who have been out of high school for several years and face despair and a bleak future. After legendary blues guitarist Robert Johnson shows up, looking for a way to undo his deal with the devil, the young friends form a rock-and-roll band and reach fame after making their own deal with the devil, who happens to be a white man. Written after Alexie himself had achieved success, the story treats the problem of the threat to American Indian identity posed by succeeding in the white world, as well as with the frustrations and dangers of Native American life. Alexie's 1996 novel *Indian Killer* is one of his few works not set on the reservation. The novel features a serial killer in Seattle who scalps his white victims, and it deals with issues of racial violence and loss of culture.

Carl L. Bankston III
Updated by David Peck

BIBLIOGRAPHY

Cox, James H. *The Muting White Noise: Native American and European American Novel Traditions.* Norman: University of Oklahoma Press, 2006. Comparative study that includes analyses of John Rollin Ridge, D'Arcy McNickle, Gerald Vizenor, Sherman Alexie, and other Native American novelists.

Hernández-Avila, Inés, ed. *Reading Native American Women: Critical/Creative Representations.* Lanham, Md.: Altamira Press, 2005. Examines Native American women's writings as "creative, cultural, and political expressions." Essays include "Relocations upon Relocations: Home, Language, and Native American Women's Writings," by Hernández-Avila, and "The Trick Is Going Home: Secular Spiritualism in Native American Women's Literature," by Carolyn Dunn.

Lincoln, Kenneth. *Native American Renaissance.* New ed. Berkeley: University of California Press, 1992. Still the most influential critical work on the Native American renaissance. Traces the writings of modern authors back to their roots in oral narrative and autobiography. Contains chapters devoted to N. Scott Momaday, James Welch, and Leslie Marmon Silko.

Lundquist, Suzanne Evertsen. *Native American Literatures: An Introduction*. New York: Continuum, 2004. Essential research tool for study of Native American literature. Includes both a broad overview of the history and scope of Native American literature as well as studies of individual authors and works. Includes excellent resources for further research.

Nabokov, Peter, ed. *Native American Testimony: A Chronicle of Indian-White Relations from Prophecy to the Present, 1492-2000*. Rev ed. New York: Penguin, 1999. In one of the best introductions to Native American history from the Indian perspective, anthropologist Peter Nabokov presents the recorded responses of Native Americans to the European and Euro-American incursion over a five-hundred-year period. Also introduces each historical period with a summary and commentary.

Parker, Robert Dale. *The Invention of Native American Literature*. Ithaca, N.Y.: Cornell University Press, 2003. Examines tradition and aesthetics in Native American literature. Includes essays examining the works of D'Arcy McNickle, Ray A. Young Bear, Leslie Marmon Silko, and others.

Porter, Joy, and Kenneth M. Roesmer, eds. *The Cambridge Companion to Native American Literature*. New York: Cambridge University Press, 2005. Dozens of essays on historical and cultural contexts and genres, as well as studies of N. Scott Momaday, James Welch, Leslie Marmon Silko, Gerald Vizenor, Louise Erdrich, and others.

Velie, Alan R., ed. *American Indian Literature: An Anthology*. Rev. ed. Norman: University of Oklahoma Press, 1991. Anthology containing a wide range of literature, including traditional tales and modern poetry and fiction, by Native Americans on Native American subjects. Useful commentaries on the different forms of literature.

Vizenor, Gerald, ed. *Native American Literature: A Brief Introduction and Anthology*. New York: HarperCollins, 1995. Collection of Native American writings assembled by an acclaimed Native American author. Part of the HarperCollins Literary Mosaic series.

Wiget, Andrew. *Native American Literature*. Boston: Twayne, 1985. Overview of Native American writing, from the earliest oral narratives to the writers of the Native American renaissance. Contains a chronology of Native American literary history from the development of agricultural myths to the publication of Leslie Marmon Silko's *Ceremony* in 1977.

SHERMAN ALEXIE

Born: Spokane Indian Reservation, Wellpinit, Washington; October 7, 1966
Also known as: Sherman Joseph Alexie, Jr.

OTHER LITERARY FORMS

Sherman Alexie initiated his literary career with an unusual collection of poems and very short stories titled *The Business of Fancydancing: Stories and Poems*, published in 1992 by a small press, Hanging Loose, in Brooklyn, New York. Of the forty-two titles in that small book, only six could be confidently described as "short stories," and the longest of these runs only nine pages. Before his thirtieth birthday, Alexie had published six more full-length books, three of which were collections of poetry, and two chapbooks of poetry. His first book of short fiction, *The Lone Ranger and Tonto Fistfight in Heaven*, was published in 1993 to considerable acclaim, and he has followed that with two other books of short fiction. Alexie's short fiction has evolved in various ways. While the average length of the twenty-four stories in *The Lone Ranger and Tonto Fistfight in Heaven* is just nine pages, the nine stories that make up *The Toughest Indian in the World* (2000) average twenty-five pages in length, and one story, the ominously allegorical "The Sin Eaters," runs almost to novella length at forty-four pages. Similarly, the first of the nine stories in his third collection, *Ten Little Indians* (2003), runs fifty-two pages and the last runs forty-eight.

Some readers admire Alexie's poetry over his prose. He has had several books of poetry published, including the limited edition chapbook *Dangerous Astronomy* (2005). Alexie has also written screenplays for two films drawn from his literary work, *Smoke Signals* (1998) and *The Business of Fancydancing* (2002).

ACHIEVEMENTS

Among other recognitions that Sherman Alexie has received for his writing, his novel *The Absolutely True Diary of a Part-Time Indian* received the 2007 National Book Award for Young People's Literature. In the fall of 2007, Alexie was honored by the Western Literature Association with its Distinguished Achievement Award. Two of his stories have appeared in *The Best American Short Stories* anthologies (1994, 2004), and one of his poems was selected for the *Best American Poetry* anthology in 1996. His first novel, *Reservation Blues*, won the American Book Award for 1996, and his second novel, *Indian Killer*, was listed as a *New York Times* Notable Book the same year. His short-story collection *The Toughest Indian in the World* was recognized with a PEN/Malamud Award for Short Fiction from the PEN/Faulkner Foundation in 2001.

BIOGRAPHY

Born with hydrocephalus (water on the brain), Sherman Joseph Alexie, Jr., grew up on the Spokane Indian Reservation in Wellpinit, Washington. His father was a member of the Coeur d'Alene tribe, his mother a Spokane. An operation when he was six months old placed him at risk of mental retardation, but Alexie survived to become a voracious reader early on. Feeling ostracized on the reservation, partly because of his intellectual pursuits, he transferred to the all-white high school in Reardan, twenty-two miles away, where he was a popular student and starred on the basketball team. After two years at Gonzaga University, Alexie transferred to Washington State University, where his initial interest in pursuing a medical career ended when he fainted in a human anatomy class. His poetry workshop teacher, Alex Kuo, encouraged his writing, and with the assistance of a Washington State Arts Commission fellowship in 1991, he finished his first books of poetry. In his review of *The Business of Fancydancing* for *The New York Times Book Review,* James Kincaid hailed Alexie as "one of the major lyric voices of our time." Following this initial acclaim, Alexie gave up drinking, and he has spoken out against alcohol abuse, particularly on the reservation, both in his public appearances and in his subsequent writings.

Alexie married Diane Tomhave, of Hidatsa, Ho-Chunk, and Potawatomi heritage, in 1995. They would have two sons, Joseph (born 1997) and David (born 2001). Alexie's move to Seattle is reflected in the shift of settings in his first two novels, from the Spokane reservation in *Reservation Blues* to Seattle in *Indian Killer,* which was published one year later. His involvement in film, which started with *Smoke Signals* in 1998, is consistent with his flair for public performance and stage presence. Alexie takes pride in having won the World Heavyweight Poetry Bout (slam poetry) in 1998 and each of the next three years as well, and his credits include stand-up comedy and various television appearances, including the Public Broadcasting Service's program *A Dialogue on Race with President Clinton* in 1998. With Colville Indian musician Jim Boyd, Alexie has also collaborated on several musical recordings.

Owing to an administrative oversight, Alexie's bachelor's degree was not awarded by Washington State University until 1994; his alma mater recognized him in 2003 with a Regents' Distinguished Alumnus Award. He also holds honorary degrees from Seattle University and Columbia College (Chicago).

ANALYSIS

In his poetry volume *Old Shirts and New Skins* (1993) Sherman Alexie offers a formula that he attributes to one of his recurring characters, Lester FallsApart: "Poetry = Anger × Imagination." The formula appears slightly altered in a story in *The Lone Ranger and Tonto Fistfight in Heaven,* where "Poetry" is replaced with "Survival." A more accurate formula might require that Anger and its multiple, Imagination, be divided by Humor or Wit, for what makes Alexie's anger tolerable for many readers is not so much his imagination, which is sometimes visionary and suggests certain features of Magical Realism, but his comic, generally satiric sensibility. Alexie's comedy is often dark, and he frequently employs insult humor, as in *Reservation Blues*, when Chess, a Flathead Indian woman, tells Veronica, an Indian wannabe, that "a concussion is just as traditional as a sweatlodge." This passage exemplifies another facet of Alexie's perspective on Indianness. He has described himself as having been influenced as much by 1970's family television program *The Brady Bunch* as by tribal traditions.

Part of what makes Alexie so popular with academic audiences is his blending of pop-culture elements with historical and literary allusion. In *The Absolutely True Diary of a Part-Time Indian*, for instance, young Arnold Spirit, Jr., reflects on the opening sentence of Leo Tolstoy's *Anna Karenina* (1875-1877). *Reservation Blues* is constructed on the Faust legend as embodied in the historical blues guitarist Robert Johnson, but the novel is also haunted by such historical figures as Colonel George Wright, who had nine hundred Spokane horses shot in 1858. Two New Age white groupies who hang out with the reservation blues band are named Betty and Veronica, straight out of the Archie comic books. Female characters figure prominently and powerfully in Alexie's fiction. He consistently assails racist and sexist attitudes, and he has taken a strong stand against homophobia and gay bashing.

Dreams and memories, sometimes historically based like the murder of Crazy Horse, tend to haunt Alexie's fiction. These combine with characters such as Big Mom, who appears to have mystical powers, to lend otherworldly or surreal overtones. A basketball game might dissolve into fantasy. A magical guitar might burst into flame. In *Flight*, the teenage protagonist experiences a series of metamorphoses, inhabiting multiple bodies, both white and Indian, before he returns to himself in the body of his runaway father, which prompts him to reflect on William Shakespeare's *Hamlet* (pr. c. 1600-1601).

With certain exceptions, as in *Indian Killer* and some of the later stories, Alexie prefers uncomplicated syntax and colloquial dialogue; short paragraphs predominate. These stylistic features combine with others, including Alexie's disinclination toward complex imagery and metaphor, to make his fiction readily accessible.

RESERVATION BLUES

The three predominant characters in his first novel, *Reservation Blues*, Alexie has described as "the holy trinity of me": Victor Joseph (angry, physical, inclined to drink), Junior Polatkin (the "intellectual" because he went to college for a couple of years), and Thomas Builds-the-Fire (the storyteller, spiritual, given to memories and dreams). When they acquire legendary blues singer Robert Johnson's magic guitar, this trio forms the nucleus of the reservation blues band, Coyote Springs, which is joined by two Flathead Indian sisters, Chess and Checkers Warm Water. Their success arouses the enmity of their fellow Spokanes, notably in the person of the tribal chair, David WalksAlong.

Thomas and Chess (predictably, the more intellectual of the sisters) form a couple, and record producers from the East, Phil Sheridan and George Wright (both named after historically renowned Indian fighters), offer them an audition with Cavalry Records. Despite Big Mom's assistance, however, the recording session ends disastrously, and when the band members return to the reservation, Junior commits suicide. Ironically, the record company finds Betty and Veronica to be "Indian enough" and signs them to a contract, the refrain to one song being "Indian in my bones." Thomas stomps on the tape.

When Thomas, Chess, and Checkers leave the reservation to move to the city of Spokane, Big Mom organizes reconciliation with the tribe at the longhouse. One important theme of the novel concerns the importance of maintaining blood quantum through the marriage of Thomas and Chess. Alexie also deals with the dangers of alcohol and violence (the beverage of choice at the longhouse is Pepsi). While he does not reject traditional tribal values (Big Mom teaches a song of survival at the end of the novel), Alexie implicitly underscores the benefits of leaving the reservation, as he himself elected to do.

INDIAN KILLER

In *Indian Killer*, a wealthy white couple from Seattle adopts an infant from an unspecified Indian reservation. John Smith (the name ironically echoes the historical Captain John Smith of Jamestown fame) consequently grows up tribeless and confused as to his identity. A loner and apparently a paranoid schizophrenic, John suffers from various delusions and violent fantasies. When a serial killer scalps victims and leaves owl feathers with their bodies, the reader tends to side with characters in the novel who suspect an Indian (likely John) is the killer.

Opposite John Smith stands Marie Polatkin, a self-assured Spokane Indian activist and University of Washington student (majoring in English), who ably puts down the arrogant professor of Native American literature, Dr. Clarence Mather. It could be argued that racial profiling or stereotyping runs throughout this often-foreboding novel. It seems unlikely, for example, that any teacher in Mather's position would offer Forrest Carter's controversial 1976 novel *The Education of Little Tree* as required reading in a college course on Indian writers, and the virulently racist shock-jock radio talk-show host Truck Schultz is as exaggerated a caricature as a Charles Dickens villain. Suzanne Evertsen Lundquist has connected the faux-Indian novelist Jack Wilson with the Paiute Ghost Dance prophet Wovoka. Daniel Grassian has observed that the novel arose from Alexie's "anger and dissatisfaction" regarding non-Indians who write "Indian books."

The killer is not identified, and although some readers may assume it is John Smith, who commits suicide by leaping from the skyscraper on which he has been working, Alexie never states for certain that the killer is in fact an Indian. Moreover, it may be debatable whether John himself is truly "Indian"; he never appears to acquire a confident sense of who he is. Reviewers have characterized *Indian Killer* as "angry" and even "ugly," but its sinister theme calls for such pejorative qualifiers: the white control, denial, even eradication of the Indian's identity or possession of self and the violence resulting from that act.

FLIGHT

Flight, a short novel (at fewer than forty thousand words, more aptly "novella"), opens with the fifteen-year-old protagonist declaring, in the mode of Herman Melville's Ishmael, from *Moby Dick* (1851), "Call me Zits." The streetwise, angry-and-sad, mixed-blood product of multiple foster homes and various types of abuse describes himself as "a blank sky, a human solar eclipse," but he adopts a darkly comic perspective and refuses to feel sorry for himself. A white boy allegorically named Justice gets Zits involved in a bank robbery armed with both a real pistol and a paint gun. When he is fatally shot during the robbery, however, Zits begins a series of five transformations (metempsychoses) in which he inhabits various male bodies, starting with that of a white agent of the Federal Bureau of Investigation (FBI) in 1975 Idaho (the action recalls events that took place at Wounded Knee, South Dakota).

As he occupies other bodies, ranging from that of a mute Indian boy at the Battle of the Little Bighorn to that of a guilt-ridden pilot who has taught a Muslim terrorist how to fly a plane, Zits participates in acts of violence, but he also witnesses compassionate and heroic behavior, notably on the part of white characters. After occupying his Indian father's body, Zits is brought to an understanding of why his father deserted his mother, who died soon afterward. When he returns to himself, Zits leaves the bank and hands his guns to a friendly white police officer named Dave, who arranges to have Zits adopted by his brother and his wife, who introduces the boy to acne medicine. In the last sentences of the novella, Zits reveals his actual name, "Michael."

In *Flight* Alexie offers readers who might have been alarmed at certain ominous aspects of *Indian Killer* a more hopeful solution to the problem of Indian identity and to an apparently inescapable cycle of violence in contemporary American (especially urban) society. Although this book has not been identified as young adult fiction, the protagonist's age and the elements of fantasy and time travel are likely to appeal to that readership.

THE ABSOLUTELY TRUE DIARY OF A PART-TIME INDIAN

Although the page count of *The Absolutely True Diary of a Part-Time Indian* is higher than that of *Flight*, this autobiographical novel runs about the same length (that is, around forty thousand words) and so might also be designated a "novella." Marketed as young adult fiction, the book features a fourteen-year-old protagonist, Arnold Spirit, Jr., who resembles Alexie in every way, including his hydrocephalic birth; his move from the reservation town of Wellpinit to Reardan, which he sees as necessary to his hopes but also as possible betrayal of his tribe; and his popularity in the white world and his success as a basketball player and as a student.

Divided into twenty-nine very short chapters and illustrated by Seattle artist Ellen

Forney (Arnold says that he draws cartoons because he finds words "too predictable" and "too limited"), the novella moves rapidly, as does most of Alexie's fiction. That is, the fast pace encountered here is not necessarily a function of the novel's intended audience. Alexie's tendency to promote dialogue as opposed to narrative paragraphs is common to most of the short stories of *The Lone Ranger and Tonto Fistfight in Heaven* and to both *Reservation Blues* and *Flight*. Only in some of the stories of *The Toughest Indian in the World* and *Ten Little Indians* and in the novel *Indian Killer* does Alexie more frequently employ paragraphs that run longer than half a page.

If *The Absolutely True Diary of a Part-Time Indian* were to be read as memoir, it would likely be described as a "success story," particularly success achieved by overcoming adversity that involves poverty and racial prejudice. Like Alexie, the adolescent Arnold chooses, at some personal risk, to redefine himself in the broader world outside the reservation. Although this decision temporarily costs him his best friend, appropriately named Rowdy, Arnold finds himself welcome (surprisingly, both for him and for the reader) in the white world of small farm-town Reardan. The hopeful story is darkened, however, by the deaths of Arnold's grandmother, his sister, and his father's best friend, all of which involve alcohol in some way. Alexie's cautionary tale for young Indian readers is clear: Avoid alcohol and accept the challenge of leaving the apparently secure but perilously limiting world of the reservation.

Ron McFarland

OTHER MAJOR WORKS

SHORT FICTION: *The Lone Ranger and Tonto Fistfight in Heaven*, 1993; *The Toughest Indian in the World*, 2000; *Ten Little Indians*, 2003; *War Dances*, 2009.

POETRY: *I Would Steal Horses*, 1992; *Old Shirts and New Skins*, 1993; *The Man Who Loves Salmon*, 1998; *One Stick Song*, 2000; *Dangerous Astronomy*, 2005.

SCREENPLAYS: *Smoke Signals*, 1998; *The Business of Fancydancing*, 2002.

MISCELLANEOUS: *The Business of Fancydancing: Stories and Poems*, 1992; *First Indian on the Moon*, 1993; *The Summer of Black Widows*, 1996 (poems and short prose).

BIBLIOGRAPHY

Alexie, Sherman. "Sherman Alexie, Literary Rebel: An Interview." Interview by John Bellante and Carl Bellante. *Bloomsbury Review* 14 (May/June, 1994): 14. Published before any of his long fiction appeared, this interview touches on important aspects of Alexie's "minimalism" (a term he does not care for), the "holy trinity of me," and various thematic issues.

Andrews, Scott. "A New Road and a Dead End in Sherman Alexie's *Reservation Blues.*" *Arizona Quarterly* 63, no. 2 (Summer, 2007): 137-152. Reflects on the ambiguities of the novel's ending, in which the blues band fails and the principal characters leave the reservation.

Chen, Tina. "Toward an Ethics of Knowledge." *MELUS* 30, no. 2 (Summer, 2005): 157-173. Discusses Alexie's *Indian Killer* as well as Cynthia Ozick's *The Shawl* (1989) and Julie Otsuka's *When the Emperor Was Divine* (2002). Advises proceeding from an ethical understanding of racial and cultural differences when dealing with these novels.

Christie, Stuart. "Renaissance Man: The Tribal 'Schizophrenic' in Sherman Alexie's *Indian Killer.*" *American Indian Culture and Research Journal* 25, no. 4 (2001): 1-19. Addresses Alexie's treatment of Native American characters and how, in Anglo-European cultural contexts, tribal identity may lead to a pathological state for Native Americans.

Grassian, Daniel. *Understanding Sherman Alexie.* Columbia: University of South Carolina Press, 2005. First book-length work offering commentary on Alexie's poetry and fiction pays ample attention to reviews and other published discussions of his writings. Provides biographical details as well as analysis and interpretation of the fiction through *Indian Killer.*

Lundquist, Suzanne Evertsen. *Native American Literatures: An Introduction.* New York: Continuum, 2004. Section on Alexie (in the chapter titled "The Best and the Best Known") includes summaries of important critiques of *Reservation Blues* and *Indian Killer* that question his representation of Native American cultural values and reservation life as well as issues of "hybridity" and "essentialism."

SAIL: Studies in American Indian Literature 9, no. 4 (Winter, 1997). Special issue devoted to Alexie's fiction includes an interview with Alexie as well as essays by such scholars as Karen Jorgensen ("White Shadows: The Use of Doppelgangers in Sherman Alexie's *Reservation Blues*"), Janine Richardson ("Magic and Memory in Sherman Alexie's *Reservation Blues*"), and P. Jane Hafen ("Rock and Roll, Redskins, and Blues in Sherman Alexie's Work").

THOMAS BERGER

Born: Cincinnati, Ohio; July 20, 1924
Also known as: Thomas Louis Berger

PRINCIPAL LONG FICTION
Crazy in Berlin, 1958
Reinhart in Love, 1962
Little Big Man, 1964
Killing Time, 1967
Vital Parts, 1970
Regiment of Women, 1973
Sneaky People, 1975
Who Is Teddy Villanova?, 1977
Arthur Rex, 1978
Neighbors, 1980
Reinhart's Women, 1981
The Feud, 1983
Nowhere, 1985
Being Invisible, 1987
The Houseguest, 1988
Changing the Past, 1989
Orrie's Story, 1990
Meeting Evil, 1992
Robert Crews, 1995
Suspects, 1996
The Return of Little Big Man, 1999
Best Friends, 2003
Adventures of the Artificial Woman, 2004

OTHER LITERARY FORMS

Thomas Berger has published numerous articles, reviews, and short stories in magazines such as the *Saturday Evening Post*, *Esquire*, *Harper's*, and *Playboy*. He has written four plays, two of which, *The Burglars: A Comedy in Two Acts* (pb. 1988) and *Other People*, have been published; *Other People* was also produced in 1970 at the Berkshire Theatre Festival in Massachusetts. Berger's radio play *At the Dentist's* was produced by Vermont Public Radio in 1981.

ACHIEVEMENTS

Thomas Berger is one of the most productive, most respected, and most challenging literary figures in the United States. His novels, including the highly acclaimed *Little Big Man* and critically and popularly successful works such as *Who Is Teddy Villanova?* and *Neighbors*, seem sure to earn for him a lasting place in American letters. His Reinhart series is one of the most singular and significant accomplishments of postwar American literature, forming as it does both a sociological epic and an index to the changing face of the American novel in the second half of the twentieth century. The Reinhart series stands—along with John Updike's Rabbit novels and Phillip Roth's Zuckerman novels—as one of the most noteworthy and respected multivolume narratives in postwar American fiction. Acknowledged as a masterful prose stylist, Berger writes novels that are aggressively intelligent without being ostentatiously "difficult," works that are often hilariously funny without losing their serious bite.

In 1970, Richard Schickel correctly identified Berger as "one of the most radical sensibilities now writing in America" and bemoaned the fact that Berger had not received the recognition he deserved. More than a decade later, Thomas R. Edwards intensified this complaint with the charge that the failure to read and discuss Berger's work is no less than "a national disgrace." Reviewing *Neighbors* for the *Chicago Tribune*, Frederick Busch may have best summed up Berger's stature as a novelist when he said, "This is a novel by Thomas Berger, and everything he writes should be read and considered." In 2003, award-winning novelist Jonathan Lethem, in his introduction to the reprint of Berger's *Meeting Evil*, added his voice to those of the readers, reviewers, and critics who celebrate Berger as "one of America's three or four greatest living novelists."

BIOGRAPHY

Thomas Louis Berger was born in Cincinnati, Ohio, on July 20, 1924, and grew up in the nearby suburban community of Lockland. Disenchanted after a short bout with college, Berger enlisted in the U.S. Army, serving from 1943 to 1946 and entering Berlin in 1945 with the first American Occupation troops; his experiences gave him some of the background for his first novel, *Crazy in Berlin*.

After the war, Berger returned to college, receiving his B.A. at the University of Cincinnati in 1948. He continued his studies as a graduate student in English at Columbia University (1950-1951), where he completed course work for an M.A. and began a thesis on George Orwell, which he never completed. Instead, Berger turned his attention to the writers' workshop at the New School for Social Research. In that workshop, under the aegis of Charles Glicksberg, Berger began to write short stories. "I produced one story a week for three months, most of them melancholy in tone, maudlin in spirit, and simple of mind," he has recounted, "Hemingway then being my model." Berger dismisses his short fiction, explaining, "The marathon is my event, and not the hundred-yard dash." Despite this assessment, Berger's short fiction has appeared in magazines ranging from the *Satur-*

day Evening Post to *Harper's*, *Esquire*, *Playboy*, and *North American Review*.

From 1948 through 1951, Berger supported his writing by working as a librarian at the Rand School of Social Science. In 1951-1952, he was a staff member of *The New York Times Index*, and the following year he was a copy editor for *Popular Science Monthly*. In 1956 Berger and his wife toured Western Europe, including France, Italy, Austria, and Germany. Revisiting the scene of his army experience in Germany allowed him the emotional distance to abandon his work in progress and to begin and complete his first published novel, *Crazy in Berlin*. Until 1964 and the publication of his third novel, *Little Big Man*, Berger had to supplement the income from his fiction with freelance editing. From 1971 to 1973, Berger wrote a characteristically idiosyncratic film column for *Esquire*, managing to discuss almost everything *but* the major motion pictures of the day.

In 1950, Berger married Jeanne Redpath, an artist he met at the New School. In the fifteen years from 1965 to 1980, Berger and his wife moved twelve times, the places they lived including New York City; Bridgehampton on Long Island; Mount Desert, Maine; Malibu, California; London, on two separate occasions; and the Hudson riverbank in Rockland County, New York. In addition to a lectureship at Yale in 1981-1982, Berger has been a distinguished visiting professor at Southampton College, and during the 1970's and early 1980's he gave readings at more than twenty universities. In 1986 he was awarded an honorary doctor of letters degree by Long Island University.

ANALYSIS

The dust-jacket blurb written by Thomas Berger for *Who Is Teddy Villanova?* reviews the general scheme of his career, pointing out that each of his novels "celebrates another classic genre of fiction: the western [*Little Big Man*], the childhood memoir [*Sneaky People*], the anatomical romance [*Regiment of Women*], the true-crime documentary [*Killing Time*], and the Reinhart books [*Crazy in Berlin*, *Reinhart in Love*, and *Vital Parts*] together form a sociological epic." *Who Is Teddy Villanova?* extended this pattern to the classic American hard-boiled detective story, *Arthur Rex* extended it to Arthurian romance, *Neighbors* traces its lineage most directly to Franz Kafka, and *Reinhart's Women* continues the Reinhart series. In similar fashion, *The Feud* offers Dreiserian slice-of-life naturalism, *Nowhere* celebrates the utopian fantasy, *Being Invisible* acknowledges its precursors in the invisibility narratives of both H. G. Wells and Ralph Ellison, *The Houseguest* revisits the banal menace of *Neighbors*, presenting a self-made hollow man in the tradition of F. Scott Fitzgerald's *The Great Gatsby* (1925), and *Changing the Past* shares assumptions with Robert Louis Stevenson's *The Strange Case of Dr. Jekyll and Mr. Hyde* (1886) and with the "three wishes" narrative tradition.

In *Orrie's Story*, Berger "reinvents" the Greek tragedy of the Oresteia, setting it in postwar America. *Robert Crews* is obviously Berger's take on Daniel Defoe's *Robinson Crusoe* (1719), and *Meeting Evil* moves from the Kafkaesque presentation of the banality of evil to the moral imperative of responding to evil that is deadly. *Suspects* renews

Berger's fascination with the interplay of law enforcement with criminals in general and with police procedurals in particular. *The Return of Little Big Man* goes back to the world and time of *Little Big Man*, updating Jack Crabb's adventures through the final vanishing of the Old West as it is replaced by the simulations of Buffalo Bill's Wild West Show and the 1893 World's Columbian Exposition. *Best Friends* is a more gentle and hopeful take on the doubling of "kicker and kickee" that has long been one of Berger's central concerns. *Adventures of the Artificial Woman*, which Berger considers a "literary conceit" rather than a true novel, blends themes from Mary Wollstonecraft Shelley's *Frankenstein* (1818) with themes from George Bernard Shaw's *Pygmalion* (pb. 1912). The mistaken notion that these "celebrations" of classic novel forms are really parodies has dogged Berger's career, but unlike parodies, his novels start from rather than aim toward literary traditions; Berger achieves a testing and broadening of possibilities rather than a burlesquing of limitations. If anything, his celebrations serve as kinds of "deparodizations," twisting genres already self-conscious to the point of parody in ways that radically defamiliarize them. The variety of Berger's novels, a range with perhaps no equal in contemporary American literature, underlines the precision of his craft while distracting readers from the steadiness and the seriousness of his purpose.

Most critics have failed to consider that Berger's manipulations of novel forms are ultimately self-exploring and reflexive literary experiments. He tries to make of each novel an "independent existence," an alternative verbal reality that he hopes the reader will approach "without the luggage of received ideas, a priori assumptions, sociopolitical axes to grind, or feeble moralities in search of support." This verbal world both owes its existence to a number of traditional and arbitrary literary conventions of representation and seeks to remind the reader that the working of those conventions is of interest and significance in itself—not only as a means to the representation of reality.

Failing to appreciate the independent existence of Berger's fictional worlds, reviewers have misread *Little Big Man* as an indictment of American abuse of Native Americans, *Regiment of Women* as a polemic for or against the women's movement, *Neighbors* as a critique of suburban life, and so on. Such a topical approach to these novels ignores the possibility that Berger's real theme is language, and that underlying the manically different surfaces of his novels is a constant preoccupation with the ways in which problems of human existence stem from the confusion of language with reality. Again and again, Berger's novels find new ways to suggest that the structures and institutions that order and give meaning to existence are much less important than the ways in which one talks about them, and that the ways one talks about those organizing beliefs inevitably have been designed by someone to influence or manipulate someone else's perception and judgment. Reinhart's ex-wife spells this out for him when she chides, "It ought to begin to occur to you that life is just a collection of stories from all points of self-interest."

Put another way, the persistent goal of Berger's novels is to shift our attention from the purportedly real world we live in to the ways in which that world is conventionally perceived as a construct of language. This effort proceeds from the assumption that what we have been told about reality (received ideas) and what we tell ourselves about reality (our personal myths) have become more "official" or persuasive than experience itself, that language has been so twisted, so manipulated as to refer more to itself than to the material world to which it ostensibly refers. It is in this sense that Berger cheerfully warns that we should not confuse fiction with life, because "the latter is false," and it is in this spirit that he reminds the readers of *Killing Time* that his novel "is a construction of language and otherwise a lie."

Accordingly, the lives of Berger's characters are affected more by words than by actions. Victimized by definitions that exclude or threaten them, by rhetoric that makes them lose sight of physical facts, and by language designed more to preclude than to encourage clear thinking, his characters are enslaved by language. For this reason, the plot of a Berger novel typically chronicles the efforts of the protagonist to free him- or herself from someone else's verbal version of reality. In this way, Jack Crabb in *Little Big Man* bounces back and forth not only between white and Plains Indian cultures but also between competing codes of conduct designed to legitimate all manner of cruelty. Berger shows how Jack's greatest problems are actually matters of definition, as he inevitably finds himself defined as white when the situation is controlled by Native Americans and as Native American when the situation is controlled by whites. All of Berger's novels explore the processes of victimization, as all of Berger's protagonists struggle, whether consciously or unconsciously, to free themselves from the inexorable tendency to think of themselves as the victims of outrages and impositions both humorously small and tragically large.

While Berger refuses to subscribe to any single codified philosophy, whether romantic, existential, or absurd, his characters do live in worlds that seem to operate largely on Nietzschean principles. As Frederick Turner has observed, Berger's moral stance is consistently "beyond sentimentality, beyond classic American liberalism," concerning itself with fundamentals rather than with surfaces. Like philosopher Friedrich Nietzsche, Berger assumes that "there are higher problems than the problems of pleasure and pain and sympathy," though few of his characters would subscribe to this view—their pleasure, their pain, and their sympathy being of paramount importance to them.

Those characters are a string of outrageously impossible but compellingly plausible individuals who seem, in Berger's words, to be "persistent liars" and "monsters of one persuasion or another." Berger is uniformly fond of these "monsters," and his characters can never be branded as "good" or "evil," since all are as appealing in their often bizarre excesses as they are sadly humorous in their deficiencies. Most important, all of Berger's characters *do their best*. They may trick, abuse, and betray one another, but in a world where understanding seems full of drawbacks and the irresponsible consistently victimize those who feel obligations, they are finally no more nor less than normal. In the courtroom of his novels, Berger refuses to become either judge or advocate, choosing instead to establish a dialectic of wildly opposing viewpoints. He explains that his job is to maintain these characters in equilibrium, a concern of "art and not politics or sociology."

No analysis of Berger's novels would be complete without mentioning the delights of his prose style. Berger is one of a handful of American writers, contemporary or otherwise, for whom the sentence is an event in itself. His style challenges the reader with precise but often elaborate or serpentine sentences, reflecting his conviction that "the sentence is the cell beyond which the life of the book cannot be traced, a novel being a structure of such cells: most must be vital or the body is dead." What sentence vitality means to Berger can be seen in the way he elaborates the commonplace metaphor of the "ham-fisted" punch in *Who Is Teddy Villanova?*

> He had struck me on the forehead, that helmet of protective bone, an impractical stroke even for such stout fingers as his, had he not turned his hand on edge and presented to my skull the resilient karate blade that swells out between the base of the smallest digit and the wrist: in his case, the size and consistency of the fleshy side of a loin of pork.

This marvelous punch knocks out Russell Wren, Berger's private-eye narrator, who comes to with this equally meticulous and mannered realization:

> My loafers were in a position just ahead of his coal-barge brogans, a yard from where I slumped; meanwhile, my feet, twisted on their edges and crushed under the crease between thigh and buttock, were only stockinged: he had knocked me out of my shoes!

Leonard Michaels described this style as "one of the great pleasures of the book . . . educated, complicated, graceful, silly, destructive in spirit," and his comment applies to all of Berger's novels. Noting that he looks for himself through the English language, Berger states that for him language is "a morality and a politics and a religion."

CRAZY IN BERLIN

In Berger's first novel, *Crazy in Berlin*, the twenty-one-year-old Carlo Reinhart, a U.S. Army medic in occupied Berlin, struggles to reconcile the conflicting claims of Nazism, Judaism, Communism, Americanism, and his own German heritage—all overshadowed by the more fundamental concepts of friendship, victimization, and survival. This first of the Reinhart novels also features the points of view of a manic series of contradictory characters, including an American intelligence officer who is an idealistic Communist, a Russian officer who wants to become a capitalist, and a cynical former Nazi now working as a Russian agent.

REINHART IN LOVE

In the second Reinhart novel, *Reinhart in Love*, Berger's bumbling protagonist is discharged from the army, in which he had been happy, and returns to civilian life, which he finds singularly disastrous. His comic misadventures are guided by Claude Humbold, a wonderfully devious real estate agent/con man for whom Reinhart reluctantly works; by the enterprising and calculating Genevieve Raven, whom he is tricked into marrying; and by Splendor Mainwaring, his black friend whose special talent is getting Reinhart into impossible situations.

LITTLE BIG MAN

Had Berger never written anything but *Little Big Man*, he would have earned a respected place in American literary history. This story of Jack Crabb's life in both the Cheyenne and white cultures of the historical as well as the dime-novel Old West has been called variously "the best novel about the West," "a Barthian western," and "a seminal event in what must now seem the most significant cultural and literary trend of the last decade—the attempt on many fronts to develop structures, styles, ways of thinking that are beyond any version of ethnocentricism." The story has been transcribed ostensibly from the tape-recorded reminiscences of "the late Jack Crabb—frontiersman, American Indian scout, gunfighter, buffalo hunter, adopted Cheyenne—in his final days upon this earth." That Jack's final days come 111 years after his first, and that he also claims to have been the sole white survivor of the Battle of the Little Bighorn, raises obvious questions about the truth of his account. Furthermore, Jack's narrative comes to the reader through the patently unreliable editorship of "Ralph Fielding Snell," a fatuous, gullible, self-professed "man of letters" who also happens to mention that he has suffered three or four nervous breakdowns in the past few years. Against these reflexive, metafictional devices, Berger balances the disarming realism of Jack Crabb's narration, its tone resonating with the wondering honesty and credibility of Huck Finn.

Frederick Turner has noted that part of the real power of this narration is derived from Jack's coming "to understand both myth and history as radically human constructs." What Turner means by "radically human constructs" can be understood from the way in which *Little Big Man* combines very different rhetorics or "codes" for talking about the Old West. Indeed, Jack's narrative consists of excerpts from and imitations of actual histories of the West, autobiographies, dime novels, Native American studies, and other codes that are mixed together in unpredictable combinations. This jumbling of codes and vocabularies (for example, Jack may mingle the crassest of frontier expressions with terms such as "colloquy," "circumferentially," "hitherto," or "tumult") exposes the perceptual biases of the "official" codes that have been developed for talking about the Old West—whether by Zane Grey, Francis Parkman, or L. A. Hoebel (an expert on Cheyenne culture). Jack begins to realize that even when his situation seems to be defined by bullets or arrows, the real conflict lies in the clash between the often antithetical ways in which he must think of himself, whether he is to define himself and act according to Cheyenne terms, cavalry terms, capitalist terms, journalistic terms, and so on.

Accordingly, the panorama of Jack's adventures, ranging from his adoption by the Cheyenne to his gunfight with Wild Bill Hickok to his being the only white survivor of Custer's Last Stand, is shadowed by the panorama of his changing narrative styles: Not only does Berger pack every classic Western theme into the novel, but he also fills it with subtly varied "codes" that make it—like all of his novels—at least in part an exploration of the workings of language. The genius of this novel is that its metafictional devices are so well woven into the fabric of Jack's fascinating story that they have eluded all but a handful of readers, reviewers, and scholars. By any standards, *Little Big Man* is a masterpiece, one of the most delightful novels ever written.

THE RETURN OF LITTLE BIG MAN

Who, remembering Ralph Fielding Snell's comment in the epilogue to *Little Big Man* that Jack Crabb's tape-recorded memories did not stop with the Battle of the Little Bighorn, would not like to know what further adventures Jack might have had, particularly as Snell hints that they included both more time witnessing the gunfighting culture of the Old West and time spent touring with Buffalo Bill's Wild West Show? Who would not want to see how Berger would return to his best-known character to tell the rest of his amazing story? In this fine sequel, Berger deftly resurrects Jack's inimitable voice and wondering vision and turns both toward chronicling the birth of a new century in which simulacra such as Buffalo Bill's Wild West Show replace the Old West, the 1893 Chicago World's Fair offers glimpses of America's technologized future, and an indomitable New Woman captures Jack's heart and his story.

KILLING TIME

Killing Time is a kind of reflexive, even self-destructive murder mystery. Based in part on accounts by Frederic Wertham in *The Show of Violence* (1949) and Quentin Reynolds in *Courtroom* (1950) of an actual sensational murder case in 1937, *Killing Time* tells the story of Joseph Detweiler, "an awfully nice guy" who is also a psychopathic murderer. The novel opens with the discovery that someone has murdered three people in an apartment. The plot seems to be developing into a routine murder mystery or police procedural as the investigative machinery goes into action, but the murderer, Joe Detweiler, turns himself in even before police suspicions about him crystallize. The balance of the novel, therefore, focuses on Detweiler's conversations with the police and his lawyer. Berger's book declines, however, to become a courtroom drama and proceeds instead through a variety of conventions, from the detective story and the psychological thriller to the courtroom drama and other well-codified genres.

Although Joe is a multiple murderer and is quite mad, all other personalities in *Killing Time* lack character in comparison. Joe is the criminal, but he alone among the policemen, lawyers, and judges truly believes in law and justice. His philosophy is bizarre, but Joe manages to change the perspectives of all those who know him. What really separates Joe from those around him is his profound mistrust of language. He sees actions as truth, while language is just "talking about talk."

To a significant extent, Berger is "talking about talk" in *Killing Time*, just as he is exploring the nature of language and the nature of fiction, for this is a supremely reflexive novel. The book is full of fictions within its larger fictional frame; all the characters apart from Joe are cast as conscious and unconscious makers of fiction. For example, Joe's lawyer derives his greatest satisfaction from "a favorable verdict returned by a jury who knew it had been hoaxed," and he explains to Joe that in the courtroom, "reality is what the jury believes." By presenting character after character whose verbal deceptions and artistry are obviously analogous to the techniques of the novelist (one character even becomes a novelist), and by putting his characters in situations analogous to that of the reader of a novel, Berger reminds his reader that the novel is just as much a hoax as any of those created by its characters. As Berger most bluntly states in the front of the book, "A novel is a construction of language and otherwise a lie."

VITAL PARTS

Vital Parts, the third Reinhart novel, picks up the adventures of its protagonist in the 1960's, as the forty-four-year-old Reinhart rapidly adds to the list of windmills with which he has unsuccessfully tilted. Bob Sweet, a flashy boyhood acquaintance, replaces Claude Humbold as Reinhart's business mentor, luring him into his most dubious venture to date: a cryonics foundation for freezing the dead. His tough-minded wife, Genevieve, and his surly hippie son, Blaine, both despise him, while Winona, his fat, unhappy, sweetly innocent daughter, worships him. Caught in a cultural crossfire, Reinhart threatens to succumb to the pressures and perversities of modern life.

REGIMENT OF WOMEN

Berger's next novel, *Regiment of Women*, managed to offend reviewers and readers on both sides of the women's movement when it was published in 1973. A dystopian novel set in America in the year 2047, the book presents a society in which traditional male and female roles have been completely reversed. Women not only control the corporate, artistic, legal, and military machinery of this society but also sexually dominate it, strapping dildos over their pants to assault men. In such an inverted society, to be "manly" is to wear dresses and makeup, to hold only powerless jobs, to have silicone breast implants, and to be emotionally incapable of rational thought or significant action. To be "effeminate" is to bind breasts, to wear false beards, to dress in pants and suits, to be rough, physical, aggressive, and to have a reduced life expectancy caused by stress.

Berger's protagonist in this future world is a twenty-nine-year-old insecurity-riddled male secretary named Georgie Cornell. An unlikely sequence of events lands him first in prison, arrested for wearing women's clothing (slacks, shirt, tie, and coat) and incorrectly suspected of being a men's liberation agent. Driven to discover accidentally that he is physically stronger than his female captors, Georgie escapes and is promptly appropriated as an agent/hero by the men's liberation underground. For the rest of the novel, Georgie struggles to discover his "natural" identity, a process that forces him to cast off received idea after received idea, discarding sexual generalizations to forge a particular definition of self. He is joined in this "rebellion" by a female FBI agent so demented that she wants only to be "masculine"—to wear dresses and makeup, to be gentle and sensitive.

Despite its topical focus, *Regiment of Women* is fundamentally concerned not with sexual roles but with the more basic problem of the hypostatizing power of language. From start to finish, the novel reminds the reader that Georgie's reality has been almost completely gloved by language, and, in so doing, also calls attention both to the way language operates in the reader's reality and to the ways in which a novelist manipulates language to create an independent "reality." At the bottom of this concern with language and rhetoric lies Berger's belief that victimization in any realm starts as a linguistic phenomenon in which the generalizations and attendant rhetoric of some self-interest part company with the particulars of immediate experience. Accordingly, *Regiment of Women* is a book much more concerned with the discovery of true individuality and freedom and with the workings of language than with sexual politics.

SNEAKY PEOPLE

Berger's seventh novel, *Sneaky People*, is easily his most gentle (although much of its action concerns plans for a murder). *Sneaky People* reveals Berger's ear for the American vernacular as it chronicles the coming-of-age of a young boy, Ralph Sandifer, in a dreamy small-town world where nothing is as bucolic as it seems. Ralph's father owns a used-car lot and plans to have one of his employees murder Ralph's mother. The drab, mousy-seeming mother secretly writes and sells pornography of the most lurid sort. Indeed, this is a book that seems to say that it is "sneaky" acts that best reveal character, and it is a book that is itself something of a sneaky act and continues Berger's obsession with the nature of language.

Berger has described *Sneaky People* as "my tribute to the American language of 1939—to be philologically precise, that of the lower-middle class in the eastern Middle West, on which I am an authority as on nothing else." The characters in this novel speak the vital, unleveled, pretelevision American vernacular of the 1930's, and the prose style of *Sneaky People* is in a sense the real subject of the book, reflecting Berger's belief that "the possibilities for wit—and thus for life—decline with the homogenization of language."

WHO IS TEDDY VILLANOVA?

Berger's mastery of and play with prose style reaches its most exuberant high in *Who Is Teddy Villanova?*, which invokes the conventions of the hard-boiled detective novel but also defies almost all of the expectations that attend those conventions. *Who Is Teddy Villanova?* gives evidence of Berger's great respect for the masters of this genre—Dashiell Hammett, Raymond Chandler, and Ross Macdonald—but it also adds a number of outlandish twists, most prominent among them being a first-person narrator who introduces himself with "Call me Russell Wren" and who tells his story "in a rococo style reminiscent by turns of Thomas De Quincey, Thomas Babington Macaulay, and Sir Thomas Malory." Wren is a former instructor of English more concerned with finding readers for the play he is writing than with finding out why a series of thugs and policemen brutalize him either in search of or in the name of a mysterious Teddy Villanova, about whom Wren knows absolutely nothing. The novel follows Wren through one misadventure after another as he pursues the elusive Villanova with Ahab's passion and some curiously "fishy" metaphors (a huge thug slips through a doorway "as deftly as a perch fins among subaqueous rocks").

In truth, Wren does confuse his own small-fish situation with that of Herman Melville's great quest, and his confusion is symptomatic of a more profound problem: When faced with experience, Wren always tries to organize it in terms of the fictional worlds of literary and television private eyes. Like Ralph Fielding Snell in *Little Big Man*, another preposterous "man of letters," Wren perpetually falls victim to his own linguistic hypostatizations as he persistently confuses the literary life of fictional detectives with his own situation. A detective who questions him observes, "I suspect you are living the legend of the private eye, which I confess I had always believed mythical." Wren's narrative style is governed by his immersion in the literary myth of the private eye, and his prose style is governed by his pseudointellectual background, producing such wonderfully incongruous lines as "This wench is my ward. . . . Toy with her fine foot if you like, but eschew her quivering thigh and the demesnes that there adjacent lie." The result is humorously self-conscious, almost forcing the reader to step back from the action of the novel and consider its implications for the act of reading and for language use itself.

ARTHUR REX

Its dust jacket announces that *Arthur Rex* is "Thomas Berger's salute to the Age of Chivalry from his own enmired situation in the Time of the Cad," and this novel has been prominently praised as "the Arthur story for our times." Berger brings to the legend of King Arthur both a profound respect for its mythic power and a modern perspective on the nature of its myth, as can be seen in a comment by Sir Gawaine, when, late in his life, he is asked if he does not long for the old days of action. Gawaine answers no, explaining,

> I am happy to have had them in my proper time, but of a life of adventure it can be said that there is no abiding satisfaction, for when one adventure is done, a knight liveth in expectation of another, and if the next come not soon enough he falleth in love, in the sort of love that is an adventure, for what he seeketh be the adventure and not the lovingness. And methinks this sequence is finally infantile, and beyond a certain age one can no longer be interested in games.

Berger's version of the Arthur legend in no way diminishes the glory of Arthur's attempt or the measure of his achievement, and it equally honors the stylistic achievement of

Sir Thomas Malory's telling of the legend. Berger does devote greater attention to the cause of Arthur's final tragedy, which centers in his account on the erosion of the innocent belief that life can be governed by the simple principle of opposing good to evil. Complexity finally overwhelms Arthur; to Launcelot, he sadly admits that "evil doing hath got more subtle, perhaps even to the point at which it cannot properly be encountered with the sword." What Arthur does not realize is that strict adherence to a rigid code of conduct may create more problems than it solves, threaten order more than ensure it. Only too late do Arthur and some of his wiser knights begin to understand that the Code of Chivalry, like any inflexible system of abstract principles, comes into conflict with itself if pursued too blindly. In Berger's hands, Arthur's most anguishing discovery is not that he has been betrayed by his queen and his most trusted knight but that his philosophy has been shallow, because "to the profound vision there is no virtue and no vice, and what is justice to one, is injustice to another."

Arthur recognizes the flaw in his great dream, but Berger makes it clear that Arthur's legend is not to be judged by the success or failure of that dream. The Lady of the Lake assures the dying Arthur that he could not have done better in his life than he did, and the ghost of Sir Gawaine offers to his king the Round Table's poignant epitaph: "We sought no easy victories, nor won any. And perhaps for that we will be remembered."

NEIGHBORS

Earl Keese, Berger's protagonist in *Neighbors*, is a quiet, reasonable, forty-nine-year-old suburbanite who tells people that his home sits "at the end of the road," because that phrase sounds less "dispiriting" than "dead end." In fact, his life has long since reached its apparent dead end, and it takes the arrival of mysterious and maddening new neighbors, Harry and Ramona, to confront Keese with a sequence of situations so outrageous that he can no longer maintain the hoax of his previously complacent life. Not only do Harry and Ramona (zany versions of Nietzsche's "free spirits") fail to observe the social amenities, but they also seem committed to deliberate provocation, pushing him to see how far he will go to avoid humiliation.

Their visits increasingly seem like motiveless assaults, as their comings and goings produce a series of off-balance events that gradually strip Keese of his easy social assumptions and habitual responses. As his bizarrely embarrassing experiences increasingly blur the line between comedy and nightmare, his relations with all those around him begin to undergo subtle changes. He realizes that his life has grown so stale that Harry and Ramona's aggravations may actually offer him a salvation of sorts—the chance to take control of and give style to his life. As Keese finally admits to Harry, "Every time I see you as a criminal, by another light you look like a kind of benefactor."

Madcap physical changes punctuate the plot—entrances, exits, fights, a damaged car, a destroyed house—but for all its action, *Neighbors* might best be described as a series of functions of language: puns, platitudes, theories, definitions, excuses, accusations, rationalizations, promises, questions, threats—all acts performed with words. Keese knows better than to trust completely what he sees (he suffers from "outlandish illusions"), but he uncritically does believe his ears, consistently confusing rhetoric with reality, mistaking verbal maps for the territory of experience. In fact, *Neighbors* may offer the most verbal world Berger has created; like *Little Big Man*, it is a book in which language becomes the only operating reality. Vocabularies from law and ethics intertwine throughout the novel, and Berger does not fail to exploit the incongruities of the two lexicons. Terms having to do with guilt, justice, punishment, revenge, motive, confession, blame, crime, and accusation appear on virtually every page, resonating at once with the rhetoric of the courtroom and with that of Franz Kafka's *The Trial* (1925). Keese's "guilt" is not unlike that of Kafka's Joseph K., and the slapstick humor of this book records a deadly serious philosophical trial.

REINHART'S WOMEN

In *Reinhart's Women*, the now fifty-four-year-old Reinhart finally discovers something he can do well: cook. The novel finds Reinhart ten years after his divorce from Genevieve, living with and supported by his daughter, Winona, now a beautiful and successful fashion model. His son, Blaine, last seen as a surly radical in *Vital Parts*, is now a surly, snobbish, and successful stockbroker, unchanged in his disdain for his father. Having finally admitted that he is hopeless as a businessman, Reinhart has withdrawn from the world and contents himself with managing his daughter's household and with cooking "in a spirit of scientific inquiry." Actually, cooking has become for him an aesthetic philosophy, and for the first time in his life he does not "feel as if he were either charlatan or buffoon." "Food," Reinhart notes, "is kinder than people."

Long completely at the mercy of unmerciful women, particularly his mother and his ex-wife, Reinhart can now even take in stride the news that his daughter is having a lesbian affair with a successful older businesswoman. Age has taught him that "the best defense against any moral outrage is patience: wait a moment and something will change: the outrage, he who committed it, or, most often, oneself."

Winona's lover (a female version of the con men who have always directed Reinhart's forays into business) contrives to lure Reinhart back into the world, first as a supermarket product demonstrator, then as a guest "chef" for a spot appearance on a local television show, and the novel closes with the strong prospect of his own show: "Chef Carlo Cooks." His apparent successes, however, are not confined to the kitchen, as Reinhart escapes the gentle and loving tyranny of his daughter, emerges unscathed from an encounter with his ex-wife, and begins a promising relationship with a young woman who seems in many ways a female version of himself—intelligent, considerate, awkward. In fact, Reinhart begins to gather around him a small band of kindred souls, hoping to buy and run a quaint small-town café. Once again the lure of business proves irresistible for Reinhart, and once again the prospect of disaster cannot be discounted, but this time the odds seem more in

Reinhart's favor. Jonathan Baumbach has summed up this addition to the Reinhart books as "Berger's most graceful and modest book, a paean to kindness and artistry, a work of quiet dazzle."

Berger's first novel, *Crazy in Berlin*, started Reinhart, "a stumbling American Odysseus," on what Berger has termed "his long career of indestructibility." The subsequent novels in the series—*Reinhart in Love, Vital Parts*, and *Reinhart's Women*—follow Reinhart as he grows older and, ultimately, wiser. Said by one critic to be "a clowning knight errant, pure of heart—that is, a custodian of our conscience and of our incongruities," Reinhart is an incurable idealist who really has no faith in idealism. Complexity, Reinhart's essence, is also his nemesis: He can always see both sides to every argument, feel responsibility for any injustice, and though he realizes that "true freedom is found only by being consistent with oneself," he has a very hard time figuring out how to do this, particularly in the novels before *Reinhart's Women*. Essentially, Reinhart seeks a consistent rationale for his unimpressive, awkward, but indomitable individuality. Combining the features of "a big bland baseball bat" with those of "an avatar of Job the beloved of a sadistic God," Reinhart can never shake the suspicion that he does not fit anywhere but is nevertheless responsible for the general confusion that surrounds and usually engulfs him.

Reinhart is as ill suited for despair, however, as he is for success. Although reminded by a successful acquaintance that he is "redundant in the logistics of life," he can never really be disillusioned, even though his dreams steadily fall prey to the practical opportunism of those around him. No match for a mother who can tell him, "If I ever thought you had truck with Filth, I'd slip you strychnine," or a shrewish wife whose advice to him is "If you're going to be an ass-kisser, then you ought to at least kiss the asses of winners," Reinhart can recognize the distinction between his secular search for a Holy Grail and the social meliorism that passes for idealism. Like all of Berger's characters, Reinhart never gives up: An indomitable toughness underlies his numerous weaknesses, and whatever the situation, he always muddles through, scarred but undaunted.

THE FEUD

In 1984, Berger almost gained the kind of critical recognition he has so long deserved as literary judges selected *The Feud* for the 1984 Pulitzer Prize—only to have their selection overruled in favor of William Kennedy's *Ironweed* (1983) by the Pulitzer administrative committee. What the vagaries and politics of literary prize determination should not obscure is the fact that Berger's twelfth novel (described by Berger as "my most modest work, a little memoir of the place and time of my youth" and "as a kind of Dreiserian slice of life") is a masterpiece of precision that posits its richly textured semblance of small-town life in 1930's America with a perfectly controlled minimum of exposition and a sense of quiet, timeless authority. In its narrowest sense, *The Feud* chronicles the sudden eruption and three-day playing out of an intense feud between two small-town families, the Beelers and the Bullards. Fueled by misunderstanding, misplaced pride, pathological insecurity, small-town xenophobia, self-serving interpretations of events, and the convergence of an incredible sequence of coincidences, this feud is finally remarkable for nothing quite so much as its representation of the way things actually happen in life. The action—both humorous and tragic—of this novel quickly reveals that the dynamics of feuding, quaint though the term may sound, is one of the received structures of human experience, a mold just waiting to be filled—whether by Montagues and Capulets, Hatfields and McCoys, or Beelers and Bullards.

CHANGING THE PAST

Berger's re-creation of the "you have three wishes but be careful what you wish for" story may be one of his most underappreciated novels and is one of his most intensely self-reflexive. Berger is a novelist known for his own approaches to "changing the past," whether it is the "historical" past of *Little Big Man* and *The Return of Little Big Man* or the legendary past of *Arthur Rex* and *Orrie's Story*. Of course, he is also a writer who programmatically changes the past of literary tradition as he consistently reinvents classic novel and literary forms. This novel allows him to imagine the consequences of an "infinitely malleable" past in which changing events seems not to free his protagonist from the larger destiny of his character.

ORRIE'S STORY

Orrie's Story re-creates much of the ambience of *The Feud* and *Sneaky People* but sets within that 1930's and 1940's small-town world the classic story of Orestes, son of Agamemnon and Clytemnestra, who must kill both Clytemnestra and her lover, Aegisthus, to avenge his father's murder by them. In the *Oresteia* (458 B.C.E.) of Aeschylus, a tragedy already recast in the American Civil War era by Eugene O'Neill's *Mourning Becomes Electra* (pr., pb. 1931), Berger has discovered another of the timeless stories of inescapable situations that have always informed and been reinterrogated by his writing. Matching the precision and control of *The Feud* and echoing its mastery of the American idiom, *Orrie's Story* may be Berger's best-written and most starkly powerful novel.

The Feud, *Being Invisible*, *The Houseguest*, and *Orrie's Story* all offer new twists to Berger's fascination with issues of discriminating "kickers" from "kickees," victims from victimizers, the disparate responses of humans confronted by the complexities of responsibility. While *Nowhere*—which continues the misadventures of Russell Wren, protagonist of *Who Is Teddy Villanova?*, as he finds himself transported to the ironic utopia of a quirky kingdom apparently modeled on American film musicals—raises issues usually larger than those facing the individual, it continues Berger's unsentimental confrontation with the essential insolubility of human problems. As Berger's protagonist in *Changing the Past* finally discovers after trying on and discarding a number of wishful alternative versions of his own past, "Life is taking your medicine."

MEETING EVIL

In his introduction to the 2003 paperback edition of *Meeting Evil*, Jonathan Lethem groups it along with *Neighbors* and *The Houseguest* as Berger's "novels of menace," provisionally adding *Best Friends* as a "gentle capstone" to these books that all explore the interplay of victim with victimizer. This may be Berger's most intensely moralistic novel, since its deadly evil provocateur, Richie, confronts solid and somewhat dull good citizen John Felton with a situation beyond the redress of language or irony, compelling him finally to act in the only way that can "meet" Richie's threat. Another way of looking at this novel would be to group it with *Orrie's Story* and with *Changing the Past* as Berger's determined attempt to free himself from the received idea among reviewers that he is a "comic" novelist. These, despite humorous moments, are grim novels, and *Meeting Evil* is possibly the most grim of them all, as it offers no wiggle room in Felton's ultimate moral responsibility.

ROBERT CREWS

For the main characters in *Robert Crews* and *Suspects*, the medicine of life, while bitter, offers the possibility of some kind of redemption. The former novel is Berger's reworking of Defoe's *Robinson Crusoe*; however, Berger's eponymous hero is a far remove from Defoe's shipwrecked Christian incipient capitalist. Crews is an alcoholic parasite who is slowly drinking himself to death. Lost in some unidentified northern woods after a plane crash, with far fewer supplies than even Crusoe is provided with, Crews slowly and surely proves himself capable of surviving in what he calls "a state of nature." He saves not only himself but also his "Friday," a woman fleeing from an abusive husband. Although not quite as blameless as some others of Berger's "kickees," Crews is able at the end to approach what one critic has called the "esteem, apparent honor, and comradeship" that some Berger victim-protagonists attain. Crews's hold on them is precarious but, one at least hopes, lasting.

SUSPECTS

In *Suspects*, Berger provides the reader with two bungling protagonists: Nick Moody, an alcoholic detective investigating a murder case, and Lloyd Howland, brother-in-law and uncle of the two victims. The novel itself takes the form of the small-town police procedural, as in books by Hillary Waugh and K. C. Constantine. In this case, however, Berger, instead of recasting or reworking the mode, deepens it, particularly in his presentation of character. Almost every character, major or minor, from the real culprit to a rookie police officer introduced near the end, is fleshed out and given three dimensions. Even so, Berger probes several characteristic concerns: the workings of fate, miscommunication between human beings, and the instability of language.

Lloyd finds himself a suspect because of a series of incongruous yet logical steps in a chain of circumstances, "an unbroken progress he was powerless to alter." He keeps losing jobs, primarily because he is a typical Berger "kickee." His victimization is caused by the misinterpretation of his actions by those around him: When he tries to return a box opener to his boss, he is perceived as wielding a threatening weapon. The main crime in the novel is also committed because the victim's actions are misconstrued by the murderer (although in this case the error is much more willfully perverse). Both Lloyd and Nick Moody find themselves in their present circumstances because they cannot come up with an adequate definition for the word "love." This imprecision of definition in Lloyd's case makes him unable to have sex with someone with whom he is friends, and in Moody's case it leads to broken marriages and a strained relationship with his son. At the end of the novel, it is Lloyd's reaching out to Moody that saves the detective from committing suicide. It is unsure whether Lloyd will make the police force or Moody will quit drinking, but at least a hint of redemption is offered.

ADVENTURES OF THE ARTIFICIAL WOMAN

In one sense, *Adventures of the Artificial Woman* is as artificial as its animatronic main character, since Berger never intended the work to be published as a novel, thinking of it as a "literary conceit," a novelette he hoped would be published with a collection of his short stories. Its ostensible protagonist is Phyllis, a robot so lifelike she can pass for human, whose striking looks and capacity for intellectual growth lead her through a series of sex-worker jobs to acting jobs and finally to her greatest and most unsustainable job as president of the United States. Phyllis's all-too-likely adventures and moral-by-design nature afford Berger the opportunity to take broad satirical swipes at a number of human vagaries and at the humbug and posturing so firmly imbricated in contemporary media and political culture—and to confront Ellery, her creator, with the age-old moral responsibility of parent to child, creator to created creature.

Brooks Landon
Updated by William Laskowski

OTHER MAJOR WORKS

PLAYS: *Other People*, pr. 1970; *The Burglars: A Comedy in Two Acts*, pb. 1988.
RADIO PLAY: *At the Dentist's*, 1981.

BIBLIOGRAPHY

Landon, Brooks. *Thomas Berger.* Boston: Twayne, 1989. First book-length study of Berger draws from the author's correspondence with Berger to support the thesis that the interpretation of Berger's novels is the study of his style. Begins with a brief overview of Berger's career and then analyzes, by conceptual grouping, Berger's first fifteen novels.

Lethem, Jonathan. Introduction to *Meeting Evil*, by Thomas Berger. New York: Simon & Schuster, 2003. Presents a brilliant analysis of Berger's career, discussing his unique strengths as a writer and his place in American letters.

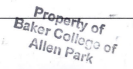

Madden, David W. *Critical Essays on Thomas Berger.* New York: G. K. Hall, 1995. Solid collection includes a valuable overview of Berger criticism by the editor, a lengthy interview with Berger, and the text of Berger's play *Other People.* Gerald Weales's 1983 essay "Reinhart as Hero and Clown," reprinted here, is perhaps still the best single discussion of the Reinhart books available.

Malone, Michael. "Berger, Burlesque, and the Yearning for Comedy." *Studies in American Humor* 2 (Spring, 1983): 20-32. One of the most instructive essays in the two-volume *Studies in American Humor* special issue on Berger, this piece offers a persuasive analysis of Berger's complexity that also considers why his achievements have not been better celebrated. Malone claims that whatever the novel form, Berger writes comedy, as opposed to comic novels.

Wallace, Jon. "A Murderous Clarity: A Reading of Thomas Berger's *Killing Time.*" *Philological Quarterly* 68 (Winter, 1989): 101-114. Offers superb analysis of the philosophical implications of Berger's use of sources in *Killing Time.* Wallace is one of the few critics to recognize the interpretive importance of Berger's style.

Wilde, Alan. "Acts of Definition: Or, Who Is Thomas Berger?" *Arizona Quarterly* 39 (Winter, 1983): 314-351. Instructive essay on Berger's work offers a phenomenology that recognizes the inseparability for the author of the concepts of freedom and self-definition. Wilde finds in Berger's novels, however, a "fear of otherness" that just as easily may be termed "fascination."

JAMES FENIMORE COOPER

Born: Burlington, New Jersey; September 15, 1789
Died: Cooperstown, New York; September 14, 1851
Also known as: James Cooper

PRINCIPAL LONG FICTION

Precaution: A Novel, 1820
The Spy: A Tale of the Neutral Ground, 1821
The Pilot: A Tale of the Sea, 1823
The Pioneers: Or, The Sources of the Susquehanna, 1823
Lionel Lincoln: Or, The Leaguer of Boston, 1825
The Last of the Mohicans: A Narrative of 1757, 1826
The Prairie: A Tale, 1827
The Red Rover: A Tale, 1827
The Wept of Wish-Ton-Wish: A Tale, 1829
The Water-Witch: Or, The Skimmer of the Seas, 1830
The Bravo: A Tale, 1831
The Heidenmauer: Or, The Benedictines—A Tale of the Rhine, 1832
The Headsman: Or, The Abbaye des Vignerons, 1833
The Monikens, 1835
Home as Found, 1838
Homeward Bound: Or, The Chase, 1838
Mercedes of Castile: Or, The Voyage to Cathay, 1840
The Pathfinder: Or, The Inland Sea, 1840
The Deerslayer: Or, The First War-Path, a Tale, 1841
The Two Admirals: A Tale, 1842
The Wing-and-Wing: Or, Le Feu-Follet, 1842
Le Mouchoir: An Autobiographical Romance, 1843 (also known as
    Autobiography of a Pocket Handkerchief)
Wyandotté: Or, The Hutted Knoll, 1843
Afloat and Ashore: A Sea Tale, 1844
Miles Wallingford: Sequel to "Afloat and Ashore," 1844
The Chainbearer: Or, The Littlepage Manuscripts, 1845
Satanstoe: Or, The Littlepage Manuscripts, a Tale of the Colony, 1845
*The Redskins: Or, Indian and Injin, Being the Conclusion of the Littlepage
    Manuscripts*, 1846
The Crater: Or, Vulcan's Peak, a Tale of the Pacific, 1847
Jack Tier: Or, The Florida Reef, 1848
The Oak Openings: Or, The Bee Hunter, 1848

The Sea Lions: Or, The Lost Sealers, 1849
The Ways of the Hour, 1850

OTHER LITERARY FORMS

Although James Fenimore Cooper was primarily a novelist, he also tried his hand at short stories, biographies, and a play. Among these works, only the biographies are considered significant. He also wrote accounts of his European travels, history, and essays on politics and society. Among his political writings, *The American Democrat* (1838) retains its appeal as an analysis of contemporary political and social issues and as an expression of Cooper's mature political and social thought. His *The History of the Navy of the United States of America* (1839, two volumes) is still considered a definitive work. Cooper was an active correspondent. Many of his letters and journals have been published, but large quantities of material remain in the hands of private collectors.

ACHIEVEMENTS

Though he is best known as the author of the Leatherstocking Tales, James Fenimore Cooper has come to be recognized as America's first great social historian. The Leatherstocking Tales—*The Pioneers*, *The Last of the Mohicans*, *The Prairie*, *The Pathfinder*, and *The Deerslayer*—are those novels in which the frontier hunter and scout Natty Bumppo is a central character. Along with *The Spy* and *The Pilot*, two novels of the American Revolution, the Leatherstocking Tales are familiar to modern readers, and critics agree that these are Cooper's best novels. Less well known are the novels he began writing during his seven-year residence in Europe, his problem and society novels. In these books, he works out and expresses a complex social and political theory and a social history of America seen within the context of the major modern developments of European civilization. Because his problem and society novels often are marred by overstatement and repetition, they are rarely read for pleasure, but they remain, as Robert Spiller argues, among the most detailed and accurate pictures available of major aspects of American society and thought in the early nineteenth century.

Cooper achieved international reputation with *The Spy*, his second novel, which was translated into most European languages soon after its publication. With this work, he also invented a popular genre, the spy novel. He is credited with having invented the Western in the Leatherstocking Tales and the sea adventure with *The Pilot*, another popular success. His ability to tell tales of romance and adventure in convincingly and often beautifully described settings won for him a devoted readership and earned a title he came eventually to resent, "The American Scott." His reputation began to decline when he turned to concerned criticism of American society. Though his goal in criticism was always amelioration through the affirmation of basic principles, Cooper's aristocratic manner and his frequent opposition to popular ideas made him increasingly unpopular with the public. The political and social atmosphere was not favorable to his opinions, and his works routinely

James Fenimore Cooper
(Library of Congress)

received scathing reviews as pretentious and aristocratic, also as politically motivated and self-serving. As Spiller argues, Cooper was too much a man of principle to use consciously his public position for personal ends. His suits against the press to establish a definition of libel, his exploration of the principles of democracy in his novels and essays, and his careful and objective research in his naval histories and biographies reveal a man who passionately sought truth and justice regardless of the effect on his popularity.

Though his popularity declined after 1833, Cooper continued writing with energy. In his thirty-year writing career, he wrote more than thirty novels, the naval history, several significant social works, and many other works as well. Howard Mumford Jones credits Cooper with early American developments of the international theme, the theme of the Puritan conscience, the family saga, the utopian and dystopian novel, and the series novel. By general agreement, Cooper stands at the headwaters of the American tradition of fiction; he contributed significantly to the themes and forms of the American novel.

BIOGRAPHY

James Cooper was born in Burlington, New Jersey, on September 15, 1789, the twelfth of thirteen children of William and Elizabeth Cooper. He added Fenimore to his name in 1826 in memory of his mother's family. Elizabeth Fenimore was an heiress whose wealth contributed to William Cooper's success in buying and developing a large tract of land on which he founded Cooperstown, New York. Cooper's father, descended from English Quakers, expressed enlightened ideas about developing wilderness lands in his *A Guide in the Wilderness* (1810). William Cooper and Cooperstown became models for Judge Temple and Templeton in *The Pioneers*. The Coopers moved to Cooperstown in 1790, and Cooper grew up there as the son of the community's developer and benefactor, a gentleman who eventually became a judge and a Federalist congressman. Cooper's conservative Enlightenment views of the frontier, of American culture, and of democracy had their roots in his Cooperstown youth.

Like many sons of the wealthy gentry, Cooper had some difficulty deciding what to do with his life. In his third year at Yale, he was dismissed for misconduct. In 1806, he began a naval career that led to a commission in the U.S. Navy in 1808, and he served on Lake Ontario, scene of *The Pathfinder*. In 1809, his father died from a blow delivered from behind by a political opponent, and Cooper came into a large inheritance. In 1811, he married Susan Augusta DeLancey, of an old and respectable Tory family, and he resigned from the Navy. For eight years he lived the life of a country gentleman, eventually fathering seven children. By 1819, however, because of the financial failures and deaths of all his brothers, which left him responsible for some of their families, Cooper found himself in financial difficulty. Cooper began writing at this time, not with the hope of making money—there was no precedent for achieving a living as an author—but in response to a challenge from his wife to write a better novel than one he happened to be reading to her. Once he had begun, Cooper found in various ways the energy and motivation to make writing his career. Susan's support and the family's continued domestic tranquillity inspired Cooper's writing and protected him from what he came to see as an increasingly hostile public.

The success of *The Spy* and of his next four novels made him secure enough in 1826 to take his family to Europe, where he hoped to educate his children and to improve the foreign income from his books. While living in Paris and London and traveling at a leisurely pace through most of Europe, Cooper involved himself in French and Polish politics and published several works. Before his return to the United States in 1833, he met Sir Walter Scott, became intimate with Marie de La Fayette, aided the sculptor Horatio Greenough in beginning his career, and cultivated his lifelong friendship with Samuel Morse. This period of travel was another turning point in his life. In *Notions of the Americans* (1828), Cooper wrote an idealized defense of American democracy that offended both his intended audiences, the Americans and the English. When he went on to publish a series of novels set in Europe (1831-1833), Cooper provided American reviewers with more reasons to see him as an apostate. Upon his return to the United States, he tended to confirm this characterization by announcing his retirement as a novelist and publishing a group of travel books, satires, and finally a primer on republican democracy, *The American Democrat*. When he returned to writing novels with *Homeward Bound* and *Home as Found* in 1838, he indicated that he had found America much decayed on his return from Europe. The promises of a democratic republic he had expressed in *Notions of the Americans* were fading before the abuse of the Constitution by demagogues and the increasing tyranny of the majority. *The American Democrat* was, in part, a call to return to the original principles of the republic.

Having resettled in Cooperstown in 1833, Cooper soon found himself embroiled in controversies over land title and libel, controversies that the press used to foster the image of Cooper as a self-styled aristocrat. He is credited with establishing important legal precedents in the libel cases he won against editors such as Thurlow Weed and Horace Greeley. By 1843, Cooper's life had become more tranquil. He had settled down to the most productive period of his life, producing sixteen novels between 1840 and 1851; among them are many marred by obtrusive discussions of political and social issues but also several that are considered American classics, such as *The Pathfinder* and *The Deerslayer*, the last two of the Leatherstocking Tales. His last five novels show evidence of increasing interest in religious ideas. Although Cooper had been active in religious institutions all his life, and although all his novels express Christian beliefs, he was not confirmed as an Episcopalian until the last year of his life. He died at Cooperstown on September 14, 1851.

ANALYSIS

James Fenimore Cooper was a historian of America. His novels span American history, dramatizing central events from Columbus's discovery (*Mercedes of Castile*) through the French and Indian Wars and the early settlement (the Leatherstocking Tales) to the Revolution (*The Spy* and *The Pilot*) and the contemporary events of the Littlepage and Miles Wallingford novels. In some of his European novels, he examines major intellectual developments, such as the Reformation, that he thought important to American history, and in many of his novels he reviews the whole of American history, attempting to complete his particular vision of America by inventing a tradition for the new nation. Modern criticism is divided concerning the meaning and nature of Cooper's tradition. Following the lead of D. H. Lawrence, a group of myth critics have concentrated on unconscious elements in Cooper's works, while Robert Spiller and a group of social and historical critics have concentrated more on Cooper's conscious opinions.

In his *Studies in Classic American Literature* (1923), Lawrence argues that Cooper's myth of America is centered in the friendship between Natty Bumppo and the American Indian Chingachgook, and in the order of composition of the Leatherstocking Tales. Of the friendship, Lawrence says, Cooper "dreamed a new human relationship deeper than the deeps of sex. Deeper than property, deeper than fatherhood, deeper than marriage, deeper than love. . . . This is the nucleus of a new society, the clue to a new epoch." Of the order of writing, Lawrence observes says that the novels "go backwards, from old age to golden youth. That is the true myth of America. She starts old, old and wrinkled in an old skin. And there is a gradual sloughing of the old skin, towards a new youth." These insightful statements have been elaborated by critics who have looked deeply into Cooper's works but have concentrated most of their attention on the Leatherstocking Tales to find in Cooper affinities with Herman Melville, Mark Twain, and others who seem to find it necessary, like Natty Bumppo, to remain apart from social institutions to preserve their integrity. Because these critics tend to focus on mythic elements in the tales, they may be better guides to American myth than to Cooper. Although Cooper contributed images and forms to what became myths in the hands of others, his own mind seems to have been occupied more with making American society than with escaping it.

Another more traditional mythic pattern pervades all of his works, including the Leatherstocking Tales. Several critics have called attention to a key passage in *The Last of the Mohicans* when Natty describes the waterfall where the scout and his party take refuge from hostile Native Americans. The pattern of a unified flow falling into disorder and rebellion only to be gathered back again by the hand of Providence into a new order not only is descriptive of the plot of this novel but also suggests other levels of meaning that are reflected throughout Cooper's work, for it defines Cooper's essentially Christian and Enlightenment worldview, a view that he found expressed, though with too monarchical a flavor, in Alexander Pope's *An Essay on Man* (1733-1734).

In *Home as Found*, Cooper sees the same pattern in the development of frontier settlements. They begin with a pastoral stage in which people of all kinds cooperate freely and easily to make a new land support them. The second stage is anarchic, for when freed of the demanding laws of necessity, society begins to divide as interests consolidate into factions and as families struggle for power and position. Though it appears painful and disorderly, this phase is the natural, providential reordering process toward a mature society. In the final phase, established, mutually respecting, and interdependent classes make possible a high civilization.

In *The American Democrat*, Cooper often echoes Pope's *An Essay on Man* as he explains that human life in this world is a fall into disorder where the trials exceed the pleasures; this apparent disorder, however, is a merciful preparation for a higher life to come. Many of Cooper's novels reflect this pattern; characters leave or are snatched out of their reasonably ordered world to be educated in a dangerous and seemingly disordered one, only to be returned after an educational probation into a more familiarly ordered world, there to contribute to its improvement. This pattern of order, separation, and reintegration pervades Cooper's thought and gives form to his conscious dream of America. He came to see America as moving through the anarchic and purifying phase of the Revolution toward a new society that would allow the best that is in fallen humankind to be realized. This dream is expressed, in part, in *The Pioneers*.

THE PIONEERS

The Pioneers is Cooper's first great novel, the first he composed primarily to satisfy himself. The popular success of *The Spy* increased both his freedom and his confidence, encouraging him to turn to what proved to be his richest source of material, the frontier life of New York state. This first novel in the Leatherstocking series has a complex double organization that is an experimental response to what Robert Spiller sees as Cooper's main artistic problem, the adaptation of forms developed in aristocratic civilized Europe to his democratic frontier material. On one hand, *The Pioneers* describes daily life in the new village of Templeton on Otsego Lake and is ordered within a frame of seasonal change from Christmas, 1793, until the following autumn. Behind this organization, on the other hand, stands a hidden order that gradually reveals itself as the story unfolds; central to this plot is the transfer of title of the largest portion of land in the district from Judge Marmaduke Temple to Edward Oliver Effingham. These two structures interact to underline the providential inevitability and significance of this transfer.

The seasonal ordering of events brings out the nature of the community at Templeton at this particular point in its development. Templeton is shown to be suspended between two forms of order. Representing the old order are the seventy-year-old Natty Bumppo, the Leatherstocking, and his aged Indian friend, John Mohegan, whose actual name is Chingachgook. The forest is their home and their mediator with divine law. Natty, through his contact with Chingachgook and his life in the forest, has become the best man that such a life can produce. He combines true Christian principles with the skills and knowledge of the best of American Indian civilization. Natty and the Indian live an ideal kind of life, given the material circumstances of their environment, but that environment is changing. Otsego Lake is becoming settled and civilized. Chingachgook remains because he wishes to live where his ancestors once dwelt. Natty stays with his friend. Their presence becomes a source of conflict.

The new order is represented at first by Judge Temple, but the form of that order remains somewhat obscure until the revealing of motives and identities at the end of the novel. Temple's main function in the community is moral. He is important as the owner and developer of the land. He has brought settlers to the land, helped them through troubled times, and, largely at his own expense, built the public buildings and established the institutions of Templeton. During the transition to civilization, Temple is a center of order, organization, and—most important—restraint. In part through his efforts, the legislature is enacting laws to restrain the settlers in the state. Restraint on two kinds of behavior is necessary. On one hand, there are characters such as Billy Kirby, whose wasteful use of community resources stems primarily from the inability to understand the needs of a settled country. These individuals live in the old forest world but without the old forest values. On the other hand, there are the settlers themselves: Some, such as Richard Jones and Hiram Doolittle, tend toward cupidity, while others, such as the community's poor, are so unaccustomed to having plenty that they waste it when they have it. These attitudes are shown in the famous scenes of pigeon shooting and lake fishing, and they are pointedly contrasted with the old values practiced by Natty and Chingachgook. The settlers need restraint; Judge Temple feels in himself the desire to overharvest the plentiful natural resources of Templeton and knows at first hand the importance of restraining laws that will force the settlers to live by an approximation of the divine law by which Natty lives.

The central conflict in the seasonal ordering of the novel is between Natty, who lives by the old law, the natural law of the forest that reflects the divine law, and the settlers, who are comparatively lawless. This conflict is complicated as the new restraining civil laws come into effect and the lawless members of the community exploit and abuse those laws in order to harass Natty. Hiram Doolittle, a justice of the peace, and Richard Jones, the sheriff, become convinced that Natty is secretly mining silver on Judge Temple's land. In reality, Natty is concealing the aged and senile original white owner of this land, Major Effingham, helping to care for the old man until his grandson, Oliver Effingham, is able to move him to better circumstances. Doolittle succeeds at maneuvering the law and its institutions so that Judge Temple must fine and jail Natty for resisting an officer of the law. Natty thus becomes a victim of the very laws designed to enforce his own highest values, underlining the weakness of human nature and illustrating the cyclical pattern of anarchy, order, and repression and abuse of the law. When Doolittle's machinations are revealed and Natty is freed, he announces his intent to move west into the wilderness that is his proper home.

The conflict between the old order and the new is resolved only in part by Natty's apparent capitulation and retreat into the wilderness. Before Natty leaves, he performs a central function in the land transfer plot, a function that infuses the values of the old order into the new order. The land to which Judge Temple holds title was given to Major Effingham by a council of the Delaware chiefs at the time of the French and Indian Wars. In recognition of his qualities as a faithful and brave warrior, Effingham was adopted into the tribe as a son of Chingachgook. In this exchange, the best of Native American civilization recognized its own qualities in a superior form in Effingham, a representative of the best of European Christian civilization. This method of transfer is crucial because it amounts to a gentleman's agreement ratified by family ties; the transfer is a voluntary expression of values and seems providentially ordained. The history of the land, as it passes from the Major to his son, illustrates these same values. The Major confidently gives his son control over his estates, knowing that his son will care for them as a gentleman should. Generosity and honor, rather than greed and violence, characterize these transfers.

For the transfer to be complete, the owners must be Americanized by means of the American Revolution. This process is a purification that brings to culmination in Oliver the traditions of American democracy and European and American Indian aristocracy. The Effinghams are a Tory family. Oliver's father and Judge Temple are brothers in honor, a civilized reflection of Natty and Chingachgook. Temple is an example of Americanized aristocracy. His aristocratic family had declined in the New World, but beginning with his father, they reemerged as democratic "aristocrats," what Cooper referred to as gentlemen. A gentleman is one whose superior talents are favored by education and comparative leisure to fit him as a moral leader of the community. The gentleman differs from the Old World aristocrat in that he has no hereditary title to political power. In the ideal republic, the gentleman is recognized for his attainments by the common people, who may be expected to choose freely their political leaders from among the gentry. The Effinghams have not undergone this Americanizing process. The process is portrayed in the novel in Oliver Effingham's resentful efforts to restore his grandfather to his accustomed way of life.

Oliver labors under the mistaken idea that Temple has usurped his family's land, but as the final revelations show, the Americanized gentleman has remained faithful, holding the land in trust for the Effinghams to take once they have become American. Oliver's deprivation, the military defeat of his family, and his working in disguise for Judge Temple are lessons in humility that reveal to him the moral equality between himself and the Temples. Without such an experience, he might well consider himself above the Judge's daughter, Elizabeth, unable to marry her and unable to bring together the two parts of the estate. The other main component of Oliver's transformation comes under the tutelage of Natty and Chingachgook, who attempt to impress on Oliver, as well as on Elizabeth, their obligations to the land and to its previous owners. Through this two-pronged education, the aristocrat becomes a gentleman and the breach caused by the American Revolution is healed. This healing is manifested most clearly in the marriage of Oliver and Elizabeth. The best of the Old World is recognized by the best of New World Indians and, by means of the Revolution, is purified of its antidemocratic prejudices; the aristocrat becomes a gentleman worthy to rule in America.

The transfer of title takes place within the context of inevitable seasonal change; its rhythm of tension and crisis reflects similar events within the seasons. The transition from the old order of Native American occupation to the new order of white democratic civilization is shown, despite local tensions and conflicts, to be providentially ordered when viewed from a sufficient distance. Within the seasons as well as in the human actions, the central theme of displacement underlines and elaborates the meaning of the overall movement.

The novel is filled with displaced persons. Remarkable Pettibone is displaced as mistress of the Temple mansion by Elizabeth. Natty and Chingachgook are displaced by white civilization. Oliver is displaced by the American Revolution, Le Quoi by the French Revolution. Finally, Judge Temple is displaced as the first power in the community. Within this thematic pattern, two general kinds of resolution occur. Oliver, Chingachgook, and Le Quoi are variously restored to their proper places, though Chingachgook must die in order to rejoin his tribe. Pettibone and Temple come to accept their displacement by their superiors. Natty is unique. His displacement seems destined for repetition until Providence finally civilizes the continent and no place is left that is really his home. For him, as for Chingachgook, only death seems to offer an end to displacement. Natty's legacy must live on, however, in those gentlemen who combine "nature and refinement," and there is some hope that in a mature American society, Natty as well as good American Indians might find a home.

Critics tend to see Natty as an idealized epic hero who is too good for any society he encounters, but this is not quite true. In each of the books in which he appears, he acts as a
conserver of essential values. This role is clearest when he teaches Elizabeth the ethics of
fishing for one's food and when he saves her and Oliver from a fire on the mountain. His
complaints about the "wasty ways" of civilization and about the laws that ought to be un-
necessary are a part of this function. Although he fails to understand the weaknesses of
civilized people and their need for the civil law, he still functions to further the best interests of civilization, not only by taming the wild but also by performing a role like that of
the Old Testament prophets. He constantly calls people's attention back to the first principles of civilized life. In this respect, Natty is much like Cooper.

The Pioneers is a hopeful novel, for in it Cooper reveals a confidence in a providential
ordering of history that will lead to the fulfillment of his ideas of a rational republic. This
novel resolves the central anarchic displacements of the native inhabitants and of the traditional European ruling class by asserting that the American republic is the fruition of these
two traditions. Though far from perfect, the American experiment seems, in this novel, to
be destined for a unique success.

THE LAST OF THE MOHICANS

The Last of the Mohicans is the best known of the Leatherstocking Tales, probably because it combines Cooper's most interesting characters and the relatively fast-paced adventure of *The Spy* and *The Pilot*. Set in the French and Indian Wars, this novel presents
Natty and Chingachgook in their prime. Chingachgook's son, Uncas, is the last of the
Mohican chiefs, the last of the line from which the Delaware nation is said to trace their origins. Although the novel moves straightforwardly through two adventures, it brings into
these adventures a number of suggestive thematic elements.

The two main adventures are quests, with filial piety as their motive. Major Duncan
Heyward attempts to escort Cora and Alice Munro to their father, commander of Fort Wil-
liam Henry on Horican Lake (Lake George). Led astray by Magua, an American Indian
who seeks revenge against Munro, the party, which comes to include a comic psalmodist,
David Gamut, encounters and enlists the help of Natty and his Indian companions. This
quest is fully successful. Magua joins the Hurons who are leagued with the besieging
French forces at William Henry and captures the original party, which is then rescued by
Natty and his friends to be delivered safely to the doomed fort. This adventure is followed
by an interlude at the fort in which Heyward obtains Munro's permission to court Alice
and learns, to his own secret pain, that Cora has black blood. Also in this interlude, Munro
learns he will get no support from nearby British troops and realizes that he must surren-
der his position. Montcalm allows him to remove his men and equipment from the fort before it is destroyed, but the discontented Native Americans, provoked by Magua, break the
truce and massacre the retreating and exposed people for booty and scalps. Magua precipitates the next quest by capturing Alice and Cora and taking them, along with David

Gamut, north toward Canada. The second quest is the rescue mission of Natty, Chingach-gook, Uncas, Heyward, and Munro. This attempt is only partly successful, for both Cora and Uncas are killed.

Cooper heightens the interest of these quests in part through a double love plot. During the first movement, Duncan and Alice come to love each other and Uncas is attracted to Cora. Though thematically important, the first couple is not very interesting. Except for the slight misunderstanding with Munro that reveals the secret of Cora's ancestry, the barriers between Heyward and Alice are physical and temporal. More complicated and puzzling is the relationship between Cora and Uncas. Whereas Alice seems to spend most of the two quests calling on her father, weeping, and fainting, Cora shows a spirit and courage that make her an interesting character and that attract the admiration of Uncas. Magua is also interested in Cora, proposing in the first capture that if she will become his wife, he will cease his persecution of the rest of the family. Magua is primarily intent on revenge against Munro, but it seems clear that his interest in Cora as a woman grows until it may even supplant his revenge motive. Near the end of the novel, Natty offers himself in exchange for Cora, but even though Natty is a much more valuable prisoner, Magua prefers to keep Cora. When the hunted Magua's last remaining comrade kills Cora, Magua turns on him. Though there is no indication that Magua's is more than a physical passion, he seems strongly attracted to Cora, perhaps in part because of her courageous refusal to fear or to submit to him.

Critics have made much of the relationship between Cora, Uncas, and Magua, suggesting that Cooper gives Cora black blood to "sanitize" her potential relationship with Uncas and the heavenly marriage between them suggested in the final funeral service of the Indians. Cora becomes an early example of "the tragic mulatto" who has no place in the world where racial purity is highly valued. Natty insistently declares that even though he has adopted American Indian ways, he is "a man without a cross"; his blood is pure white. On the other hand, the three-part pattern that seems to dominate Cooper's historical vision might imply a real fulfillment in the Indian funeral that is intended to bring Cora and Uncas together in the next life. This incident may be as close as Cooper came to a vision of a new America such as Lawrence hints at, in which even the races are drawn together into a new unity. The division between races is a symptom of a fallen and perverse world. Natty more than once asserts that there is one God over all and, perhaps, one afterlife for all.

The first meeting of Heyward's party with Natty's party in the forest has an allegorical quality that looks forward to the best of Nathaniel Hawthorne and begins the development of the theme of evil, which—in Cooper's vision—can enjoy only a temporary triumph. Lost in the forest, misled by the false guide, Magua, this party from civilization has entered a seemingly anarchic world in which they are babes "without the knowledge of men." This meeting introduces two major themes: the conception of the wilderness as a book one must know how to read if one is to survive, and the conception of Magua and his

Hurons as devils who have tempted Heyward's party into this world in order to work their destruction. Though Magua is represented in Miltonic terms as Satan, he is not so much a rebel angel as he is a product of "the colonial wars of North America." Magua's home is the "neutral territory" that the rival forces must cross in order to fight each other; he desires revenge on Munro for an imprudent act, an act that symbolizes the whites' disturbance of Magua's way of life. As Magua asserts, Munro provided the alcohol that unbalanced him, then whipped him for succumbing to that alcohol. Magua has most of the qualities of the good men: courage, cunning, the ability to organize harmoniously talent and authority, and highly developed skills at reading the book of nature. He differs from Natty and his Native American companions, however, in that he allows himself to be governed by the evil passion of revenge rather than by unselfish rationality. Of his kind, the unselfishly rational men must be constantly suspicious. Montcalm's failure to control his Indian forces demonstrates that only the most concerted efforts can prevent great evil. The novel's end shows that ultimately only divine Providence can fully right the inevitable wrongs of this world.

Within this thematic context, a crucial event is David's response to Natty's promise to avenge his death if the Hurons dare to kill him. David will have no vengeance, only Christian forgiveness. Natty acknowledges the truth and beauty of the idea, but it is clear that his struggle is on another level. Those he fights are devils, the dark side of himself, of Chingachgook and Cora and Uncas—in fact, of all the main characters—for Magua is doubled with each of the main characters at some point in the novel. Magua comes to represent the evil in each character. In this forest world, the dark self takes shape in passionate savages who must be exterminated absolutely, like those who first capture Heyward's party. To show them pity is to endanger oneself; to neglect killing them is to open one to further jeopardy, such as the "descent into hell" to rescue the captured maidens, which is one element of the second quest. Only under the rule of civil law in civilization does human evil become a forgivable weakness rather than a metaphysical absolute.

THE PRAIRIE

Critics have noted the improbable plot of *The Prairie* while acknowledging its powerful and moving episodes. Ishmael Bush, an opponent of land ownership and of the civil law, has led onto the vast western prairie his considerable family, including a wife, seven sons, and an unspecified number of daughters; his brother-in-law, Abiram White; a well-educated and distantly related orphan, Ellen Wade; Obed Battius, a comic naturalist and doctor; and Inez Middleton, whom Abiram has kidnapped for ransom. Bush's ostensible motive is to escape the various restraining regulations of civilization and, particularly, to set up his farm far from the irksome property law. It is never made clear why he has consented to join the kidnapping or how anyone expects to collect a ransom. This expedition draws in its wake Paul Hover, a secret suitor of Ellen, and a party of soldiers led by Duncan Uncas Middleton, who seeks to recover his bride, who was snatched between the ceremony and the consummation. On the prairie, they all meet the eighty-seven-year-old Natty, who has forsaken human-made clearings in order to avoid the sound of the axe and to die in a clearing made by God. The situation is complicated by the presence of feuding American Indian bands: the bad Indians, the Hurons of the plains, are the Sioux, led by the treacherous Mahtoree; the good Indians are the Pawnee, led by the faithful Hard Heart. With these melodramatic materials, Cooper forges a moving tale that he makes significant in part by bringing into play issues of law and morality.

During the captivities and escapes that advance the novel's action, the white characters divide into two alliances that are then associated with the two Native American tribes. Both alliances are patriarchal, but their characters are significantly different. Bush is the patriarch of physical power. He lives by the "natural law" that "might makes right," establishing his dominance over his family through physical strength and his conviction of his own power and rectitude. This alliance is beset by internal danger and contradiction. The second alliance is a patriarchy of wisdom and virtue. Bound together by the faith of its members, it grows under the leadership of Natty to include Paul, Duncan, Ellen, Inez, and Dr. Battius. The conflict between these two groups is prefigured in the first confrontation between Natty and Ishmael. Ishmael is represented in the opening of the novel as being out of place on the prairie, for he is a farmer who has left the best farmland to take the route of those who, "deluded by their wishes," are "seeking for the Eldorado of the West." In one of the many great tableaux of this novel, Ishmael's group first sees Natty as a gigantic shadow cast toward them by the setting sun. He is a revelation who suggests to them the supernatural. Bush has come to the prairie in the pride of moral self-sufficiency, but Natty is an example of humble dependence on the wisdom of God. In part, through Natty's example, Ishmael finally leads his "wild brood" back to civilization at the novel's end.

Pride on the prairie, as in the wilderness of New York, leads to the subjection of reason to passion, to precipitate actions and death, whereas humility, though it may not save one from death, leads to the control of passion, to patience and probable survival. Natty teaches this lesson repeatedly to the group of which he becomes father and leader. Ishmael and the Sioux, "the Ishmaelites of the American deserts," learn the lesson through more bitter experience. The narrator implies that both Ishmael and Mahtoree, in attempting to be laws unto themselves, are playing God. In the central dialogue of the novel, Natty tells Dr. Battius, in terms that echo *Essay on Man*, that humankind's "gifts are not equal to his wishes . . . he would mount into the heavens with all his deformities about him if he only knew the road. . . . If his power is not equal to his will, it is because the wisdom of the Lord hath set bounds to his evil workings." Mahtoree, unrestrained by the traditional laws of his tribe, seeks through demagoguery to manipulate his people to effect his selfish desire for Inez. He and his band are destroyed in consequence. Bush's lesson comes when he discovers that Natty is not actually the murderer of Bush's eldest son, Asa.

The lesson Bush learns is always present to him. When his sons learn the well-kept secret that Ishmael is assisting Abiram in a kidnapping, they become indignant and rebellious.

Cooper uses this conflict to demonstrate the precariousness of arbitrary power. Bush knows that he deserted his parents when he felt strong enough, and he is aware that only his strength keeps his sons with him in the present danger from American Indians. This knowledge of instability becomes complete when he learns that Abiram has returned the blow he received from Asa by shooting the boy in the back. It is difficult to determine how fully Bush understands this revelation. He feels his dilemma, for he admits that while he suspected Natty, he had no doubt that the murderer deserved execution, but when he learned of his brother-in-law's guilt, he became unsure. The wound to his family can hardly be cured by killing another of its members. For the first time in his life, Bush feels the waste and solitude of the wilderness. He turns to his wife and to her Bible for authority. He feels the extent to which Abiram has carried out Ishmael's own desire to punish his rebellious son, and thus he himself suffers as he carries out the execution of Abiram. This bitter lesson humbles him and sends him back to settled country and the restraints of civil law.

For Natty's informal family, there are gentler lessons. Paul and Duncan learn to be humble about their youthful strength, to realize their dependence on others, and to become better bridegrooms. Battius learns a little intellectual humility from Natty's practical knowledge of the wilderness. The center of Natty's teaching is that the legitimate use of power is for service rather than for self. This lesson arises out of the relationship between Natty and Hard Heart. Natty and the faithful Pawnee chief adopt each other when it appears the Sioux will kill Hard Heart. Natty later asserts that he became Hard Heart's father only to serve him, just as he becomes the figurative father of the more civilized fugitives in order to serve them. Once their relationship is established, it endures. Natty lives the last year of his life as a respected elder of the Pawnee and dies honored in their village. Having learned their lesson on the humble use of power in God's wilderness, Paul and Duncan carry their wisdom back to the high councils of the republic, where they become respected family men, property owners, and legislators. Like the Effinghams at Otsego Lake, the Hovers and the Middletons—the latter descending from the Heywards of *The Last of the Mohicans*—infuse the wisdom of the wilderness into the social order of America.

Cooper believed he had ended his Leatherstocking Tales when he completed *The Prairie*. Probably for this reason, he brought together his themes and characters and clarified the importance of Natty Bumppo to American civilization. Most critics have agreed that Cooper was drawn toward two ideals, the ability to exist in the wilderness and the ideal of a "natural aristocracy" of social and political order. It may be, however, that the first three of the Leatherstocking Tales are intended in part to create a history of America in which the wisdom of the wilderness is transferred to the social and political structure of the republic. Natty distrusts written tradition because "mankind twist and turn the rules of the Lord to suit their own wickedness when their devilish cunning has had too much time to trifle with his commands." Natty's experience provides a fresh revelation that renews the best of the Christian tradition and calls people back to basic Christian principles. That revelation consists essentially of a humble recognition of human limitations, justifying Cooper's vision of a republic where rulers are chosen for wisdom and faithfulness, where the tradition is not rigidly controlled by a hereditary elite but is constantly renewed by the unfettered ascendancy of the good and wise.

Throughout his career, Cooper worked within a general understanding of human history as a disordered phase of existence between two orders and a particular vision of the contemporary United States as a disordered phase between the old aristocratic order and the new order to be dominated by the American gentleman. In the first three of the Leatherstocking Tales, Cooper reveals a desire to naturalize the aristocratic tradition through exposure to the wilderness and its prophet, the man who reads God's word in the landscape. The result of this process would be a mature natural order that, though far from divine perfection, would promise as much happiness as is possible for fallen humankind. In his later novels, Cooper gives increasing attention to the ways in which American society failed to understand and to actualize this purified tradition. He looks back often, especially in *The Deerslayer*, to the purity and goodness of those basic values. Although they are rarely read today, novels such as *Satanstoe* and *The Oak Openings* among his later works are well worth reading, as is *The Bravo* from among his problem novels. In all these works, Cooper continues to express his faith in the possibility of a high American civilization.

Terry Heller

OTHER MAJOR WORKS

NONFICTION: *Notions of the Americans*, 1828; *A Letter to His Countrymen*, 1834; *Sketches of Switzerland*, 1836; *Gleanings in Europe: England*, 1837; *Gleanings in Europe: France*, 1837; *The American Democrat*, 1838; *Chronicles of Cooperstown*, 1838; *Gleanings in Europe: Italy*, 1838; *The History of the Navy of the United States of America*, 1839 (2 volumes); *Ned Meyers: Or, A Life Before the Mast*, 1843; *Lives of Distinguished American Naval Officers*, 1845; *New York*, 1864 (wr. 1851; unfinished; reprinted as *New York: Being an Introduction to an Unpublished Manuscript, by the Author, Entitled "The Towns of Manhattan,"* 1930); *The Letters and Journals of James Fenimore Cooper*, 1960-1968 (6 volumes; J. F. Beard, editor).

BIBLIOGRAPHY

Barker, Martin, and Roger Sabin. *The Lasting of the Mohicans: History of an American Myth*. Jackson: University Press of Mississippi, 1995. Discusses how Cooper's novel has acquired mythic status through numerous adaptations to film and television. Argues that each adaptation provides a new interpretation of the idea of the American frontier.

Clark, Robert, ed. *James Fenimore Cooper: New Critical Essays*. Totowa, N.J.: Barnes & Noble Books, 1985. Eight essays cover different aspects of Cooper's fiction, with most contributors focusing on specific novels. Includes detailed index.

Darnell, Donald. *James Fenimore Cooper: Novelist of Manners.* Newark: University of Delaware Press, 1993. Explores the themes of manners and customs in fifteen of Cooper's novels. Includes bibliographical references and index.

Fields, W., ed. *James Fenimore Cooper: A Collection of Critical Essays.* Boston: G. K. Hall, 1979. Presents both nineteenth century reviews of Cooper's novels and essays by modern critics. Valuable as a beginning point for students of Cooper's work.

Franklin, Wayne. *James Fenimore Cooper: The Early Years.* New Haven, Conn.: Yale University Press, 2007. Well-written, informative work—the first part of a planned two-volume biography—covers Cooper's life from birth until his move to Europe in 1826. Describes his personal life as well as the events surrounding the writing and publishing of *The Last of the Mohicans.*

_____. *The New World of James Fenimore Cooper.* Chicago: University of Chicago Press, 1982. Examines Cooper's attitude toward the frontier through a close reading of five of his novels—*The Pioneers, The Wept of Wish-Ton-Wish, Wyandotté, The Crater,* and *The Last of the Mohicans.* Maintains that for Cooper the wilderness begins as a place of hope and promise but ends as the source of tragedy.

Long, Robert Emmet. *James Fenimore Cooper.* New York: Continuum, 1990. General study of Cooper and his fiction touches on all the major works. Bibliography lists the most important studies of Cooper up to the 1990's.

McWilliams, John P. *"The Last of the Mohicans": Civil Savagery and Savage Civility.* New York: Twayne, 1995. Provides a general introduction to Cooper's most widely read novel as well as a particular approach to it. Divided into two sections: The first explores the literary and historical context of *The Last of the Mohicans,* and the second is devoted to analysis of the style of the novel as well as what Cooper was attempting to say about race, gender, history, and imperialism.

Peck, H. Daniel, ed. *New Essays on "The Last of the Mohicans."* New York: Cambridge University Press, 1992. Collection of essays begins with an introduction that provides information about the composition, publication, and contemporary reception of the novel as well as the evolution of critical opinion concerning it. Each of the five original essays that follow places the novel in a particular context, thus providing readers with an array of interesting perspectives from which to view Cooper's masterpiece.

Person, Leland S., ed. *A Historical Guide to James Fenimore Cooper.* New York: Oxford University Press, 2007. Collection of essays includes a brief biography by Wayne Franklin and a survey of Cooper scholarship and criticism. Among the works examined are the multivolume *Gleanings in Europe,* the four novels about the Revolutionary War, and the five Leatherstocking novels. Also features an illustrated chronology of both Cooper's life and important nineteenth century historical events.

Ringe, Donald A. *James Fenimore Cooper.* Updated ed. New York: Twayne, 1988. Provides a succinct and helpful introduction to Cooper's life and work. Includes complete chronology and index.

Tawil, Ezra F. *The Making of Racial Sentiment: Slavery and the Birth of the Frontier Romance*. New York: Cambridge University Press, 2006. Examines the frontier romance, a popular genre of nineteenth century American fiction, focusing on how novels by Cooper and Harriet Beecher Stowe helped to redefine the concept of race. Two chapters concentrate on Cooper's early fiction and *The Wept of Wish-Ton-Wish*.

LOUISE ERDRICH

Born: Little Falls, Minnesota; June 7, 1954
Also known as: Karen Louise Erdrich

OTHER LITERARY FORMS

In addition to long fiction, Louise Erdrich (UR-drihk) has published poetry, books for children, nonfiction, and short fiction. Many chapters in her novels were originally published as short stories in various periodicals. Her early books of poetry *Jacklight* (1984) and *Baptism of Desire* (1989) present vivid North Dakota vignettes as well as personal reflections on Erdrich's relationships with her husband and children. Several of the poems in these volumes, together with nineteen new ones, are included in *Original Fire: Selected and New Poems* (2003). Erdrich's memoir of her daughter's birth, *The Blue Jay's Dance: A Birth Year*, was published in 1995, and her travel memoir *Books and Islands in Ojibwe Country* appeared in 2003.

ACHIEVEMENTS

A poet and poetic novelist, Louise Erdrich learned to draw on her Ojibwa (also known as Chippewa) and German-immigrant heritage to create a wide-ranging chronicle of Native American and white experience in twentieth century North Dakota and Minnesota. She received fellowships from the MacDowell Colony in 1980 and from Dartmouth College and Yaddo Colony in 1981. Since she began to publish her fiction and poetry in the early 1980's, her works have garnered high critical praise, and her novels have been best sellers as well.

Erdrich was awarded a National Endowment for the Arts Fellowship in 1982, the

Pushcart Prize in 1983, and a Guggenheim Fellowship in 1985-1986. Her first novel, *Love Medicine*, won the National Book Critics Circle Award in 1984, and three stories that became chapters in that book were also honored: "The World's Greatest Fishermen" won the 1982 Nelson Algren Fiction Award, "Scales" appeared in *The Best American Short Stories 1983*, and "Saint Marie" was chosen for *Prize Stories 1985: The O. Henry Awards* (1985). Two of the stories included in the novel *Tracks* also appeared in honorary anthologies: "Fleur" in *Prize Stories 1987: The O. Henry Awards* and "Snares" in *The Best American Short Stories 1988*. Erdrich's 2001 novel *The Last Report on the Miracles at Little No Horse* was a finalist for the National Book Award for fiction, and her children's book *The Game of Silence* (2005) received the Scott O'Dell Award for Historical Fiction.

Erdrich's works often focus on the struggles of Native Americans for personal, familial, and cultural survival. Her treatment of white characters and of characters of mixed Native American and white blood, however, reveals an empathetic understanding of the ways in which people of all races long for closer connection with one another and the land.

BIOGRAPHY

Karen Louise Erdrich, whose grandfather was tribal chair of the Turtle Mountain Band of the Ojibwa Nation, grew up in Wahpeton, a small town in southeastern North Dakota. Both of her parents—Ralph Erdrich, the son of a German immigrant, and Rita Gourneau Erdrich, who is three-quarters Ojibwa—taught at the Wahpeton Indian Boarding School. Erdrich's mixed religious and cultural background provided a rich foundation for her later poetry and fiction.

Erdrich earned two degrees in creative writing, a B.A. from Dartmouth College in 1976 and an M.A. from Johns Hopkins University in 1979. In 1981, she married Michael Dorris, a professor of anthropology and head of the Native American Studies Program at Dartmouth. Erdrich and Dorris devoted much of their married life to ambitious family, literary, and humanitarian goals. Dorris, who was three-eighths Modoc Indian, had previously adopted three Lakota Sioux children; together Erdrich and Dorris had three daughters. Professionally, they collaborated on virtually all the works that either one published—whether fiction, poetry, or nonfiction. Erdrich has thus acknowledged Dorris's important contribution to her earlier fiction; similarly, she collaborated with him on his first novel, *A Yellow Raft in Blue Water* (1987), and on his study of fetal alcohol syndrome (FAS), *The Broken Cord* (1989). Erdrich and Dorris donated money and campaigned for legislation to combat FAS, which afflicts the lives of many Native American children born to alcoholic mothers.

Unfortunately, their private lives became difficult. All of their adopted children were permanently affected by the alcoholism of their mothers and led troubled lives as adults. One son attempted to extort money from Dorris and Erdrich, and their daughter became estranged from them. Their oldest adopted child, Abel (renamed Adam in *The Broken Cord*), was struck by a car and killed in 1991, an event that deeply affected the marriage.

Erdrich and Dorris eventually moved from New Hampshire to Minneapolis and later separated after fifteen years of marriage. During subsequent divorce proceedings, Dorris, who had been profoundly depressed since the second year of their marriage, attempted suicide twice. He succeeded on April 11, 1997.

In 2000, Erdrich established Birchbark Books, a small independent bookstore in Minneapolis; she gave birth to another daughter the following year. She continues to incorporate her study of the Ojibwa language and culture into her writing.

ANALYSIS

In a 1985 essay "Where I Ought to Be: A Writer's Sense of Place," Louise Erdrich states that the essence of her writing emerges from her attachment to her North Dakota locale. The ways in which Erdrich has brought this region to literary life have been favorably compared by critics to the methods and style of William Faulkner, who created the mythical Yoknapatawpha County out of his rich sense of rural Mississippi. Like Faulkner, Erdrich has created a gallery of diverse characters spanning several generations, using multiple points of view and shifting time frames. Erdrich's fiction further resembles Faulkner's in that the experiences of her characters encompass a broad spectrum, ranging "from the mundane to the miraculous," as one critic has put it.

Erdrich's stories generally begin with realistic bases of ordinary people, settings, and actions. As the tales develop, however, these people become involved in events and perceptions that strike the reader as quite extraordinary—as exaggerated or heightened in ways that may seem deluded or mystical, grotesque or magical, comic or tragic, or some strange mixture of these. Thus, one critic has described Erdrich as "a sorceress with language" whose lyrical style intensifies some of the most memorable scenes in contemporary American fiction.

LOVE MEDICINE

Erdrich's first novel, *Love Medicine*, spans the years 1934-1984 in presenting members of five Ojibwa and mixed-blood families, all struggling in different ways to attain a sense of belonging through love, religion, home, and family. The novel includes fourteen interwoven stories; though the title refers specifically to traditional Ojibwa magic in one story, in a broader sense "love medicine" refers to the different kinds of spiritual power that enable Erdrich's Native American and mixed-blood characters to transcend—however momentarily—the grim circumstances of their lives. Trapped on their shrinking reservation by racism and poverty, plagued by alcoholism, disintegrating families, and violence, some of Erdrich's characters nevertheless discover a form of "love medicine" that helps to sustain them.

The opening story, "The World's Greatest Fishermen," begins with an episode of "love medicine" corrupted and thwarted. Though June Kashpaw was once a woman of striking beauty and feisty spirit, by 1981 she has sunk to the level of picking up men in an oil boomtown. Unfortunately, June fails in her last attempts to attain two goals that other characters will also seek throughout the novel: love and home. Although she appears only briefly in this and one other story, June Kashpaw is a central character in the novel, for she embodies the potential power of spirit and love in ways that impress and haunt the other characters.

The second part of "The World's Greatest Fishermen" introduces many of the other major characters of *Love Medicine*, as June's relatives gather several months after her death. On one hand, several characters seem sympathetic because of their closeness to June and their kind treatment of one another. Albertine Johnson, who narrates the story and remembers her Aunt June lovingly, has gone through a wild phase of her own and is now a nursing student. Eli Kashpaw, Albertine's granduncle, who was largely responsible for rearing June, is a tough and sharp-minded old man who has maintained a time-honored Ojibwa way of life as a hunter and fisherman. Lipsha Morrissey, who, though he seems not to know it, is June's illegitimate son, is a sensitive, self-educated young man who acts warmly toward Albertine. In contrast to these characters are others who are flawed or unsympathetic when seen through the eyes of Albertine, who would like to feel that her family is pulling together after June's death. These less sympathetic characters include Zelda and Aurelia (Albertine's gossipy mother and aunt), Nector Kashpaw (Albertine's senile grandfather), and Gordon Kashpaw (the husband whom June left, a hapless drunk). Worst of all is June's legitimate son King, a volatile bully. King's horrifying acts of violence—abusing his wife Lynette, battering his new car, and smashing the pies prepared for the family dinner—leave Albertine in dismay with a family in shambles.

Love Medicine then shifts back in time from 1981, and its thirteen remaining stories proceed in chronological order from 1934 to 1984. "Saint Marie" concerns a mixed-blood girl, Marie Lazarre, who in 1934 enters Sacred Heart Convent and embarks on a violent love-hate relationship with Sister Leopolda. In "Wild Geese," also set in 1934, Nector Kashpaw is infatuated with Lulu Nanapush, but his affections swerve unexpectedly when he encounters Marie Lazarre on the road outside her convent. By 1948, the time of "The Beads," Marie has married Nector, had three children (Aurelia, Zelda, and Gordie), and agreed to rear her niece June. Nector, however, is drinking and philandering, and June, after almost committing suicide in a children's hanging game, leaves to be brought up by Eli in the woods. "Lulu's Boys," set in 1957, reveals that the amorous Lulu Lamartine (née Nanapush) had married Henry Lamartine but bore eight sons by different fathers. Meanwhile, in "The Plunge of the Brave," also set in 1957, Nector recalls the development of his five-year affair with Lulu and tries to leave his wife Marie for her, but the result is that he accidentally burns Lulu's house to the ground.

The offspring of these Kashpaws and Lamartines also have their problems in later *Love Medicine* stories. In "A Bridge," set in 1973, Albertine runs away from home and becomes the lover of Henry Lamartine, Jr., one of Lulu's sons, a troubled Vietnam War veteran. "The Red Convertible," set in 1974, also involves Henry, Jr., as Lyman Lamartine tries unsuccessfully to bring his brother out of the dark personality changes that his time in Vietnam has wrought in him. On a lighter note, "Scales," set in 1980, is a hilarious account of the romance between Dot Adare, an obese clerk at a truck weighing station, and Gerry Nanapush, one of Lulu's sons who is a most unusual convict: enormously fat, amazingly expert at escaping from jail, but totally inept at avoiding capture. "Crown of Thorns," which overlaps with the time of "The World's Greatest Fishermen" in 1981, traces the harrowing and bizarre decline of Gordie Kashpaw into alcoholism after June's death.

Though in these earlier *Love Medicine* stories the positive powers of love and spirit are more often frustrated than fulfilled, in the last three stories several characters achieve breakthroughs that bring members of the different families together in moving and hopeful ways. In "Love Medicine," set in 1982, Lipsha Morrissey reaches out lovingly to his grandmother Marie and to the ghosts of Nector and June. In "The Good Tears," set in 1983, Lulu undergoes a serious eye operation and is cared for by Marie, who forgives her for being Nector's longtime extramarital lover. Finally, in "Crossing the Water," set in 1984, Lipsha helps his father, Gerry Nanapush, escape to Canada and comes to appreciate the rich heritage of love, spirit, and wiliness that he has inherited from his diverse patchwork of Ojibwa relatives—especially from his grandmother Lulu, his great-aunt Marie, and his parents, June and Gerry.

THE BEET QUEEN

In *The Beet Queen*, her second novel, Erdrich shifts her main focus from the American Indian to the European-immigrant side of her background, and she creates in impressive detail the mythical town of Argus (modeled on Wahpeton, where she was reared, but located closer to the Ojibwa reservation) in the years 1932-1972. The opening scene of *The Beet Queen*, "The Branch," dramatizes two contrasting approaches to life that many characters will enact throughout the novel. On a cold spring day in 1932, two orphans, Mary and Karl Adare, arrive by freight train in Argus. As they seek the way to the butcher shop owned by their Aunt Fritzie and Uncle Pete Kozka, Mary "trudge[s] solidly forward" while Karl stops to embrace a tree that already has its spring blossoms. When they are attacked by a dog, Mary runs ahead, continuing her search for the butcher shop, while Karl runs back to hop the train once again. As the archetypal plodder of the novel, Mary continues to "trudge solidly forward" throughout; she is careful, determined, and self-reliant in pursuit of her goals. On the other hand, Karl is the principal dreamer—impressionable, prone to escapist impulses, and dependent on others to catch him when he falls.

The Adare family history shows how Karl is following a pattern set by his mother, Adelaide, while Mary grows in reaction against this pattern. Like Karl, Adelaide is physically beautiful but self-indulgent and impulsive. Driven to desperation by her hard luck in the early years of the Great Depression, Adelaide startles a fairground crowd by abandoning her three children (Mary, Karl, and an unnamed newborn son) to fly away with the Great Omar, an airplane stunt pilot.

In Argus, Mary tangles with yet another beautiful, self-centered dreamer: her cousin Sita Kozka, who resents the attention that her parents, Pete and Fritzie, and her best friend, the mixed-blood Celestine James, pay to Mary. Mary prevails, however, and carves a solid niche for herself among Pete, Fritzie, and Celestine, who, like Mary, believe in a strong work ethic and lack Sita's pretentious airs.

A number of episodes gratify the reader with triumphs for Mary and comeuppances for the less sympathetic characters Karl, Adelaide, and Sita. Mary becomes famous for a miracle at her school (she falls and cracks the ice in the image of Jesus), gains Celestine as a close friend, and in time becomes manager of the Kozka butcher shop. By contrast, Karl becomes a drifter who finds only sordid momentary pleasure in his numerous affairs. Meanwhile, Adelaide marries Omar and settles in Florida, but she becomes moody and subject to violent rages. Similarly, Sita fails in her vainglorious attempts to become a model and to establish a fashionable French restaurant; she escapes her first marriage through divorce and becomes insane and suicidal during her second.

Even as Erdrich charts the strange and sometimes grotesque downfalls of her flighty characters, however, she develops her more sympathetic ones in ways that suggest that the opposite approach to life does not guarantee happiness either. Mary is unsuccessful in her attempt to attract Russell Kashpaw (the half brother of Celestine), and she develops into an exotically dressed eccentric who is obsessed with predicting the future and controlling others. Like Mary, Celestine James and Wallace Pfef are hardworking and successful in business, but their loneliness drives each of them to an ill-advised affair with Karl, and he causes each of them considerable grief. In addition, the union of Celestine and Karl results in the birth of Dot Adare (who grows up to be the ill-tempered lover of Gerry Nanapush in the *Love Medicine* story "Scales"); since Celestine, Mary, and Wallace all spoil the child, Dot turns out, in Wallace's words, to have "all of her family's worst qualities." As a teenager, Dot herself comes to grief when she is mortified to learn that the well-meaning Wallace has rigged the election for queen of the Argus Beet Festival so that she, an unpopular and ludicrously unlikely candidate, will win.

In addition to the defeats and disappointments that all the characters bear, Erdrich dramatizes the joy that they derive from life. The compensations of family and friendship—ephemeral and vulnerable as these may be—prove to be significant for all the characters at various times in the story, particularly at the end. The irrepressible vitality of these people, troublesome as they often are to one another, keeps the reader involved and entertained throughout the novel.

TRACKS

Erdrich's third novel, *Tracks*, is concentrated, intense, and mystical. It is shorter than the previous novels, covering a time span of only twelve years and alternating between only two first-person narrators. This compression serves the story well, for the human stakes are high. At first, and periodically throughout the novel, the Ojibwa characters fear for their very survival, as smallpox, tuberculosis, severe winters, starvation, and feuds with mixed-blood families bring them close to extinction. Later in the novel, government taxes and political chicanery threaten the Ojibwas' ownership of family and tribal land. In response, Erdrich's Ojibwa characters use all the powers at their command—including the traditional mystical powers of the old ways—to try to survive and maintain their control over the land.

Nanapush, one of the novel's two narrators, is an old Ojibwa whom Erdrich names for the trickster rabbit in tribal mythology who repeatedly delivers the people from threatening monsters. In *Tracks*, Erdrich's Nanapush often does credit to his mythological model, Nanabozho, by wielding the trickster rabbit's powers of deliverance, wiliness, and humor. He saves Fleur Pillager, a seventeen-year-old girl who is the last but one of the Pillager clan, from starvation. Later he delivers young Eli Kashpaw from the sufferings of love by advising him how to win Fleur's heart. Also, Nanapush is instrumental in saving the extended family that forms around Fleur, Eli, and himself. This family grows to five when Fleur gives birth to a daughter, Lulu, and Eli's mother, Margaret Kashpaw, becomes Nanapush's bedmate. As these five come close to starvation, Nanapush sends Eli out to hunt an elk; in one of the most extraordinary passages of the novel, Nanapush summons a power vision of Eli hunting that the old man imagines is guiding Eli to the kill. Nanapush also demonstrates the humor associated with his mythological model in his wry tone as a narrator, his sharp wit in conversation, and the tricks that he plays on his family's mixed-blood antagonists, the Morrisseys and the Lazarres.

Foremost among these antagonists is the novel's other narrator, Pauline Puyat. A "skinny big-nosed girl with staring eyes," Pauline circulates in Argus from the Kozkas' butcher shop to the Sacred Heart Convent, and on the reservation from the Nanapush-Pillager-Kashpaw group to the Morrissey and Lazarre clans. At first attracted to Fleur by the beauty and sexual power that she herself lacks, Pauline later takes an envious revenge by concocting a love potion that seems to drive Fleur's husband, Eli, and Sophie Morrissey to become lovers. Ironically, though one side of her believes in a Catholic denial of her body, Pauline later gives birth out of wedlock to a girl named Marie, and at the end of her narrative Pauline enters the convent to become Sister Leopolda—the cruel nun who later torments her own daughter, Marie Lazarre, in *Love Medicine*.

Though Erdrich clearly feels passionately about the sufferings visited on her Ojibwa characters in *Tracks*, she treats this politically charged material with her usual disciplined restraint. Her dispassionate, deadpan use of first-person narrators (never broken by authorial commentary) matches the understated, stoic attitude that Nanapush adopts toward the numerous waves of hardship and betrayal that the Ojibwas must endure.

If in some ways *Tracks* seems to conclude with a feeling of fragmentation and defeat, in other ways it strikes positive notes of solidarity and survival, especially when considered in relation to *Love Medicine* and *The Beet Queen*. Fleur disappears, leaving her husband and daughter, but Nanapush uses his wiliness to become tribal chairman and then to retrieve Lulu from a distant boarding school. At the end, the reader is reminded that Nanapush has addressed his entire narrative to Lulu: The old man hopes that his story will convince Lulu to embrace the memory of Fleur, "the one you will not call mother." Further, the reader familiar with *Love Medicine* will realize how this young girl, who becomes Lulu Lamartine, carries on the supernaturally powerful sexuality of her mother Fleur and the wily talent for survival of Nanapush, the old man who gave her his name and reared her.

THE BINGO PALACE

The Bingo Palace takes place roughly ten years after the end of *Love Medicine* and follows several characters introduced in Erdrich's first three novels. Primary among these is June Kashpaw's luckless son Lipsha Morrissey, back on the reservation after a series of failed jobs. His uncle, shrewd businessman Lyman Lamartine, offers Lipsha a job at his bingo parlor as a part-time bartender and night watchman. After his dead mother June appears with bingo tickets that are destined to change his luck significantly, gentle Lipsha not only wins a prize van but also pockets more of Lyman's money by continuing to win. A further complication in their relationship is Shawnee Ray Toose (Miss Little Shell), champion jingle-dress dancer, with whom Lipsha is promptly smitten, even though she has had a son by Lyman.

This loosely structured novel recounts Lipsha's sweet but faltering courtship of Shawnee, who rebuffs both of her suitors; Lyman's schemes to erect a splendid bingo palace on the last bit of Pillager land; and a joint vision quest that is serious for Lyman but comic for Lipsha, whose vision animal turns out to be a skunk that really sprays him. Lipsha has another abortive reunion with his father, escaped convict Gerry Nanapush, and is left stranded in a stolen car in a blizzard until his great-grandmother Fleur Pillager steps in. Erdrich employs techniques of Magical Realism as the dead speak and the lake monster Misshepeshu continues to strike terror into the hearts of all except the dauntless Fleur.

THE ANTELOPE WIFE

Erdrich's seventh novel, *The Antelope Wife*, shifts to a new set of characters and a new locale, Minnesota. A young cavalry private, Scranton Roy, is sent to quell an American Indian uprising but mistakenly attacks a neutral Ojibwa village. Realizing his error, he manages to rescue a baby whom he then nurses with his own miraculous milk and raises to adulthood. In this way the white Roy family begins a relationship that spans five generations with two Ojibwa families.

The infant's grieving mother marries a man named Showano and bears twin girls. Her twin granddaughters Zosie and Mary Showano figure prominently as the wife and the lover of Scranton Roy's grandson and as the two mothers of Rozina Roy Whiteheart Beads, herself the mother of twin daughters. Rozina wants to leave her husband Richard for a Minneapolis baker, Frank Showano. Although this novel was completed just before

Michael Dorris's death, it is uncomfortably prescient in its account of the unhappy marriage between Rozina and her suicidal husband.

This is a novel of repeated family patterns (lost mothers, lost daughters), emphasized by the linking imagery of the archetypal beaders that introduce each section. In this subtle and seamless blending of Ojibwa myth with contemporary life, Magical Realism becomes even more pronounced. Frank Showano's brother Klaus is nearly destroyed by his infatuation with a seductive, shape-shifting antelope woman. The windigo, a cannibal hunger spirit, is a very real presence and threat, and some chapters are narrated by a talking dog named Almost Soup. *The Antelope Wife* affirms the vitality of Ojibwa culture on and off the reservation.

THE LAST REPORT ON THE MIRACLES AT LITTLE NO HORSE

Erdrich's darkly comic eighth novel, *The Last Report on the Miracles at Little No Horse*, revisits several of the characters from earlier books, particularly Father Damien Modeste, the mild old priest at Little No Horse reservation in North Dakota. Erratically spanning the years from 1910 to 1996, this book offers an account of his unusual history, including the revelation that he is not only a woman, Agnes DeWitt, but a former nun and farm wife to whom a piano, even a simple Chopin nocturne, presents an occasion of sin. Swept in by the flooding Red River, he arrives on the reservation to assume the identity of a recently drowned priest and begin a life of service. As Father Damien, he enjoys a deepening friendship with the Ojibwa elders Kashpaw and Nanapush as well as with their extended families. He also endures the unwelcome visit of a foul black dog that thrusts its paw into his soup, bargains for his soul, and presents him with an irresistible temptation.

A second story line involves an initial inquiry into purported miracles that were worked by the late Sister Leopolda (formerly Pauline Puyat), as the first step toward her possible canonization. Enigmatic Leopolda, skeletal and bone-white, appears only briefly as a figure from the past, although her memory looms large in the present. Prior to entering the novitiate, Pauline had tirelessly attended the sick and dying during the devastating influenza epidemic of 1918. On the reservation, people still recall stories of her stigmata, the imprints of Christ's wounds on her body, and a mysterious paralysis that caused her to fold like a jackknife. As the nun's only surviving contemporary, Father Damien supposedly knows the real truth about her and has been writing desperate, unanswered letters to the Vatican ever since his arrival.

At last the Vatican sends Father Jude Miller to investigate. Eager to discover a new saint, Father Jude embarks on a series of interviews with various residents who offer guarded recollections of Sister Leopolda. Father Damien, on the other hand, has developed serious misgivings about the nun's sanctity and harbors no illusions about his own. His hard-earned wisdom leads him to a question that Erdrich has implied before: He fears that all his good intentions have been futile, that the government schools and forced conversion of the Ojibwas to Christianity have been horrible mistakes, offering the people little more than a destructive, alcohol-soaked alternative to their own culture.

Erdrich's books are seldom predictable, but life at Little No Horse offers more surprises than most with its splendid procession of mystery, mysticism, gravity, and humor. The hilarious account of Nanapush's death at the mercy of a runaway moose (and his subsequent resurrection) is one of the highlights of the novel.

THE PLAGUE OF DOVES

Erdrich returns to the familiar plains of North Dakota for *The Plague of Doves*, but, as in *The Antelope Wife*, with completely new characters whose lives are intertwined. This time her setting is near Argus, in the fictional town of Pluto, whose sparse population consists of Germans, Norwegians, and Ojibwas from the neighboring reservation. The present is filled with dizzying relationships, interspersed with tales from the past that reveal the origins and history of the community.

The novel opens in 1911, immediately after the horrific slaughter of a whole family, save for an infant, then shifts back fifteen years to the time when a sudden plague occurred. Invading doves blackened the skies like locusts and settled over the land, devouring everything. In desperation, people attempted to drive them away, while the local Catholic priest organized a procession of the mixed-blood population to pray for deliverance. During this event a young altar boy, Seraph Milk, took advantage of the confusion to run off with his future wife, to become the progenitor of the Milk-Harp family around which the story centers.

In this novel, Erdrich employs three main narrators as well as several minor ones. The first is Evelina (Evey) Harp, the granddaughter of Seraph Milk, who is now called Mooshum (Grandfather). Evey reveals her childhood crushes on a mischievous classmate, Corwin Peace, and on her sixth-grade teacher, whom the children call Sister Godzilla. Later, Evey becomes a psychiatric aide in the state mental hospital, eventually signing herself in as a patient after a bad experience with some LSD that Corwin has given her. (In an Erdrich novel, at least one character is always slightly mad.) Other narrators include a judge whose grandfather, as a member of an ill-fated surveying party, had a hand in the founding of Pluto, and a naïve teenager who marries Corwin's charismatic uncle, an evangelist who founds a dangerous cult.

Mooshum is another of Erdrich's delightfully roguish old men, as is his crippled brother Shamengwa, who plays a magical violin in spite of his damaged arm. The two elders relish teasing Mooshum's daughter by sneaking forbidden whiskey past her, which they manage whenever an unpopular priest, Father Cassidy, comes calling in another attempt to save their souls. Because Shamengwa long ago left the Catholic Church to return to traditional beliefs, any hope of his conversion is doomed, but Mooshum enjoys sparring with the frustrated priest.

One of the tales that Mooshum relates to Evey is a shameful secret widely known in the community yet seldom repeated—the story of an Ojibwa youth who was a distant relative.

Dying from tuberculosis, the boy's pious mother nailed wooden crosses to her son's boot soles to protect him from the disease, so that his footprints revealed crosses, a holy track, which then became his nickname. Holy Track, whom Erdrich modeled on a historical figure of the same name, was one of four innocent Ojibwas hanged by an angry mob of Pluto's white citizens, believing that the men were responsible for murdering the baby's family.

Like most of Erdrich's work, this is a story of connections, mixing regional and human history with fiction and elements of the supernatural. Descendants of the lynch mob and of their victims now live side by side in Pluto. Erdrich exposes the underlying wounds between Ojibwas and whites that still remain, but silence helps to preserve the amenities of everyday living, and even reconciliation, in a town where some secrets are not spoken yet are shared by all.

If Louise Erdrich had been born two hundred years earlier, she might have become a traditional Ojibwa storyteller, whose tales would have reminded her listeners of their unchanging relationship to the land and to the mythic and legendary characters who inhabited it. Several generations removed from such a stable and undamaged culture, Erdrich nevertheless has been able to create a richly neotribal view of people and place. Her novels testify to the profound interrelatedness of her characters—Native American and white, contemporaries and ancestors—both with one another and with their midwestern homeland.

Terry L. Andrews
Updated by Joanne McCarthy

OTHER MAJOR WORKS

SHORT FICTION: "The Red Convertible," 1981; "Scales," 1982; "American Horse," 1983; "Destiny," 1985; "Saint Marie," 1985; "Fleur," 1987; "Snares," 1987; "Matchimanito," 1988; *The Red Convertible: Selected and New Stories, 1978-2008*, 2009.

POETRY: *Jacklight*, 1984; *Baptism of Desire*, 1989; *Original Fire: Selected and New Poems*, 2003.

NONFICTION: *The Blue Jay's Dance: A Birth Year*, 1995; *Books and Islands in Ojibwe Country*, 2003.

CHILDREN'S LITERATURE: *Grandmother's Pigeon*, 1996 (illustrated by Jim LaMarche); *The Birchbark House*, 1999; *The Range Eternal*, 2002; *The Game of Silence*, 2005.

EDITED TEXT: *The Best American Short Stories 1993*, 1993.

BIBLIOGRAPHY

Beidler, Peter G., and Gay Barton. *A Reader's Guide to the Novels of Louise Erdrich*. Columbia: University of Missouri Press, 1999. Informative handbook for students of Erdrich's fiction covers geography, chronology, and character relationships in her novels through *The Antelope Wife*.

Brehm, Victoria. "The Metamorphoses of an Ojibwa *Manido*." *American Literature* 68 (December, 1996): 677-706. Traces the evolution of the legendary Ojibwa water monster Micipijiu (Misshepeshu), with a fascinating section on the symbolism and significance of the monster in Erdrich's *Love Medicine, Tracks,* and *The Bingo Palace.*

Chavkin, Allan, ed. *The Chippewa Landscape of Louise Erdrich.* Tuscaloosa: University of Alabama Press, 1998. Collection of original essays focuses on Erdrich's writings that are rooted in the Ojibwa experience. Premier scholars of Native American literature investigate narrative structure, signs of ethnicity, the notions of luck and chance in Erdrich's narrative cosmology, and her use of comedy in exploring American Indians' tragic past.

Chavkin, Allan, and Nancy Feyl Chavkin, eds. *Conversations with Louise Erdrich and Michael Dorris.* Jackson: University Press of Mississippi, 1994. Collection contains several articles and twenty-five interviews with the couple, including an interview conducted by Abenaki author and storyteller Joseph Bruchac.

Ferguson, Suzanne. "The Short Stories of Louise Erdrich's Novels." *Studies in Short Fiction* 33 (1996): 541-555. Provides an excellent discussion of four short stories—"Saint Marie," "Scales," "Fleur," and "Snares"—and how Erdrich modified them when they became chapters in her novels. Argues that the short stories should be read differently when they stand on their own compared with when they are presented as chapters in novels.

Smith, Jeanne Rosier. *Writing Tricksters: Mythic Gambols in American Ethnic Literature.* Berkeley: University of California Press, 1997. Presents a thorough examination of ethnic trickster figures as they appear in the works of Erdrich, Maxine Hong Kingston, and Toni Morrison. Chapter 3 explores the trickster characteristics of Old Nanapush, Gerry Nanapush, Lipsha Morrissey, Fleur Pillager, and others found in Erdrich's novels.

Stookey, Lorena Laura. *Louise Erdrich: A Critical Companion.* Westport, Conn.: Greenwood Press, 1999. Study of Erdrich's works presents biographical information, an examination of Erdrich's place in literary tradition, and analysis of each novel through *The Antelope Wife.* Includes bibliographical references and index.

Treuer, David. *Native American Fiction: A User's Manual.* St. Paul, Minn.: Graywolf Press, 2006. An Ojibwa author offers an intriguing perspective on the work of several contemporaries, including Erdrich. The chapter "Smartberries" praises Erdrich's modern literary techniques in *Love Medicine,* but in other chapters Treuer questions what in fact constitutes "authentic" Native American writing.

Wong, Hertha D. Sweet. *Louise Erdrich's "Love Medicine": A Casebook.* New York: Oxford University Press, 2000. Presents documents relating to the historical importance of *Love Medicine,* representative critical essays, and excerpts from several interviews with Erdrich and Michael Dorris.

HAMLIN GARLAND

Born: West Salem, Wisconsin; September 14, 1860
Died: Hollywood, California; March 4, 1940
Also known as: Hannibal Hamlin Garland

PRINCIPAL LONG FICTION

Jason Edwards: An Average Man, 1892
A Little Norsk, 1892
A Member of the Third House, 1892
A Spoil of Office, 1892
Rose of Dutcher's Coolly, 1895
The Spirit of Sweetwater, 1898 (reissued as *Witch's Gold*, 1906)
Boy Life on the Prairie, 1899
The Eagle's Heart, 1900
Her Mountain Lover, 1901
The Captain of the Gray-Horse Troop, 1902
Hesper, 1903
The Light of the Star, 1904
The Tyranny of the Dark, 1905
The Long Trail, 1907
Money Magic, 1907 (reissued as *Mart Haney's Mate*, 1922)
The Moccasin Ranch, 1909
Cavanagh, Forest Ranger, 1910
Victor Ollnee's Discipline, 1911
The Forester's Daughter, 1914

OTHER LITERARY FORMS

Hamlin Garland published in nearly every literary form—short story, biography, auto-biography, essay, drama, and poetry. Several of his short stories, such as "Under the Lion's Paw," "A Soldier's Return," and "A Branch Road," were much anthologized. His autobiographical quartet, *A Son of the Middle Border* (1917), *A Daughter of the Middle Border* (1921), *Trail-Makers of the Middle Border* (1926), and *Back-Trailers from the Middle Border* (1928), is a valuable recounting of life during the latter part of the nineteenth century through the early twentieth century. Garland also wrote about psychic phenomena in such books as *Forty Years of Psychic Research: A Plain Narrative of Fact* (1936).

ACHIEVEMENTS

Hamlin Garland was a pioneer in moving American literature from Romanticism to realism. His early works of frontier life on the Middle Border (the midwestern prairie states

Hamlin Garland
(Library of Congress)

of Wisconsin, Iowa, Minnesota, and Nebraska, as well as the Dakotas) made his reputation, and even today he is best known for his strongly regional, unpretentious pictures of the brutalizing life on the farms and in the isolated communities of the monotonous prairie lands.

Even though his reception as a writer did not afford him the financial rewards he sought, Garland was an active participant in the literary scene in Chicago and New York. He traveled widely in the United States and made the obligatory trip to Europe. He counted among his friends and acquaintances such literary giants as William Dean Howells, Mark Twain, George Bernard Shaw, and Rudyard Kipling, and others such as Bliss Carmen, Kate Wiggins, George Washington Cable, and Frank Norris (whom he regarded as a promising young writer).

While Garland published stories in magazines such as *The Arena*, *Circle*, and *Century*, he augmented his income by lecturing, often at the University of Chicago. He was instrumental in organizing and perpetuating literary clubs and organizations such as the National Institute of Arts and Letters, the MacDowell Club, The Players, and the Cliff Dwellers Club. When his fiction-writing skills began to abate in his late middle age, Garland wrote plays, articles about psychic phenomena in magazines such as *Everybody's*, and his memoirs. The popular reception of his autobiographical quartet on the Middle Border region revived his confidence in his writing ability, and he won the Pulitzer Prize for the second of the quartet, *A Daughter of the Middle Border.*

Though Garland wrote several novels after his critically noteworthy Middle Border novel *Rose of Dutcher's Coolly*, they were mostly set in the Far West and dealt with cowboys, American Indians, and rangers; compared to his earlier work, they can be considered strictly commercial potboilers.

Primarily a gifted short-story writer, Garland had difficulty sustaining a narrative for the length of a novel. With the exception of *Rose of Dutcher's Coolly*, Garland is to be remembered more for what he accomplished as a writer of short stories and autobiography than for what he produced as a novelist. He was elected to the board of directors of the American Academy of Arts and Letters in 1918 and, in 1922, he won the Pulitzer Prize for biography and autobiography.

BIOGRAPHY

Hamlin Garland's early years were spent on an Iowa farm. As soon as he was big enough to walk behind a plow, he spent long hours helping to plow the acres of land on his father's farm. After twelve years of springs, summers, and early falls working at the ceaseless toil of farming, Garland came to realize that education was the way out of a life of farm drudgery. He attended and graduated from Cedar Valley Seminary. He next held a land claim in North Dakota for a year but mortgaged it to finance a trip to Boston, where he intended to enroll at Boston University. Once in Boston, he was unable to attend the university but continued his education by reading voraciously in the Boston Public Library. He also began to write at that time.

Garland's instincts for reform were ignited in Boston, where he joined the Anti-Poverty Society and, introduced to the work of Henry George, came to believe that the single tax theory was a solution to many contemporary social problems. He eventually returned to North Dakota and began to see some of his stories, sketches, and propagandistic novels published. By 1894, he had formulated in a series of essays his theory of realism, which he called "veritism."

Garland married Zulime Taft in 1899, and the couple had two daughters (in 1904 and 1907). He continued to write, but by 1898, he had begun to feel that he had exhausted "the field in which [he] found *Main-Travelled Roads* and *Rose of Dutcher's Coolly*." He believed that he had "lost perspective" on the life and characters of the Middle Border and had found new "creative strength" in the Colorado Hills, where he visited frequently.

By 1911, Garland believed that he had "done many things but nothing which now seems important." His various literary and cultural activities seemed to him to have been "time killers, diversions [adding] nothing to [his] reputation." At age fifty-two, he knew he had "but a slender and uncertain income." His home was mortgaged, his ranch unproductive, his health not particularly good, and he had "no confident expectation of increasing [his] fortune." Then, after rejections from six editors, Garland finally sold *Son of the Middle Border* to *Collier's* magazine. His reputation was firmly established by 1918 with his election to the board of directors of the American Academy of Arts and Letters and then later with winning the Pulitzer Prize. In 1930, he built a home in the Laughlin Park area of Los Angeles, probably to be near his two married daughters. He died in 1940 of a cerebral hemorrhage.

ANALYSIS

Hamlin Garland's theory of literature, detailed in his book *Crumbling Idols: Twelve Essays on Art* (1894), grew out of two concepts formulated early in his writing career: "that truth has a higher quality than beauty, and that to spread the reign of justice should everywhere be the design and intent of the artist." This theory of veritism obligated him to write stories early in his career that he said were "not always pleasant, but . . . [were] generally true, and always provoke thought."

Garland wrote about "truth" that, for the most part, he had himself experienced. The "justice" he sought to perpetuate was simplified by a reformer's zeal. As a result, he produced a series of didactic early novels that often retell his life experiences in thin disguise. Later on, when he began to view writing as a business, churning out books and shorter pieces that were intentionally commercial, he wrote a series of safely inoffensive novels that were more romantic than realistic and that are consequently of little importance today.

A SPOIL OF OFFICE

In his first novel, *A Spoil of Office*, Garland set out to write propaganda, or social protest. In it, he achieved greater continuity of plot than in many subsequent books, he included fewer digressions, and he realized his indisputable though not lofty aim. *A Spoil of Office* is one of his better novels.

It is the story of a hired man, Bradley Talcott, who, inspired by political activist Ida Wilbur, decides to make something of himself, to become more than he is. He goes back to school, then on to law school, and becomes in succession a lawyer, an Iowa state legislator, and ultimately a Congressman in Washington, D.C. He falls in love with and marries Ida, and together they work in the crusade for equal rights for everyone.

Garland showed in *A Spoil of Office* that corruption and inequality prevail in the legislative process. Prejudiced against the moneyed classes, Garland laid much of the injustice against the poor and average folk at the door of the well-to-do: Brad implies that the financially poorer legislators are the more honorable ones; that while living in a hovel is no more a guarantee of honesty than living in a brownstone is a "sure sign of a robber," it is a "tolerably safe inference."

Garland's own experiences and interests are reflected in Brad's fondness for oratory and Ida's alliances with various reform movements and organizations (the Grange, women's rights, the Farmers Alliance). In his youth, Garland had entertained the notion of an oratorical career; his reform activities under the influence of Benjamin O. Flowers, editor of the radical magazine *The Arena*, are well documented.

A LITTLE NORSK

The "truth" of prairie living, its harshness and its prejudices, is seen in Garland's short novel of realistic incident, *A Little Norsk*. The story is about a Norwegian girl, Flaxen, adopted and reared by two bachelors. She grows up, well-loved by her adopted "father" and "uncle." When the two men find their paternal feelings changing to more romantic love, they wisely send her off to school. Flaxen, called so because of her blond hair, meets and marries an irresponsible young man and they soon have a child. The young man, hounded by gambling debts, flees them and his family; a drowning accident removes him permanently from Flaxen's life. She moves back with the older, fatherly bachelor, taking her baby daughter with her. The novel ends with the strong implication that she will marry the younger bachelor.

In spite of a contrived plot, the novel is a realistic portrayal of the harshness of life on the prairie. Garland describes the blizzard that kills Flaxen's parents, conveying the terror that uncontrollable natural phenomena brought to the hapless prairie settlers. Although often romanticized for the benefit of those who had never experienced it, a blizzard on the isolated prairie was the harbinger of possible death. When a death occurs, as it does in *A Little Norsk*, there is the gruesome prospect of the dead bodies being attacked by hungry mice and even wolves—a prospect that Garland does not fail to dramatize.

Garland shows how Scandinavian women were treated by "native-born" American men when Flaxen occasionally encounters the village men who wink at her and pinch her. The two bachelors are aware that "the treatment that the Scandinavians' women git from the Yankees" is not nearly as respectful as that which Yankee women can expect. Ironically, Garland himself was probably guilty of such prejudices, because many of his fictional and autobiographical works reveal a condescending, patronizing attitude toward blacks, a disregard for hired hands (unless they are main characters, such as Brad Talcott), and an apparent dislike for immigrants such as Germans, Scandinavians, and Jews. (In *Rose of Dutcher's Coolly*, a character says of another, "he's a Jew, but he's not too much of a Jew.") *A Little Norsk* thus documents both the harsh physical realities and the purely human harshness and prejudice of prairie life.

ROSE OF DUTCHER'S COOLLY

Garland's most sustained novel is *Rose of Dutcher's Coolly*. At the time of its publication in 1895, it was a most daring book, primarily because it treats rather openly the sexual misdemeanors of adolescents. To a modern reader, however, Garland's treatment of this subject will appear markedly restrained and even genteel, hardly in keeping with his resolve to tell the truth without evasion or prettification.

Rose, a motherless child, spends her infancy and early childhood with her father on their farm. She grows up hearing and seeing things that many children are never confronted with: the "mysterious processes of generation and birth" with a "terrifying power to stir and develop passions prematurely"; obscene words among the farm hands; "vulgar cackling of old women"; courtship, birth, and death. She goes to her father with all her questions and he, with sometimes blundering answers, manages to keep her from becoming too curious too soon. When the time comes in her teenage years when she can no longer hold her feelings in check, she, like other youngsters, experiments with sex. She tells her father, and he, by appealing to her love for him and his wish that she be a good girl, staves off further episodes.

Rose is interested in reading and writing, and Doctor Thatcher, who visits her school, is so impressed by her that he promises to try to help her get into a college-preparatory school. Though her father is reluctant, she is finally allowed to go. Once there, she—now a beautiful young woman—has many suitors but is not interested in them beyond friendship. She wishes for a life of intellectual activity and creative writing. Finishing the seminary, she goes to Chicago, again with her father's reluctant approval. There she meets and falls in love with Mason. After overcoming his disinclination to marry, Mason finally proposes to Rose.

Rose of Dutcher's Coolly has been called Garland's best novel. He dared to speak frankly about natural, common occurrences in a sincere, sensible way. This blunt approach was perhaps what shocked his first readers; apparently they were unprepared to face in print those things about which they hardly talked and never in mixed company. Libraries ruled out the book, calling it "unsafe reading." Yet, even with these realistic elements, the book does not live up to its promise because Garland, as usual, romanticizes his "beautiful" heroine. Rose is nevertheless, a heroine fit to share the stage with Stephen Crane's Maggie and Theodore Dreiser's Sister Carrie.

THE CAPTAIN OF THE GRAY-HORSE TROOP

One of Garland's most successful novels is a romanticized story of the Far West, *The Captain of the Gray-Horse Troop*. Captain George Curtis, surveying the mountainous land he has come to love, sums up the novel's plot elements when he says to his sister Jennie, "Yes, it's all here, Jennie . . . the wild country, the Indian, the gallant scout, and the tender maiden." Add the noble captain and the villainous ranchers, and the mix that makes the story is complete.

Unlike Garland's earlier novels set in the Middle Border, *The Captain of the Gray-Horse Troop* is realistic primarily in the sense that it deals with a genuine problem (the encroachment on Native American lands and rights by avaricious Caucasians). Intentionally or not, it also reveals the whites' attitude of superiority in regard to the American Indian. Curtis is a good and honorable man, yet he can say, having learned of a barbaric execution of an Indian, "It's a little difficult to eliminate violence from an inferior race when such cruelty is manifested in those we call their teachers." Earlier he remarks of the Indians that "these people have no inner resources. They lop down when their accustomed props are removed. They come from defective stock."

This "superiority" is reflected elsewhere throughout the novel: in the unintentionally ironic comment describing "a range of hills which separate the white man's country from the Tetong reservation," and in comments such as "A Mexican can't cook no more'n an Injun." Yet Garland has Captain Curtis, unaware of his own prejudice, remark about another character who is blatantly anti-Native American that she is "well-schooled in race hatred." Written in the stilted style more reminiscent of the genteel tradition than of the veritism Garland espoused in his earlier years, *The Captain of the Gray-Horse Troop* truthfully depicts relations between American Indians and Caucasians in the nineteenth century. Interestingly enough, all the white characters, even those who, like Curtis, want to help the Indians and thwart their persecutors, seem to believe that the Indians are at best very low on the social scale.

The significance of this novel today may well lie not in the story of one white man's attempt to secure justice for the oppressed Indians but rather in its revelation of the bigoted attitudes of whites toward nonwhites. In its time, the book sold very well, going into several editions. It ultimately sold nearly 100,000 copies, Garland's largest sale. (Thirty years after publication it was still selling.) It received better reviews than Garland had hoped for, even from critics who had condemned his earlier books.

Apparently it was the success of this book (which had been considered during the height of its popularity for a motion-picture production) that convinced Garland that his earlier Middle Border stories would never bring him financial success. It is not difficult to understand why the remainder of his novels were like *The Captain of the Gray-Horse Troop*, though less successful.

Garland's subsequent literary output offers little that is memorable. His reputation in American literature rests primarily on his work as a short-story writer and autobiographer. An early realist, he also had a naturalistic bent. His earlier works, up to and including *Rose of Dutcher's Coolly*, show that individuals are controlled by the "outer constraints of environment and circumstance" as well as by the "inner constraints of instinct and passion." Garland uses local color not to caricature or make fun of his characters but to make his work more realistic and true to nature. The social elements he includes help to provide the significance he felt all literature must have to survive. The impressionistic tendencies seen in certain very subjective descriptions indicate a concern for "individualism as the coloring element of a literature." His minor lapses into romantic sentimentality and genteel restraint (typified by his habit of referring to "legs" as "limbs") are in themselves evidence of this same individualism; his restraint demonstrates his personal reluctance to be unnecessarily graphic in describing certain aspects of life. Still he was forthright in delineating most of his subjects. Garland's early novels are, for the most part, fine examples of his veritistic theory.

American literature is indebted to Garland for the stronger realism and the wealth of social history he contributed. It is not difficult to applaud Garland's early novels. He set out to show truth in time, place, people, and incident. He sought to bring social significance to his work. He succeeded in several novels before succumbing to commercialism and the desire or need to be not only a good writer but also a financially successful one.

Jane L. Ball

OTHER MAJOR WORKS

SHORT FICTION: *Main-Travelled Roads: Six Mississippi Valley Stories*, 1891; *Prairie Folks*, 1893; *Wayside Courtships*, 1897; *Other Main-Travelled Roads*, 1910; *They of the High Trails*, 1916; *The Book of the American Indian*, 1923.

PLAY: *Under the Wheel: A Modern Play in Six Scenes*, pb. 1890.

POETRY: *Prairie Songs*, 1893.

NONFICTION: *Crumbling Idols: Twelve Essays on Art*, 1894; *Ulysses S. Grant: His Life and Character*, 1898; *Out-of-Door Americans*, 1901; *A Son of the Middle Border*, 1917; *A Daughter of the Middle Border*, 1921; *Trail-Makers of the Middle Border*, 1926; *The Westward March of American Settlement*, 1927; *Back-Trailers from the Middle Border*, 1928; *Roadside Meetings*, 1930; *Companions on the Trail: A Literary Chronicle*, 1931; *My Friendly Contemporaries: A Literary Log*, 1932; *Afternoon Neighbors*, 1934; *Joys of the Trail*, 1935; *Forty Years of Psychic Research: A Plain Narrative of Fact*, 1936; *Selected Letters of Hamlin Garland*, 1998 (Keith Newlin and Joseph B. McCullough, editors).

BIBLIOGRAPHY

Foote, Stephanie. "The Region of the Repressed and the Return of the Region: Hamlin Garland and Harold Frederic." In *Regional Fictions: Culture and Identity in Nineteenth-Century American Literature*. Madison: University of Wisconsin Press, 2001. Garland is among several novelists whom Foote defines as a "regionalist." She argues that Americans' conceptions of local identity originated with Garland and other regional fiction writers of the late nineteenth and early twentieth centuries.

Joseph, Philip. "The Artist Meets the Literary Community: Hamlin Garland, Sarah Orne Jewett, and the Writing of 1890's Regionalism." In *American Literary Regionalism in a Global Age*. Baton Rouge: Louisiana State University Press, 2007. Joseph analyzes works of literary regionalism, including Garland's novel *A Spoil of Office* and some of his short stories and nonfiction, to determine if these works remain relevant in the modern global world. He concludes that Garland and other regionalists share a belief that local communities can benefit from global contact.

Kaye, Frances. "Hamlin Garland's Feminism." In *Women and Western Literature*, edited by Helen Winter Stauffer and Susan Rosowski. Troy, N.Y.: Whiston, 1982. Kaye discusses Garland's feminism, identifying him as the only male author of note at the end of the nineteenth century who spoke in favor of women's rights, including suffrage and equality in marriage.

McCullough, Joseph. *Hamlin Garland*. Boston: Twayne, 1978. This study follows Garland through his literary career, dividing it into phases, with major attention to the first phase of his reform activities and the midwestern stories. Includes a primary bibliography and a select, annotated secondary bibliography.

Nagel, James, ed. *Critical Essays on Hamlin Garland*. Boston: G. K. Hall, 1982. Nagel's introduction surveys the critical responses to Garland's work. This volume is especially rich in reviews of Garland's books, and it also includes twenty-six biographical and critical essays.

Newlin, Keith. *Hamlin Garland: A Life*. Lincoln: University of Nebraska Press, 2008. Newlin's biography of Garland, the first to be published in more than forty years, is based in part on previously unavailable letters, manuscripts, and family memoirs. Discusses Garland's contributions to literature and places Garland's work within the artistic context of its time. Includes notes, an index, a list of Garland's works, and illustrations.

Petty, Leslie. "Expanding the Vision of Feminist Activism: Frances E. W. Harper's *Iola Leroy* and Hamlin Garland's *A Spoil of Office*." In *Romancing the Vote: Feminist Activism in American Fiction, 1870-1920*. Athens: University of Georgia Press, 2006. Petty analyzes Garland's book and several other novels about politically active women and discusses how these books influenced the women's rights movement of the late nineteenth and early twentieth centuries.

Pizer, Donald. *Hamlin Garland's Early Work and Career*. Berkeley: University of California Press, 1960. Pizer treats in careful detail Garland's intellectual and artistic development during the first phase of his literary and reformist career, from 1884 to 1895. He discusses Garland's development of his creed, his literary output, and reform activities in society, theater, politics, and the arts. Includes a detailed bibliography of Garland's publications during these years.

Silet, Charles, Robert Welch, and Richard Boudreau, eds. *The Critical Reception of Hamlin Garland, 1891-1978*. Troy, N.Y.: Whitston, 1985. This illustrated volume contains thirty-three essays that illustrate the development of Garland's literary reputation from 1891 to 1978. The introduction emphasizes the difficulty critics have had trying to determine the quality of Garland's art.

Taylor, Walter Fuller. *The Economic Novel in America*. 3d ed. New York: Octagon Books, 1973. Taylor examines Garland's work in the context of fiction that reflects economic issues and trends. He sees in Garland's literary career a reflection of the fall of pre-American Civil War agrarian democracy with the halting of the advance of the frontier and the decline of populism.

JIM HARRISON

Born: Grayling, Michigan; December 11, 1937
Also known as: James Thomas Harrison

PRINCIPAL LONG FICTION

Wolf: A False Memoir, 1971
A Good Day to Die, 1973
Farmer, 1976
Legends of the Fall, 1979 (collection of three novellas: *Revenge, The Man Who Gave Up His Name*, and *Legends of the Fall*)
Warlock, 1981
Sundog: The Story of an American Foreman, 1984
Dalva, 1988
The Woman Lit by Fireflies, 1990 (collection of three novellas: *Brown Dog, Sunset Limited*, and *The Woman Lit by Fireflies*)
Julip, 1994 (collection of three novellas: *Julip, The Seven Ounce Man*, and *The Beige Dolorosa*)
The Road Home, 1998
The Beast God Forgot to Invent, 2000 (collection of three novellas: *The Beast God Forgot to Invent, Westward Ho*, and *Forgot to Go to Spain*)
True North, 2004
The Summer He Didn't Die, 2005 (collection of three novellas: *The Summer He Didn't Die, Republican Wives*, and *Tracking*)
Returning to Earth, 2007
The English Major, 2008

OTHER LITERARY FORMS

To appreciate fully the lyrical voice that dominates Jim Harrison's best novels, it is helpful to bear in mind that he began his career as a poet. His first two volumes of poetry, *Plain Song* (1965), written under the name James Harrison, and *Locations* (1968), received very little attention, and the reviews were mixed. With the publication of *Outlyer and Ghazals* (1971), critics began to give Harrison his due, but his next two volumes, *Letters to Yesenin* (1973) and *Returning to Earth* (1977), both issued by small publishing houses, were again overlooked, even after they were reissued in a single volume in 1979. *Selected and New Poems: 1961-1981* (1982), a volume that included the best of his previous work, demonstrated Harrison's range and complexity and established his as a major voice in American poetry. His collection *The Theory and Practice of Rivers: Poems* (1985) only served to demonstrate more fully both his breadth of interests and his mastery of the poetic form. *The Shape of the Journey: New and Collected Poems* (1998) restores to

Jim Harrison
(Library of Congres)

print lyrics and protest poems of *Plain Song*, the effusive *Letters to Yesenin*, and the Zen-inspired *After Ikkyu, and Other Poems* (1996).

In addition to novels and poetry, Harrison has published numerous essays, predominantly in *Sports Illustrated* and *Esquire*. In many of his essays, Harrison emerges as an amateur naturalist who denounces those who violate fish and game laws, sings the praises of seasoned guides and ardent canoe racers, and laments the passing of the wilderness in the face of urban development. Harrison has also published some food-related nonfiction, including *The Raw and the Cooked: Adventures of a Roving Gourmand* (2001), and the memoir *Off to the Side* (2002).

ACHIEVEMENTS

Jim Harrison, a venturesome and talented writer, proved himself an able poet, novelist, and journalist by revitalizing the territories and boundaries explored by others. Along with Nebraska, the territory of Ted Kooser and Willa Cather, both northern Michigan and Key West, the Hemingway provinces, are re-created in Harrison's work. Also present are the subterranean worlds and the connecting roads that the Beats had earmarked, the relatively unsullied outback celebrated by Edward Abbey and Theodore Roethke, and the predominantly masculine worlds explored by writers such as Harrison's friend and fellow hunter Thomas McGuane and Larry McMurtry.

However, it was Denise Levertov who helped Harrison publish his first book of poetry, *Plain Song*. It was not long after that when he received the first of three grants from the National Endowment for the Arts in 1967 and a Guggenheim Fellowship in 1969. These helped him to settle down in the Leelenau Peninsula in northern Michigan and to focus on poetry and finally fiction in the early 1970's. After steadily developing a literary following over two decades, and having his work published in twenty-seven languages, in 1999 Harrison was a finalist for the Los Angeles Times Book Prize, and he was awarded the *Colorado Review*'s Evil Companions Award, along with Michigan State University's College of Arts and Letters Distinguished Alumni Award. In 2000, he received the Spirit of the West Literary Achievement Award and the Michigan State University Distinguished Alumni Award, and in 2007, he was elected to the American Academy of Arts and Letters.

Harrison's greatest achievement, however, might be the fact that he has never changed his approach to theme, style, setting, and characterization to suit anyone but himself, his friends, and his readers. He has held fast to his vision of art as nature, all as real and true as a birch tree or brown trout, and let the scholars and journalists come to him. In fact, the same things for which reviewers criticized him in his first novel, *Wolf*, were the things that reviewers applauded about his 2007 novel *Returning to Earth*. By refusing to limit himself to a single genre and by attending to "audible things, things moving at noon in full raw light," Harrison appeals to a diversified audience and portrays an integrated vision that reflects the subtler nuances of the physical and natural world. While his references are often esoteric, he is a masterful storyteller who easily blends primitive and naturalistic images with arcane literary allusions. The reader is thus able to hear and feel simultaneously the meaning and motion of objects and experiences.

BIOGRAPHY

James Thomas Harrison was born December 11, 1937, in Grayling, Michigan; soon after his birth, his family moved to Reed City and then to Haslett, near the Michigan State University (MSU) campus, when Harrison was twelve. While he has repeatedly stated that his childhood was unremarkable, he clearly assimilated the spirit of the land and people found in northern Michigan and was deeply affected by the emotional bonds that held his family together. Perhaps because so much of this land has been ravaged by development, northern Michigan, and certainly its Upper Peninsula, has come to constitute Harrison's version of William Faulkner's fictional Yoknapatawpha County, peopled by figures drawn from his German and Swedish ancestral lines along with the Finns and Chippewa who populate the Upper Peninsula.

After a short period of enrollment at MSU in 1956, Harrison dropped out. Convinced that "you couldn't be an artist in Michigan," he made a number of treks to New York City, San Francisco, and Boston in search of the "right setting" in which to write; not surprisingly, these forays, described in *Wolf*, were unsuccessful. Inevitably, he returned to MSU; he received his B.A. in English in 1960, enrolled in graduate school, and made two key lifelong friendships with writers Thomas McGuane and Dan Gerber. McGuane persuaded Harrison to diversify his work by pursuing long fiction. McGuane also connected him with actor Jack Nicholson, who funded Harrison's writing, after his grant money was spent, in 1978-1979. It was in 1979, with the very successful publication of *Legends of the Fall*, that Harrison began to make a living on his writing alone. Beginning in 1968, Gerber and Harrison coedited the literary journal *Sumac*, in which they published a number of successful poets, such as Diane Wakoski, Charles Simic, Hayden Carruth, Barbara Drake, Adrienne Rich, Gary Snyder, Galway Kinnell, Carl Rokosi, and Denise Levertov.

Tragedy struck Harrison early in life, when he lost sight in one eye after being cut with a broken laboratory beaker. Later, his fourteen-year-old niece died. It was not until after his father and sister were killed in a head-on automobile collision in 1962 that he began to write in earnest. These personal losses, all the greater because they were unexpected, inform several of his novels and poems.

As the allusions that pepper Harrison's writing make clear, he became a prodigious reader early on. Not surprisingly, his graduate work was in comparative literature, and he has called himself an "internationalist" in terms of his literary tastes and influences. An outspoken and somewhat outrageous man, Harrison experienced bouts with severe depression that drove him periodically to the woods of Michigan, where he would write until exhausted, then play, hunt, and wander the beloved fields near his farmhouse near Lake Leelenau, where he lived from 1968 to 2002. In time this setting did not provide enough seclusion, so he purchased a modest cabin on the coast of Lake Superior; this served as a writing retreat until he sold it in 2004, when he finally gave up Michigan life to spend his time between Livingston, Montana, and Patagonia, Arizona.

An avid outdoorsman, Harrison adopted fishing as a counterweight to his time devoted to writing, being committed to a code of ethics and a way of life that discourage superfluous self-indulgence and encourage husbanding of resources. This earthy, well-read man is known for shunning the literary associations so expected of famed authors, preferring instead a simpler existence of sharing the backwoods with friends when not engaged in verse.

ANALYSIS

What is perhaps most striking about Jim Harrison's novels is the range of emotions they encompass. While in his early fiction he assumes a masculine point of view and revels in violence and debauchery, he is able to capture the romantic spirit that energizes his protagonists. He also avoids the bathetic trap that undermines the artistry of so many novels written from an aggressively male perspective. His central characters, in works such as

Brown Dog, *Legends of the Fall*, and *Wolf*, though often wantonly callous in their attitudes toward women, are propelled by a youthful wanderlust and are always extremely affable. In his later novels, some of his characters display a type of compassion, love, and generosity that provide readers with a sense of hope in the human spirit. While many writers have described the purpose of literature as exploring the dark side of the human condition, Harrison attempts to provide ways to escape this darkness. There is always a solution in his work if the reader cares to recognize it, and it often parallels the Buddhist path to Nirvana, the Chinese Dao, and the Gospels of the New Testament.

In his novels, Harrison often routinely suspends the narrative sequence and deletes causal explanation. In this way, he constructs a seamless web and traps reader and character alike in a world inhabited by legendary figures who are attuned to primeval nuances and thrive on epic adventure. His penchant for the episodic is complemented by his metaphorical language and lyric sensibilities, which enhance his ability to shift scenes rapidly without sacrificing artistic control or obscuring the qualitative aspects of his various milieus.

Harrison is willing to tackle topics that some other artists may consider too pedestrian. He is willing to experiment and to risk the wrath of his critics. While in terms of his allusions he is very much an artist's artist, he is also very much a people's artist—willing to confront the dilemmas of aging that confront us all and make us look ridiculous on more than one occasion. More important, Harrison is capable of conveying a sense of loss and dispossession as it relates to the wilderness. What saves this sense from overwhelming his writing is his capacity for wonder and his ability to capture the mystery resident in the land and to imagine in life legendary figures whose exploits make life bearable. If one accepts Waldo Frank's definition of a mystic as being one "who *knows* by immediate experience the organic continuity between himself and the cosmos," then Harrison is a mystic. He is a superlative storyteller who is attuned to the rhythms of the earth and a poet whose lyrical voice can be heard on every page.

WOLF

By giving *Wolf* the subtitle *A False Memoir*, Harrison properly alerts the reader to the poetic license that he has taken in reconstructing his biography. Much of what is included is factual, but he has embellished it and transformed it into art. The work is "false" in that it merges time and place in such a way as to convey a gestalt of experiences rather than a sequence of events. It is also "false" because he succumbs to his "constant urge to reorder memory" and indulges himself in "all those oblique forms of mental narcissism." What results is a compelling odyssey of Swanson's impetuous flirtation with decadence and debauchery.

In his relatively obtuse author's note, Harrison provides some biographical data to flesh out the Swanson persona. Also included is an admission that the romance he is about to unfold is somewhat of a self-indulgence that, like his desire to see a wolf in broad daylight, is central to no one but himself. Having thus offered his apologia, he proceeds to enmesh the reader in the tangles of people and places that have affected his narrator, Swanson. When Swanson is introduced, he is on a weeklong camping trip in northern Michigan's Huron Mountains. In the course of the novel, he is alternately lost in the woods and lost in his own mental mires as he reflects on the "unbearably convulsive" life he had led between 1956 and 1960.

Swanson's wilderness excursions constitute a correlative for his sallies into the mainstream. When he is in the woods, his hikes produce a configuration resembling a series of concentric circles; he is guided largely by his instincts and his familiarity with certain reference points. Similarly, his treks to Boston, New York City, and San Francisco have a cyclical cadence, and his itineraries are dictated more by his primal emotions than by conscious planning. In both environments, he assumes the stance of a drifter who is searching, against the odds, to discover an ordering principle around which to unscramble his conflicting longings.

A careful reading of *Wolf* reveals that the tension between the freewheeling and nostalgic selves energizes the entire book. By coming to the woods, Swanson is attempting somehow to resolve the dualistic longings that have colored his first thirty-three years, to "weigh the mental scar tissue" acquired during his various rites of passage. While in the woods, he is constantly recalling the head-on crash that killed both his father and his sister; the pain of this memory is undisguised and serves as a counterweight to the bravado with which he depicts his adventuring.

Appropriately, the dominant chord in *Wolf*, as in most of Harrison's work, is a sense of dispossession and loss. Throughout the book, he emphasizes the ways in which greed, technology, and stupidity have led to the despoliation of the wilderness and endangered not only species but ways of life as well. Noting that the "continent was becoming Europe in my own lifetime," Swanson recognizes that the "merest smell of profit would lead us to gut any beauty left." It is this understanding that leads him to depict governments as "azoological beasts," to conceive of the history of the United States in terms of rapine and slaughter, and to indulge himself in fantasies of depredation that come to fruition in *A Good Day to Die*.

When one reaches the end of the novel, however, one senses that Swanson has resolved very little. During his week in the woods, he has not only failed to see the wolf but also failed to illuminate a route "out of the riddle that only leads to another"; even as he labels his urban adventures "small and brutally stupid voyages" and accepts the fact that he longs for the permanence once provided by the remote family homesteads, he acknowledges that he will continue to drift, to "live the life of an animal" and to "transmute my infancies, plural because I always repeat never conquer, a circle rather than a coil or spiral."

A GOOD DAY TO DIE

A Good Day to Die, as William Crawford Wood observes, constitutes the second part of the song begun in *Wolf*. The novel, which takes its title from a Nez Perce Indian saying regarding war, chronicles the journey of the nameless narrator (who bears a marked resemblance to Swanson) from Key West to northern Arizona and on to Orofino, Idaho. As in *Wolf*, Harrison relies heavily on flashbacks and melds the narrator's memories with ongoing events; the novel is then less a correspondence between two periods than the route by which the narrator comes to accept life's capriciousness as a matter of course.

The nascent urge to avenge nature present in *Wolf* comes to fruition in *A Good Day to Die*. While the narrator, in retreat from his domestic woes, is vacationing and fishing in Key West, he is befriended by Tim, a Vietnam War veteran whose philosophy of life is fatalistic and whose lifestyle is hedonistic. In the midst of an intoxicating evening, the two formulate a vague plan to go west and save the Grand Canyon from damnation. En route, they stop in Valdosta, Georgia, to pick up Sylvia, Tim's childhood sweetheart, who is the epitome of idealized womanhood—beautiful, innocent, and vulnerable—and who, in the course of the journey, unwittingly evokes the basest emotions and reactions from both of her cohorts.

The improbability that such a threesome could long endure is mitigated by Harrison's ability to capture the conflicting urges and needs of all three. While Sylvia may be too homey to be entirely credible, she does assume a very real presence. Throughout the novel, she functions as a counterweight to her companions and serves to underscore the risks inherent in not controlling one's romanticism. While all three have a tendency to delude themselves, she seems the most incapable of grounding herself and perceiving her situation clearly.

FARMER

In *Farmer*, Harrison frees himself from his tendency to write false memoirs in lieu of novels. There are passing references to a nephew who resembles the author, but these serve to underscore Harrison's familiarity with the people and the milieu he is depicting. The portraits are especially sharp and clear in the cases of Joseph, a forty-three-year-old farmer and schoolteacher, and Dr. Evans, a seventy-three-year-old country physician. Equally crystalline is Harrison's portrayal of the northern Michigan environs in which Joseph's long overdue "coming-of-age" occurs.

Against the advice of his twin sister, Arlice, and his best friend, Orin, Joseph has remained on the family homestead in northern Michigan "not wanting to expose himself to the possible cruelties of a new life." Crippled in a farm accident at the age of eight, he has used various pretexts to avoid travel; he has lived through books rather than opening himself to firsthand experience. While his reading has kept him abreast of events in the world, it has done little to sate his hunger for a fuller existence. In fact, his preference for books dealing with the ocean, marine biology, distant wars, and the Orient has contributed to his growing dissatisfaction; he longs to visit the ocean, to partake more fully of the life about which he has only read and dreamed.

Against this backdrop Harrison develops a strain that is present in both of his previous novels: the counterpointing of characters. In this case, the restrained but steadfast Rosealee is set in contrast to the urbanized and impetuous Catherine. Rosealee and Joseph, both reared in the provincial backwaters, have been about to be married for approximately six years. Joseph, who has made love to only a few women in his lifetime, impulsively enters into an affair with Catherine, his seventeen-year-old student, who is attractive, experienced, and willing.

Structurally, the novel moves from June, 1956, back to the events that transpired between October, 1955, and the following June. The affair begins as a self-indulgence, but Joseph becomes increasingly light-headed and childlike, reveling in a swell of sensations and previously unknown emotions; he becomes embroiled in the kind of sexual morass that he had previously associated with the fictional worlds of Henry Miller and D. H. Lawrence. Only in retrospect does he understand the risks he has taken in order to free himself from his spiritual torpor; he has nearly destroyed Rosealee's love.

In the hands of a lesser writer, the story that Harrison unfolds could quickly become melodrama, the tone maudlin. That it does not is a measure of Harrison's talent. *Farmer*, far from lacking ironic distance, as some critics have charged, constitutes a parody of the Romantic novel; throughout the book, Harrison burlesques Joseph's inability to attain "a peace that refused to arrive" and with mock seriousness describes self-pity as "an emotion [Joseph] had never allowed himself." Using Dr. Evans as a foil, Harrison unearths Joseph's buried resentments and fears and concludes the novel in such a way as to confirm the doctor's earlier statement that Catherine "is not even a person yet" and that the dallying has simply served as a diversion for both of them. The fact that Joseph cannot come firmly to this conclusion on his own clearly distinguishes him from the protagonists in *Legends of the Fall*.

LEGENDS OF THE FALL

Legends of the Fall, a collection of three novellas, confirms Harrison's fascination with those elemental and primal emotions that defy logic, are atavistic, and propel one into the "nether reaches of human activity" despite the attendant risks. Cochran in *Revenge*, Nordstrom in *The Man Who Gave up His Name*, and Tristan in *Legends of the Fall* operate in defiance of consensual reality; each builds his own fate, guided more by inner compulsions and a taste for the quintessential mystery of existence than by rational planning.

All three of the main characters are blessed with "supernatural constitutions" and a wariness that allows them to survive against the odds and to perform feats of strength and cunning. Running like a chord through all three of these novellas is Harrison's sense of the gratuitousness of any life plan, his belief that events are "utterly wayward, owning all the design of water in the deepest and furthest reaches of the Pacific." There are countless chance meetings and abrupt turns of plot and any number of catalytic conversions. Whereas in longer works such confluences might strain readers' ability to suspend disbelief, in these novellas one is swept along and becomes a willing coconspirator.

Revenge is, in some respects, the weakest of the three pieces because the reader is asked to believe that Cochran, who spent twenty years in the Navy as a fighter pilot, is so transported by his affair with Miryea that he is blind to the warnings issued by her husband, whose nickname, Tibey, means shark. In the service, Cochran had earned a reputation for being "enviably crazier and bolder than anyone else," but he had also maintained the instinctual mindfulness of the Japanese samurai, insisting on understanding "as completely as possible where he was and why." Once he meets Miryea, however, his circumspection is superseded by his romanticism and his "visionary energy." He conceives of her in terms of an Amedeo Modigliani painting, the quintessence of female beauty and charm; he is plummeted into a "love trance" that "ineluctably peels back his senses." Failing to comprehend the meaning of Tibey's gift of a one-way ticket to Madrid and seven thousand dollars, Cochran sets out heedlessly for a weekend tryst in Agua Prieta, where he and Miryea are beaten unmercifully by Tibey and his henchmen.

Opening with a visage of the badly wounded Cochran lying in the desert, Harrison neatly discounts the pertinence of biographical data and summarily explains how Cochran arrived at his unenviable state. The focus of *Revenge* then comes squarely to rest on Cochran's attempts to avenge himself and recover Miryea. Despite the novella's sparsity, the reader is given sufficient information to comprehend the separate agonies that Cochran, Miryea, and Tibey are experiencing and to understand the emotional flux that resulted in the die being "cast so deeply in blood that none of them would be forgiven by their memories."

The events that transpire, a mix of the comic and the deadly serious, come to a head when Miryea, succumbing to her own agony, becomes comatose—a development that allows Cochran to discover her whereabouts. The denouement follows quickly; Cochran and Tibey journey together to perform what amounts to a deathwatch. The epilogue is deftly understated so as to capture the enormity of Cochran's loss—he mechanically digs a grave "with terrible energy, methodical, inevitable"—and the meaning of the Sicilian adage "Revenge is a dish better served cold" becomes clear and indisputable.

Harrison's ability to write economic and yet sufficiently comprehensive novellas is more fully realized in *The Man Who Gave up His Name.* While again Harrison provides minimal biographical data to explain how Nordstrom, once a prominent Standard Oil executive, has come to be a cook in a modest restaurant in Islamorada, Florida, he focuses the work in such a way as to make Nordstrom's conversion convincing and compelling. Nordstrom, like Joseph in *Farmer,* gradually awakens to his lassitude and, unlike Joseph, decides to do something positive to change his life and to get back in touch with the elemental pleasures that had sustained him when he was growing up in Reinlander, Wisconsin. What enables Nordstrom to make the transition is the fact that he has retained a healthy capacity for wonder. The novella opens with the image of Nordstrom dancing alone so as to recapture the metaphysical edginess that his years of success have denied him. Harrison then provides an overview of the pivotal experiences that have left Nordstrom dissatisfied with himself "for so perfectly living out all of his mediocre assumptions about life." In the course of two short chapters, Harrison introduces Laura, Nordstrom's former wife, and their daughter Sonia, who, when she was sixteen, had jolted Nordstrom out of his lethargy with the observation that he and Laura were both "cold fish." This observation prompted Nordstrom to resign his Standard Oil job and take a less demanding job as vice president of a large book wholesaler and to seek fulfillment through any number of expensive purchases and avocations.

Nordstrom's quest for the "volume and intensity" that had been lacking in his corporate existence is accelerated when his father unexpectedly passes away in October of 1977. As he is grappling with his own sense of loss and "the unthinkable fact of death," he is compelled to question why he has conformed to all the normative expectations that have so little to do with the essence of life. To the amazement and horror of friends and family, he resigns his position and tries to give his money away, even making a contribution of twenty-five thousand dollars to the National Audubon Society, "though he had no special fascination for birds." At the behest of his broker and his ex-wife, he sees a psychiatrist, and it becomes clear that he has exchanged the inessential insanities fostered by the American Dream for the essential insanities that will allow him to free himself from stasis and fulfill personal desires.

The defiance of social expectations that lies at the heart of Nordstrom's transition is even more central to an understanding of Tristan, the main character in *Legends of the Fall*. Unlike Nordstrom, however, Tristan has never paid obeisance to anyone. Having abandoned any sense of cosmic justice at the age of twelve, Tristan has steadfastly made his own rules and run his life according to personal design. He emerges as a legendary voyager, propelled by a seemingly genetic compulsion to wander; spiritually he is the direct descendant of his grandfather, who at the age of eighty-four is still engaged in high-seas adventuring. Like Cochran and Nordstrom, Tristan has chosen to "build his own fate with gestures so personal that no one in the family ever knew what was on his seemingly thankless mind." Accordingly, Tristan is fated to live out certain inevitabilities.

Legends of the Fall is an episodic saga with perimeters that are staggering in their breadth. In the course of eighty-one pages, Harrison manages to imagine into being a multigenerational extended family, recount several complete cycles of events, and examine the ramifications of these sequences as they affect each member. The action spans several decades and several continents, and it is a measure of Harrison's mastery that he can cover this range without sacrificing context or character delineation.

The tale opens in 1914 with the departure of Tristan and his brothers, Alfred and Samuel, from the family homestead in Choteau, Montana; accompanied by One Stab, they travel to Canada to enlist in the war effort. Using several complementary techniques, Harrison economically contrasts the personalities of the three brothers; it quickly becomes clear that Tristan and Alfred are polar opposites and that Samuel, a romantic naturalist in the tradition of Louis Agassiz, is fated to die in World War I.

Just how opposed Tristan and Alfred are becomes a central thread in the novella. After Samuel is killed, Harrison makes a point of underlining the grief and guilt experienced by Tristan and Ludlow, their father; Alfred's response is virtually nonexistent, since "as a child of consensual reality" he alone escaped feelings of guilt. Equally important for understanding the distance between the two is that Tristan's career moves him from the status of horse wrangler to outlaw, while Alfred goes through all the "proper" channels, beginning as an officer and ending as a U.S. senator. Finally, the response of Susannah, who is first married to Tristan and then to Alfred, is telling; her breakdown and ultimate suicide are responses, in part, to the impossibility of ever regaining Tristan's love.

The "legends" that constitute the heart of the novella are Tristan's, but the dominating spirit is One Stab's "Cheyenne sense of fatality." Samuel's death is the first turning point, and, while Ludlow is consumed by his own powerlessness, Tristan is compelled to act. That Samuel's death was the product of the Germans' use of mustard gas serves not only to justify Tristan's revenge—scalping several German soldiers—but also to convey Harrison's antipathy for the grotesqueries justified in the name of modernization.

Tristan's legendary status is enhanced by his joining and then succeeding his grandfather as the pilot of a schooner that traffics in munitions, ivory, and drugs. Rather than dwelling on the specifics of the seven years that Tristan spends at sea, Harrison merely provides a glimpse of the first year and an outline of the next six, noting that the substance of these years is known only to Tristan and his crew. The next leg of Tristan's journey is also neatly understated. It begins when he returns home, "still sunblasted, limping, unconsoled and looking at the world with the world's coldest eye." It soon becomes evident, however, that the wounds that the sea could not assuage are virtually washed away by his marriage to Two, the half-American Indian daughter of Ludlow's foreman, Decker. The seven-year grace period that Tristan experiences is elliptically treated because "there is little to tell of happiness"; Harrison quickly shifts to the coup de grâce that kills Two and leaves Tristan inconsolable, "howling occasionally in a language not known on earth."

With a growing realization that he could never even the score with the world, that his losses have far exceeded his ability to avenge the capriciousness of either Samuel or Two's death, Tristan nevertheless becomes embroiled in a final sequence of death-defying events. Again the denouement is quick, but it involves an unexpected turn as Ludlow assumes the active role. As in the other novellas, the epilogue adds a sense of completeness and juxtaposes the modernized ranch owned by Alfred's heirs with the family graveyard in the canyon where they once had found "the horns of the full curl ram." It comes as no surprise that, "always alone, apart, somehow solitary, Tristan is buried up in Alberta." So ends the legend.

WARLOCK

In his 1981 novel *Warlock*, Harrison melds the tone and techniques of the "false memoir" with those associated with the genre of detective fiction; what initially appears to be a marked unevenness in the pacing of the book is a direct result of this unconventional wedding. The first part of the novel contains minimal action and is used primarily to develop the central characters; the second and third parts, on the other hand, are packed with action and abrupt turns of plot. What unifies the work is Harrison's adept use of several comic devices, including a great deal of what Sigmund Freud called "harmless" wit and humor.

When he is introduced, Warlock, at the age of forty-two, has recently lost his well-paid position as a foundation executive and expends much of his time in self-indulgent reverie and experiments in creative cookery. He is a Keatsian romantic who began his career as an artist "on the tracks of the great Gauguin," finds resonance in the nobility and idealism of works such as Boris Pasternak's *Doctor Zhivago* (1957) and Miguel de Cervantes' *Don Quixote de la Mancha* (1605, 1615), and spends countless hours dreaming of a new beginning. He and Diana have moved north to Michigan's Lake Leelanau Peninsula to maintain "the illusion that one lived in a fairy tale, and everything would work out," a motive that makes him an unlikely candidate for top-secret sleuthing.

Diana, on the other hand, appears to be relatively stable, with a nature almost antithetical to Warlock's. It becomes clear, however, that she is not really any more able to decode the enigmas of reality than he. Although she is repeatedly depicted as a pragmatist, this trait is counterbalanced by her affinity for Asian mysticism and her infatuation with genius. While she is an ardent feminist and an excellent surgical nurse, she is equally drawn to the charades that animate their sexual life and constitute a variant of the living theater in which Warlock later becomes the unwitting star.

It is the dynamic tension between Diana and Warlock that leads him to accept a position as a troubleshooter for Diana's associate, Dr. Rabun; while both acknowledge that Rabun is an eccentric, neither knows the extent of his idiosyncrasies. From the onset, Rabun lets it be known that he does not like to reveal all that he knows; it is his very elusive nature that energizes the last two parts of the novel. How little either Diana or Warlock knows about him becomes clear only after both have been sufficiently beguiled to prostitute themselves and do his bidding.

The initial meeting between Warlock and Rabun and its immediate aftermath resemble slapstick comedy. In addition to the absurdist context into which Harrison implants their clandestine meeting, there is the brusque repartee and the importance each attaches to the inessentials. The contents of a briefcase that Rabun entrusts to Warlock are telling; in addition to two folders outlining Rabun's holdings, there are copies of *Modern Investigative Techniques*, a guide to tax law regulations, and a sensationalized, paperback best seller on business crime. Warlock is given two days to study the material and write a brief reaction to it. Warlock's behavior is no less comic; he arrives home and promptly secretes the briefcase in the refrigerator for safekeeping and deludes himself with grandiose dreams that his life is beginning to merge "with a larger scheme of affairs," a truth that, unknown to him, constitutes a pithy double entendre.

Warlock's father, a top detective in Minneapolis, tries to warn his son away from the position with Rabun and, failing at that, offers a good deal of advice and assistance. Their conversations are peppered throughout and serve to infuse the novel with a droll midwestern humor and to underline Warlock's comic naïveté. Warlock's unpreparedness and vulnerability quickly become a dominant chord; while he conceives of himself as one of the "knights of the surrealistic age," the author makes it clear that, as a knight-errant, he lacks the purity of motive that spurred Don Quixote and the equivalent of a Sancho Panza. Instead, he has only his most unfaithful dog, Hudley, as his "Rozinante though without saddle or snaffle."

Part 2 opens with an image of Warlock setting north on his first mission, completely undaunted despite the fact that he is en route to walk a two-thousand-acre area in the Upper Peninsula in search of lumber poachers. While he has the appropriate sense of adventure for the mission he undertakes, his idealism repeatedly blinds him to clues that should be obvious to the most amateur sleuth. During the third part of the novel, Warlock abruptly discovers that reality is far more evanescent than even the most fleeting of dreams. Sent to Florida to "get the goods" on Rabun's estranged wife and his ostensibly homosexual son, who appear to be cheating Rabun out of millions of dollars, and on a society dame who has filed a seemingly outrageous suit against Rabun for injuries incurred when one of his health spa machines went wild, Warlock finds himself in a veritable house of mirrors.

The events that transpire during his Florida sally are unexpected and outrageously comedic. Again, Harrison relies on "harmless" humor and evokes compassion for the hapless hero. As a result of Warlock's adventures, Harrison abruptly turns the tables and destroys his preconceptions by unmasking Rabun as a perverted swindler and forcing Warlock to the realization that he has been "played for the fool" by almost everyone, including the charmed Diana.

After recovering a modicum of equilibrium, Warlock takes the offensive; reading only children's books, "to keep his mind cruel and simple," he launches a counterattack that is simultaneously programmatic and impulsive, the former aspects resulting from the work of his father and the latter from Warlock's own primal energies. There is a good deal of mock-heroic action on Warlock's part, but in the end, Rabun is brought to justice and Warlock and Diana are reunited. Like his spiritual heir who returns to La Mancha after having been bested by the Knight of the White Moon, Warlock rejects a job offer to track down a Moonie and returns to his pursuit of Pan.

While *Warlock* is not a "representative" novel, it contains many of the elements that unify Harrison's oeuvre. Warlock, like Swanson in *Wolf* and Joseph in *Farmer*, is a romantic and a dreamer; he is a man ruled by elemental desires who repeatedly becomes embroiled in ill-conceived liaisons and who "belongs" in northern Michigan despite the fact that he has a habit of getting lost in the woods. All of Harrison's central characters seem to have a "capsulated longing for a pre-Adamic earth" and a nostalgia for the unsullied woodlands of their childhoods.

SUNDOG

With the publication of *Sundog*, Harrison returned to his technique of employing the almost all-too-present narrator. The novel hopscotches between revealing the life of Robert Corvus Strang and chronicling the misadventures of the narrator, who bears a strong resemblance to the persona Harrison created in his earlier works.

The narrator meets Strang during what he describes as a "long voyage back toward Earth," a voyage that would put him in touch with the quintessential American. Strang pursued the American Dream only to be crippled in a fall down a three-hundred-foot dam. His experiences, no less than his persistent refusal to accept defeat, make Strang worth knowing. He is, as Harrison describes him, "a man totally free of the bondage of the appropriate."

It becomes clear that Strang and the narrator are kindred spirits—two sides of a single being. Both have more than average appreciation and respect for the forces of nature, even if the narrator is far less willing to plunge heart, soul, and body into its incomprehensible eddy. Both have unbounded passions and lusts, even if the narrator seems less in control of his anima or animus than Strang and more prone to succumb to melancholy, confusion, and despair. Both harbor a deep need to make sense of their own biographies and to plumb the depths of forgotten events that have unmistakably marked their personalities and approaches toward life. The hint of a biographical connection only strengthens their correspondences.

Robert Corvus Strang, as the reader comes to know him, is a man who has been involved on an international scale, building bridges, dams, and irrigation systems since his debut involvement in the construction of the Mackinac Bridge, despite the fact that he developed epilepsy after he was struck by lightning at the age of seven. His has been a life influenced by the polar personalities of his father, who traveled the revival circuit, and his older brother, Karl, who viewed truth as largely situational. His understanding of mechanical and electrical principles is balanced by his understanding of people, most of whom suffer, in his estimation, "because they live without energy" and can accomplish nothing. Strang, on the other hand, even as he attempts to recover from the side effects of a local remedy for his epilepsy, lives with great energy and maintains his commitment to regain his health and resume his career as a contractor on an upcoming project in New Guinea.

His self-imposed cure requires him to regress to a preadolescent state so as to "repattern his brain and body," the physical corollary to what the narrator asks him to do on a more personal and emotional level. At the novel's conclusion, Strang's attempts to begin again can be seen both as a therapeutic renewal process and as an exorcism through which he conquers the artificial barriers imposed by both modern medicine and those who profess to care for him.

Among the personal dramas of Strang's early life and his current battles, Harrison interweaves a sense of wonder that also serves as a leitmotif in each of his earlier works, again claiming the Upper Peninsula as his own. Against this setting, Harrison offers counterpoints of urban violence, corporate greed and venality, and the unbridled insensitivity and martyrdom of missionaries. The novel's ambiguous denouement only serves to underline Harrison's conviction that life resembles a "crèchelike tableau, a series of three-dimensional photographs of the dominant scenes, the bitterest griefs and the accomplishments." Harrison captures these images in his portrayal of Strang, whose life is keynoted by "love, work, and death . . . held together by wholeness, harmony and radiance."

DALVA

Despite its multiple plot lines, *Dalva* is also held together by a wholeness and a humanitarian spirit. The novel, in some ways, is Harrison's most ambitious undertaking. It is ambitious not only because it seeks to communicate a multigenerational family history but also because two-thirds of the novel is told from a woman's perspective. Harrison's use of Dalva as the primary narrator, no less than his use of Clare as the major force in *The Woman Lit by Fireflies*, demonstrates his capacity to transcend the masculine point of view and enter into a world that, according to the majority of critics, he has never even conceptualized. Dalva, like her mother Naomi, emerges as a woman capable of acting and reacting with equal amounts of certitude.

From the beginning it is clear that, despite caprice and mistreatment, Dalva is not about to "accept life as a brutal approximation." Having lost her only child to adoption, and Duane, the only man she ever loved, to circumstances (and later death), Dalva is caught amid conflicting emotions—knowing what she has to do to earn her own freedom but fearing the consequences and the pain she could cause others. She is also mired in a family matrix that defies easy explanation.

Harrison structures *Dalva* as a three-part novel, centering the first book on Dalva's longings and aspirations, the second on Michael's misbegotten attempts at scholarship, and the third on the events leading up to Dalva's eventual reintegration of the various aspects of her biography. While each of the books has a completeness on a superficial level, the three are ineluctably associated with Dalva's grandfather and his allegiance to the American Indians.

Grandfather's journals allow the reader to comprehend a period of history that has long been whitewashed in American history textbooks, and his sage advice allows Naomi, Dalva, Rachael, and others to make sense out of the tragedies that pepper their lives. His attitude is one born of pragmatism and necessity; having seen the less seemly side of American culture, he fully understands that "each of us must live with a full measure of loneliness that is inescapable and we must not destroy ourselves or our passion to escape this aloneness." It was this same uncanny understanding of the human condition that allowed Grandfather to coexist with the Sioux, who found his ethic toward the land and his rapport with people akin to their own.

THE WOMAN LIT BY FIREFLIES

The ongoing vulnerability of the American Indians is a theme that dominates *Brown Dog*, the first of the three novellas that constitute Harrison's 1990 publication *The Woman Lit by Fireflies*. Harrison's tone, however, is distinctly different. Rather than delving into the historical record, Harrison highlights the insensitivity of modern Americans to Native American traditions and culture and lampoons a legal system that defends the denigrators of history. While his sympathies remain the same as in his earlier works, the approach he takes is more reminiscent of *Warlock* than of *Dalva*.

Because of the seriocomic tone of the work, the book is dominated by characters (both living and dead) who are not entirely believable and who serve, instead, to buttress an assault against the materialism and insensitivity of the modern world. That Harrison casts his story through the filtered lens of Shelly, an aspiring anthropology graduate student, tips his hand from almost the first page. While it is clearly apparent that Brown Dog may well need an editor, Shelly serves as a deflector rather than an editor.

Brown Dog, as a typical Harrison protagonist, is a man trying to cope with middle age. When he finds a three-hundred-pound American Indian chief at the bottom of Lake Superior, he responds with the same degree of maturity that destines Warlock to his misadventures. Like Warlock, he stumbles through life, but unlike Warlock, he lacks an intelligent counterpart. Instead, Brown Dog is teamed with the female equivalent of Dalva's Michael. Shelly is opportunistic and insensitive to the values that make certain areas off-limits to outsiders. She is not unlike Brown Dog, however, as both are comic characters obviously unprepared to deal with the modern world. What she has over Brown Dog is that she comes from a wealthy family and can generally extract the results that she desires.

The ability to buy oneself out of trouble is also a theme that dominates *Sunset Limited*, the second novella in *The Woman Lit by Fireflies*. *Sunset Limited*, unlike *Brown Dog*, reads as a parable in which one is forced to reconsider the parable of the camel and the eye of the needle. It is an abbreviated retrospective akin to Thomas Pynchon's *Vineland* (1989), in which the reader is reacquainted with 1960's radicals and forced to deal with the ways in which their pasts have shaped their presents. Gwen, who seems like an unlikely revolutionary, is teamed with two individuals who have clearly abandoned any insurrectionary thoughts and another who has merely retreated from the fray. That their quest is to gain the freedom of a tired gadfly of a revolutionary who has been hanging on long after his time is both relevant and beside the point. Harrison rather heavy-handedly points out in the final chapter that this is a fable, and, as in most fables, there is a moral that has to do with basic values and the risks of renouncing those values at the expense of the immediate community. Hence, once Billy confesses to his past complicity with the authorities, it comes as no surprise that if a life must be spared, it will be his. Riches, in the elemental world in which Harrison dwells, guarantee very little.

As if to reinforce this point, but from a very different perspective, Harrison closes this set of novellas with *The Woman Lit by Fireflies*, which leaves the reader with no illusions about the protections offered by money. *The Woman Lit by Fireflies* may silence those critics who cannot see Harrison as a universal novelist. His appreciation for the lot of women—their failed expectations, existential angst, and lack of challenge—comes through quite clearly. Clare is a woman wearied from "trying to hold the world together, tired of being the living glue for herself, as if she let go, great pieces of her life would shatter and fall off in a mockery of the apocalypse."

Clare is not an extraordinary character, yet she has the courage to abandon a marriage that has betrayed her expectations decades before. The impetuous escape that she half-consciously orchestrates constitutes a psychic rebirth, a coming to terms with her childhood, adulthood, and future. In relinquishing the creature comforts to which she had always been accustomed, Clare finds new sources of strength as she conquers the dangers of finding shelter, water, and mental balance in a world that is dominated by elemental urges and necessities. Clare is not renouncing money or creature comforts, although along the way she does prove that she can live without them; instead, she is renouncing the predatory ethic of dominance. As she says at one point, "I want to evoke life and [Donald] wants to dominate it."

JULIP

Julip expands Harrison's manly image by leaping past the tradition of maleness to address tender life issues. Like *Legends of the Fall*, *The Woman Lit by Fireflies*, *The Beast God Forgot to Invent*, and *The Summer He Didn't Die*, the book is composed of three novellas. The title story focuses on the stressful attempts by Julip to retrieve her brother Bobby from jail. Surrounded by adversity, an alcoholic father, a cold, calculating mother, a crazy brother, and a nymphomaniac cousin, the tough and resourceful Julip resorts to the gentleness of training dogs and reading Emily Dickinson's poetry to gain solace from the madness surrounding her. Julip attempts to convince her incarcerated sibling to plead insanity as a ploy to be released from his sentence, the result of his killing three men—Julip's past lovers. The ever-continuing conflict between her parents creates a young woman full of doubts and confusion.

In *The Seven Ounce Man*, Harrison renews themes and characters from earlier works. Brown Dog, the epitome of the American existential hero, reminisces of his love for an anthropologist who attempts to desecrate an American Indian burial ground. Somewhat like Harrison, Brown Dog prefers the quiet rhythm of nature to the roaring pace of humanity. He cannot seem to avoid trouble, haphazardly bumbling through incidents, revealing the ridiculous folly that ultimately entangles him with American Indian rights groups.

Harrison selects a fifty-year-old professor accused of having a tryst with a young student as the focus in *The Beige Dolorosa*. Satiated with accusations of impropriety and campus politics, Phillip, the professor, retreats from campus life to the relaxed cadence of the Latino Southwest, where he discovers serenity. Like Julip and Brown Dog, Phillip surrenders to nature as both a form of survival and a restoration of the soul.

THE ROAD HOME

The Road Home, a deep, complex, and spiritually oriented work, demonstrates Harrison's maturity. The novel offers five compelling stories told through the multigenerational characters of *Dalva*'s Northridge family. Harrison's strong narrative weaves fantasy with reality and Native American perspectives with midwestern mentality. The novel opens in the 1950's, with the half-Sioux patriarch John remorsefully recounting his youth, his attempts at art, and his final acceptance of a way of life as a horse rancher in Nebraska. Ruthless at times in business, John amasses land, status, and a legacy, but he bemoans not achieving artistic fulfillment. Nelse, Northridge's grandson and Dalva's son, given up at birth for adoption to a wealthy family, portrays himself as a loose wanderer whose passion for birding chips away at his opportunity for a "normal" existence. Nelse targets an abused wife whom he learns to love—and who loves him. Dalva's mother, Naomi, who motivates Nelse into rejoining the family, and Paul, son of Naomi and John, offer rich viewpoints on the intriguing tale from their perspective. Finally, Dalva, the strong, willful one, faces a life-threatening illness and the turmoil of understanding the man who was the baby she gave away at birth.

Harrison uses death as a metaphor for the concept of home, but home also is the Nebraska lands surrounding the Niobara Valley and River, which courses through all the characters in the novel. The author's attention to detail, melding of familiar characters, and masterful storytelling make *The Road Home* a strong sequel to *Dalva*.

TRUE NORTH

True North is set mainly in the city of Marquette of Michigan's Upper Peninsula. It is a first-person narrative told by David Burkett in three parts: the 1960's, the 1970's, and the 1980's. The plot is driven predominantly by David's personal journey to escape the horrible deeds of his ancestors, mainly the lumber barons of his father's family in the middle to late nineteenth century who stole thousands of acres from the Native Americans, raped Michigan's Upper Peninsula, and fostered logging practices that left thousands of men maimed or dead.

David's internal conflict is that he is extremely afraid that he will turn out like his father, and early on there are some similarities between himself and his father. For example, his first two loves, Laurie and Vera, are possibly too young for him and are lusted after by his father as well. Also, there is the hint that David sees the relationship between his sister Cynthia and Donald, the son of the family's gardener, as being in bad taste. On the other hand, his father's inherent problems make David seem very admirable. David's father is a World War II hero turned alcoholic and pedophile who spends his days and nights at the country club when he is not driving to Duluth, Minnesota, to see one of his fifteen-year-old girlfriends or flying to Key West to "fish." One can assume that money is no object on these trips to Key West, as the Burketts have inheritance from both paternal and maternal sides; David's mother comes from a family that became wealthy in the shipping of iron ore from the Upper Peninsula to

Gary, Indiana, and Cleveland. As scholar Patrick A. Smith has observed, David's internal conflict is that he is transfixed and possibly doomed by the weight of history.

Typical of a Harrison novel, the protagonist is not a passive victim of circumstance. Consequently, David's external conflict is that he has to create a reality for himself in order to break away from his father's influence and, more important, the type of existence that can only be described as purposeless, living in the doldrums of his ancestors' greed. This manifests itself in many ways. First, the reader learns that David has converted from his parents' Episcopalian faith to the Baptist faith, and he now attends a Baptist church by himself. (He believes that his parents use religion to justify their privileged existence.) He eschews the family tradition of attending Yale by choosing Michigan State University, and he follows that with a stint at seminary school in Chicago. He refuses to socialize with the children of his parents' upper-class friends, preferring to spend his time with Glenn, a handyman's son. He also accepts the black sheep of the family, his uncle Fred (his mother's brother) as a father figure, if not also the family's live-in accountant, Jesse, and gardener, Clarence. David learns about alternatives to his parents' corrupt version of a Protestant upbringing through Jesse, who is from Mexico; through Clarence, who tends toward the beliefs of his Chippewa ancestors; and through Fred, a religious man who does not believe in organized religion. Most important, instead of killing his father and himself in order to end his bloodline, of which he fantasizes, David decides to write a book about the history of logging in the Upper Peninsula.

Much as Harrison has done in his body of fiction, David aims to put faces, names, and pictures to the people who built the United States and then were left out of the American narrative. The result is that he works on his book for twenty years without much hope for its publication, and, by all accounts, he is unable to balance the quantitative facts with qualitative descriptions. However, his pursuit of this goal and the nontraditional life he leads in the process, mainly in a cabin on the coast of Lake Superior, give him enough knowledge of the past that he is able to throw it away if he pleases. By learning the truth, he is eventually enlightened enough to transcend the past as well as his own futile convictions. Also typical of Harrison's work, David seems to find this truth in nature, where the reality of life, and his place in it, is more apparent.

RETURNING TO EARTH

In *Returning to Earth*, a sequel to *True North*, Harrison explores several themes and ideas that are common in his previous novels: nature as the harbinger of truth, the nontraditional family as a positive alternative to a traditional family that breaks itself upon unrealistic expectations, taboo love relationships, and alternate perspectives on reality and the American Dream, along with trying to make sense of the past and one's place in America. In addition, *Returning to Earth* meditates on the multiple ways of coping with death.

The story is told in four parts by four first-person narrators: Donald, Kenneth (much like a young Henry David Thoreau or Jack Kerouac), David Burkett, and David's sister,

Cynthia. We learn from Donald in the beginning that he has amyotrophic lateral sclerosis (ALS, or Lou Gehrig's disease) and has only a short time to live. His purpose for writing is to pass along some of his past to his children, Herald and Clare. The fact that he has dyslexia, which probably went completely untreated because he was educated in the 1960's, makes this task a courageous one—it also serves Harrison's artistic need to give a voice to the working class and the working poor. Donald is not a poor man, however; he has been steadily employed as a mason for twenty-five years, and his wife, Cynthia, worked as a teacher on the Bay Mills Indian Reservation right up until he was diagnosed. In fact, Donald and Cynthia could have been wealthy, but she has refused to use her parents' inheritance because her father's money was gained through the actions of his corrupt ancestors.

Donald, like his father, Clarence, in *True North*, is half Finn and half Chippewa. Harrison always uses the parenthetical "(Anishinabe)" after the word "Chippewa." Anishinabe is what the "Chippewa" called themselves; it means the original people. Donald tries his best to give his audience an idea of his family's history, and, in effect, his story conveys some of the humanity that David could not convey in his manuscript on the history of logging in *True North*. Donald's American Dream, at this point, is to die as he pleases. His life, in comparison to that of the Burketts of *True North*, has been ironically profound, but it is the way that he chooses to die and be buried that causes the novel's major conflict.

It is clear that, through *True North* and *Returning to Earth*, Harrison means to compare the lives of the more irresponsible "old money" Americans to those of the working class. The moral is that the honest life of a man and woman who nurture their family, even if their love was once taboo and even if they have to break from traditional expectations, can have a more positive effect on America than a family that allows the deeds of the past to ruin its descendants.

C. Lynn Munro; Craig Gilbert
Updated by Troy Place

OTHER MAJOR WORKS

POETRY: *Plain Song*, 1965; *Locations*, 1968; *Outlyer and Ghazals*, 1971; *Letters to Yesenin*, 1973; *Returning to Earth*, 1977; *Selected and New Poems, 1961-1981*, 1982; *Natural World*, 1983 (includes sculpture by Diana Guest); *The Theory and Practice of Rivers: Poems*, 1985; *The Theory and Practice of Rivers, and New Poems*, 1989; *After Ikkyu, and Other Poems*, 1996; *The Shape of the Journey: New and Collected Poems*, 1998; *Braided Creek: A Conversation in Poetry*, 2003; *Saving Daylight*, 2006.

SCREENPLAYS: *Cold Feet*, 1989 (with Thomas McGuane); *Revenge*, 1989; *Wolf*, 1994 (with Wesley Strick).

NONFICTION: *Just Before Dark: Collected Nonfiction*, 1991; *The Raw and the Cooked: Adventures of a Roving Gourmand*, 2001; *Conversations with Jim Harrison*, 2002 (Robert DeMott, editor); *Off to the Side: A Memoir*, 2002.

CHILDREN'S LITERATURE: *The Boy Who Ran to the Woods*, 2000.

BIBLIOGRAPHY

Davis, Todd F., and Kenneth Womack. "Embracing the Fall: Wilderness and Spiritual Transformation in the Novels of Jim Harrison." In *Postmodern Humanism in Contemporary Literature and Culture: Reconciling the Void*. New York: Palgrave Macmillan, 2006. Essay examining Harrison's fiction is part of a larger discussion of contemporary writers' attempts to find meaning and value in a postmodern world. Valuable for an understanding of Harrison's tendency toward resolution.

DeMott, Robert, ed. *Conversations with Jim Harrison*. Jackson: University Press of Mississippi, 2002. Collection of interviews with Harrison spans the years from 1976 to 1999. Includes an informative editor's introduction, chronology, and index.

Harrison, Jim. "The Art of Fiction: Jim Harrison." Interview by Jim Fergus. *The Paris Review* 107 (1988): 53-97. Fergus asks Harrison the right questions about life, literature, and art, and the author's responses are personal and enlightening, giving the reader a variety of interesting insights into the craft of fiction and poetry.

Jones, Allen M. "Six Short Essays About Jim Harrison." *New West*, May 16, 2006. Discusses many topics a Harrison admirer would want to know about the author, including his life in Montana, his friends, and some background stories on his work.

McClintock, James I. "*Dalva*: Jim Harrison's 'Twin Sister.'" *Journal of Men's Studies* (Spring, 1998): 319-331. Examines *Dalva* from a post-Jungian perspective, exploring the feminine side of masculinity as influenced by psychologist James Hillman.

Pichaske, David R. *Rooted: Seven Midwestern Writers of Place*. Iowa City: University of Iowa Press, 2006. In exploring the writing of authors, including Harrison, who have spent their careers expounding on one or two distinct locations, Pichaske provides insight into how geography can shape all facets of fiction and how these writers' works have transcended their respective regions.

Reilly, Edward C. *Jim Harrison*. New York: Twayne, 1996. A good introduction to Harrison's work, discussing, among other topics, the ways in which Harrison uses fiction as a medium for social commentary. Includes brief biographical section and chronology.

Rohrkemper, John. "'Natty Bumppo Wants Tobacco': Jim Harrison's Wilderness." *Great Lakes Review* 8 (1983): 20-28. Suggests that Harrison's poetic treatment of nature is closer to a "dark romantic" view, such as that of Herman Melville, than it is to an Emersonian transcendentalist outlook. Asserts that Harrison's fiction is based on the tradition of his "literary parents and grandparents," the modernists, but with one significant twist: The modernists show the "pristine beauty of nature first, and then nature spoiled," while Harrison shows how nature exists in spite of human influence.

Smith, Patrick A. *"The True Bones of My Life": Essays on the Fiction of Jim Harrison*. East Lansing: Michigan State University Press, 2002. Explores Harrison's fiction in terms of such ideas as the American myth, the American Dream, postmodernism, and the importance of place. Includes several photographs, a critical bibliography, a bibliography of Harrison's work that lists many of his published essays, and an index.

JAMAKE HIGHWATER

Born: Place unknown; 1930's(?)
Died: Los Angeles, California; June 3, 2001
Also known as: J. Marks; Jay Marks; Jack Marks

OTHER LITERARY FORMS

Published under the name J. Marks, the early works of Jamake Highwater include *Rock and Other Four Letter Words* (1968) and *Mick Jagger: The Singer, Not the Song* (1973). *Moonsong Lullaby* (1981), relating the importance of the moon in American Indian culture, is a tale for young children. Highwater also published books on Native American painting, artists, and history through art as well as on Native American dance and ceremonies. Other book-length publications include five editions of *Europe Under Twenty-five: A Young Person's Guide* (1971) and *Indian America: A Cultural and Travel Guide* (1975). This latter book, the first Fodor's guide on American Indians, is important as not only a guide for tourists but also a study of the history and cultures of American Indians. Highwater also wrote short fiction, magazine articles, and scripts for television shows.

Highwater published the nonfiction work *The Language of Vision: Meditations on Myth and Metaphor* in 1994. *Songs for the Seasons* (1995) is a children's book in which Highwater tells a tale of two red-tailed hawks. He interprets the lifestyle changes facing the hawks during different seasons. Illustrations in the book are by Sandra Speidel. *The Mythology of Transgression: Homosexuality as Metaphor* (1997) is a weighty essay focused on the homophobia of Western culture.

ACHIEVEMENTS

Jamake Highwater was recognized for a variety of talents. Novelist John Gardner said of Highwater that "he is one of the purest writers at work—a clean, clear voice." In addition to writing books and articles, Highwater hosted, wrote, and narrated *Songs of the Thunderbird* (1979) for the Public Broadcasting Service. In the field of music, Highwater's interests were diverse and included rock, American Indian, and classical music; he was a contributing editor of *Stereo Review* and classical music editor of the *Soho Weekly News*.

Highwater was called "a writer of exceptional vision and power" by Anaïs Nin. He was named a consultant to the New York State Council on the Arts, and at one time he served on the art task panel of the President's Commission on Mental Health. He also was named an honorary citizen of Oklahoma.

Among the honors that Highwater received, one of the most important to him personally was awarded at the Blackfeet Reserve in Alberta, Canada. Ed Calf Robe, elder of the Blood Reserve of Blackfeet, gave Highwater the name Piitai Sahkomaapii, which means Eagle Son. This honor, Calf Robe stated, was given because Highwater "soars highest and catches many truths which he carries to many lands." In spite of Highwater's genuine talents and achievements, after the mid-1980's he was viewed less favorably by some critics because his long-standing claim of American Indian ancestry was found to be essentially insupportable.

BIOGRAPHY

Portions of the biography of Jamake Highwater are open to question. Until the mid-1980's, Highwater maintained that he was born in Glacier County, Montana, on February 14, 1942, and that his mother, Amana Bonneville, was of the Blackfeet Nation (or was part Blackfoot and part French Canadian) and his father, Jamie, was a Cherokee. His early years, he said, were spent on the Blackfeet Indian Reservation in Montana and in Alberta, Canada, where the Blackfeet people held their summer encampments. At the age of eight, Highwater went to Hollywood with his father, a founding member of the American Indian Rodeo Association and a stunt man in Western films. Highwater said he lived in an orphanage after his father was killed in an automobile accident until his mother remarried. His stepfather, Alexander Marks, a white man, adopted him.

In the mid-1980's, this version of Highwater's life story was called into question by journalists and scholars. Highwater himself eventually intimated that he had invented some of the details. As a result, a new effort was made to construct his biography. The following represents a general consensus.

Highwater was born probably between 1930 and 1933. The place and date of his birth are unknown because he was given up for adoption by his mother. He was adopted when he was about five years old and lived most of his childhood in the San Fernando Valley in Los Angeles. He was known as Jay or Jack Marks, Marks being the last name of his adoptive parents. In the 1950's, he was inspired to continue to pursue a writing career by a correspondence with writer Nin. He also became interested in modern dance. He moved to San Francisco, where, with others, he formed a dance company called the San Francisco

Contemporary Dancers. Highwater moved to New York in 1967.

Events such as the 1969 takeover of Alcatraz Island by American Indian activists bolstered his already strong interest in Native American issues and culture. Highwater said that in the mid-1970's his adoptive mother and foster sister told him they believed he had at least some "Indian blood." Around 1974 he changed his name to Jamake Highwater. In the 1970's and 1980's, Highwater lived primarily in the Soho section of Manhattan. He founded the Native Land Foundation to promote world folk art and its influence on the modern visual and performing arts.

In the 1980's, Highwater's American Indian identity was publicly called into question, and some Indian activists and writers, among them Vine DeLoria, Jr., stated their belief that he was not Native American. Highwater was undoubtedly disappointed in a lack of support from his associates regarding his claim to Indian ancestry. In 1992, he moved back to Los Angeles and relocated the Native Land Foundation there. His writing generally began to move away from specifically Native American topics.

ANALYSIS

In much of his fiction and nonfiction, Jamake Highwater attempts to convey basic American Indian beliefs and presuppositions. When he emphasizes the differences between contemporary American values and those of American Indians, he stresses that there is more than one reality and that one is not necessarily more valid than another. Each reality has its own truths. By expressing the truths of various Indian cultures as he understands them, Highwater attempts to foster the understanding that must precede peaceful coexistence.

ANPAO

Anpao, a Newbery Honor Book in 1978, has perhaps received less attention than it deserves. Recognition as an outstanding book for children suggests to some critics that a book is intended only for a young audience. Like Mark Twain's *Adventures of Huckleberry Finn* (1884), however, *Anpao* may be enjoyed by those of all ages. As an odyssey of the American Indian, *Anpao* is a compilation of legends, an oral history of Indian tribes. Highwater chooses a number of versions from recorded accounts of these legends, giving credit to his sources. The book's hero, Anpao, is his own creation.

The novel begins with Anpao's falling in love with the beautiful Ko-ko-mik-e-is, who agrees to marry him if he will journey to the Sun and get the Sun's permission for her to marry. The quest begins; Anpao, also called Scarface, sets forth. On his journey, he learns that Anpao means "the Dawn" and that his father is the Sun. Anpao's mother was a human who went to the World-Above-the-World without dying. After the birth of her son, Anpao, she becomes homesick and attempts an escape with her son, but she manages to get only part way to Earth because the rope that she has woven from sinew is not long enough. When the Sun is taunted by his jealous first wife, the Moon, he becomes angry. He follows the footsteps of his human wife to a hole in the sky. Seeing her dangling just above the trees on Earth, he makes a hoop from the branch of a willow tree and orders the hoop to kill the woman but to spare the child. The Sun is not quick enough to snatch the rope when the root that holds the rope in the World-Above-the-World sags because of pity for the dead mother of Anpao. When the child falls onto the dead body of his mother, blood from her body causes a scar to appear on his face. The child, Anpao, lives on Earth, and his journey toward the Sun involves the learning of basic truths of American Indian culture. The legends that he learns on his travels are imparted primarily through traditional storytelling, a mode of teaching used not only by Native Americans but also by ancient Greeks and Romans.

Like Homer in the *Iliad* (c. 750 B.C.E.; English translation, 1611) and the *Odyssey* (c. 725 B.C.E.; English translation, 1614), Highwater states his theme in the short opening chapter and then moves to the story in medias res. Anpao and his twin brother (created when Anpao disobeyed the warning of the Spider Woman, with whom he lived, not to throw his hoop into the air) are poor youths who arrive in the village where the beautiful young girl Ko-ko-mik-e-is lives. After Anpao sets forth on his journey to the Sun, he meets an old woman who tells him the story of the beginning of the world, of the death of the creator Napi, and of his own birth. Then the creation of Oapna, the contrary twin brother of Anpao, is accounted for, and his death is also told. The Clown/Contrary is a familiar figure in American Indian legends.

In another typical Indian legend, Anpao meets with a sorceress, a meeting that invites comparison with Odysseus's meeting with Circe. One of the most important obstacles that Anpao has to overcome is the intense dislike of the Moon, who, as the first wife of the Sun, despises the child born to the human responsible for the Sun's misalliance. Anpao, however, earns the love of the Moon when he saves her son, Morning Star, from death; thus, Anpao becomes the first person to have the power of the Sun, Moon, and Earth.

As a result of his journey to the Sun, Anpao has the ugly scar removed from his face, thus enabling him to prove to Ko-ko-mik-e-is that he did indeed make the journey. The marriage of Anpao (the Dawn and the son of the Sun) and Ko-ko-mik-e-is (Night-red-light, which is related to the Moon) takes place, and Anpao begs the people of Ko-ko-mik-e-is's village to follow the couple as they leave to escape the death, sickness, and greed that are coming to their world. The people will not follow; instead they laugh at Anpao. (This action suggests the lack of unity among American Indians, a lack that may have been crucial to the course of Indian history.) Undaunted, Anpao, taking his beautiful bride with him, goes to the village beneath the water. Ko-ko-mik-e-is is assured by Anpao that what is happening will not be the end, because they and their people are the rivers, the land, the prairies, the rocks—all of nature. This unity with nature is fundamental to American Indian culture.

Most of the legends in *Anpao* belong to times long ago, but Highwater also has included some more modern tales that tell of the arrival of whites with their horses, weapons, and diseases. The legends selected by Highwater are, as American Indian writer N.

Scott Momaday says, "truly reflective of the oral tradition and rich heritage of Native American story-telling." The legends, old and new, are the cornerstone of Indian culture.

JOURNEY TO THE SKY

After writing *Anpao*, essentially a mythical journey, Highwater turned to recorded events for material for his next novel, *Journey to the Sky*. This journey is a fictionalized account of the actual explorations of two white men, John Lloyd Stephens, a New York attorney, and Frederick Catherwood, a British artist and architect. Stephens and Catherwood began their first trip in search of the lost cities of the Mayan kingdom in October, 1839. The men made two extended trips to the kingdom of the Mayan peoples, but Highwater confines his tale to the first exploration, which ended late in July, 1840.

Journey to the Sky is a suspense-filled adventure story that displays Highwater's writing talents more effectively than does his first novel. Although the narrative is interrupted occasionally by Highwater's accounts of later archaeological findings, the suspense and excitement of the journey are sustained throughout. Particularly impressive is Highwater's narrative skill in selecting highlights from the historical account of the Stephens-Catherwood expedition (Stephens did the writing, while Catherwood provided illustrations). Like a number of novels that appeared in the 1970's, including E. L. Doctorow's *Ragtime* (1975) and Aleksandr Solzhenitsyn's *Lennin v Tsyurikhe* (1975; *Lenin in Zurich*, 1976), *Journey to the Sky* is a new kind of historical fiction.

Having been appointed by President Martin Van Buren as U.S. diplomatic agent to the Central American Confederacy, Stephens fulfills his public duties as a diplomat, but his true interest is in the search for ruins. He meets with leaders of various colonies in Central America, paying courtesy calls and extending greetings from the U.S. government. Although Stephens finds the performance of his official duties pleasurable, he is in a hurry to begin explorations.

Early in the trip, while in Belize, the two explorers hire a young cutthroat, Augustin, as their servant. Although they seriously doubt that he will serve them well, by the end of the journey, they realize the rightness of their choice; he proves to be a loyal and valuable servant and friend. They also hire men to help transport their belongings, which include tools, food (including live chickens), and clothing. From time to time, and for differing reasons, new employees must be found.

The trip over Mico Mountain is extremely hazardous because of jungle, rocks, mud, and treacherous gullies. The rough terrain is only one of many natural hazards that they encounter during their explorations in Central America. Insects, climate, earthquakes, and malaria are some of the other forces of nature that they encounter. In addition, they meet such varied characters as the double-dealing Colonel Archibald MacDonald, superintendent of the English colonies in Central America, the petty tyrant Don Gregorio in Copan, good and bad padres, and hospitable and inhospitable people. The explorers are imprisoned, threatened with murder, and surrounded by an active rebellion in Central America.

Highwater captures the enthusiasm of Stephens and Catherwood as they discover the "lost city" just outside Copan. They are the first white men to see these tumbling pyramids and idols, evidence of the religion of the Mayas. Stephens and two helpers begin removing the foliage from rock piles that the people of Copan have been ignoring as piles of rubbish, and Catherwood sets to work documenting their discovery by making drawings of each of the fallen figures. To Stephens, this desolate city with its many magnificent works of art is evidence that the Mayas were master craftspersons.

Having located and documented the ruins at Copan, Stephens and Catherwood move to other sites, where they find further evidence of the Mayan culture. Even illness cannot deter them. From one site to another, the explorers continue their amazing trip. Although warned not to go to Palenque because of the danger to whites as a result of political upheaval, they go. There they find ruins that are quite different from those in Copan. After documenting the Palenque ruins, they go to Uxmal. Many times during the journey in Central America, the New York attorney and the British artist are warned about the hostile Indians, yet the Indians are often more hospitable than the white people they encounter. Stephens and Catherwood's discoveries of a Mayan civilization that rose and fell prior to the Spanish invasion corroborate a basic thesis of Highwater's—that American Indian cultures are meaningful and remarkable.

THE SUN, HE DIES

In *The Sun, He Dies*, Highwater once again turned to recorded history to provide a firm base for his story. The conquering of Montezuma II, ruler of the Aztec nation, by the Spaniard Hernando Cortés with a small contingent of men is perplexing to some historians, who sometimes credit Cortés with an unusual amount of tactical knowledge and ability. Highwater, on the other hand, looks carefully at the character of Montezuma and the religious beliefs of this powerful figure and concludes that these elements were the basic causes of his downfall.

Although the downfall of Montezuma is the backdrop for *The Sun, He Dies*, the novel is also an initiation story, a history of an important Aztec ruler, a history of the Aztec people, and an immersion into Native American culture. Highwater creates a narrator, Nanautzin, to tell the story: This narrative voice unifies the episodic material drawn from the oral traditions of American Indian peoples.

Beginning with "Call me Nanautzin," echoing the opening sentence of Herman Melville's *Moby Dick* (1851), *The Sun, He Dies* unfolds in chronological order. In the epic tradition, Nanautzin, the outcast woodcutter, despised by his people, announces his intention to sing of the great Aztec nation. Like Ishmael in *Moby Dick*, he alone is left to tell the story of all that happened.

Nanautzin briefly tells of his early life in his native village, where he is taunted by the children, cast away by his father, and loved by his mother. The ugly scars that signal the beginning of the unhappy life of the narrator are created by his fall, as a small child, into a cooking fire. The resultant deformities cause his father to abandon him and the villagers to name him the Ugly One. Unlike Oedipus, Nanautzin is not physically cast away; he is given an ax, called a woodcutter, and forgotten. He grows up lonely and friendless.

Nanautzin goes to Tenochtitlan for the installation of Montezuma II as the Great Speaker, even though the people of his village, Tlaxcala, loathe the lord of the greatest city in Mexico. Although Nanautzin feels honor for this great man, the trip does nothing to win for him honor or friends among his people. Because of his physical appearance, he remains the Ugly One, despised and rejected.

Eventually, Nanautzin wanders into a marvelous forest, where, although he knows he should not, he begins to chop firewood. Soon a man appears and questions him, demanding to know why he is cutting wood in the forest. The young man blurts out that, since Montezuma has become ruler, the people of Tlaxcala have not been permitted to cut dead wood wherever they wish and life has become very difficult for his people. Instead of being punished, Nanautzin is ordered to appear at the Palace of Tenochtitlan on the following day.

Fearing for his life, yet obedient, Nanautzin goes to the palace, where he discovers that the stranger he met in the forest is the Great Speaker himself. Instead of receiving punishment for his honest reply to Montezuma on the preceding day, Nanautzin is transformed into the Chief Orator because of his honesty. Then he is taken to the ruins at Tula, the once great city of the ancient Toltecs, where he, along with young boys, is taught by the priests and where he learns that here the greatest of all men once lived. This experience at Tula is both an initiation and a religious experience.

After his experience at Tula, Nanautzin becomes the confidant of Montezuma, who tells him the many legends of his people. Montezuma also confides that, according to his horoscope, his life is balanced between the war god, Huitzilopochtli, who fills the body of Montezuma with power, and the gentle god, Quetzalcoatl, who fills Montezuma's body with love. The Toltecs were the wise people created by the gentle Quetzalcoatl, who, like the Norse god Odin, was a benefactor to his people. Evil people loathed Quetzalcoatl, the tall, noble, holy white god who would not permit his people to be sacrificed. The evil men managed to trick this loving god with a mirror; drunk with pulque, Quetzalcoatl, who had seen his body in the mirror, became passionate and slept with a forbidden priestess. Evil came into the land and Quetzalcoatl went into exile in the land of Yucatan, but promised to return in the year One Reed, at which time he would recapture his throne and bring peace forevermore. Montezuma believes that Quetzalcoatl will return.

Although believing in the return of Quetzalcoatl, Montezuma also believes the horoscope, thus making him susceptible to doubt about himself: Is he one of the evil ones who destroyed this great god or one of the faithful who follow him? On one hand, he demands tributes and sacrifices from the people, ruling much of the time by force, thus acceding to Huitzilopochtli and alienating many of the tribes. On the other hand, he honors the gentle Quetzalcoatl and longs for his return.

During his early years as Chief Orator, Nanautzin learns the beliefs of this mighty leader and the history of the people. He recognizes the goodness in the Great Speaker of Tenochtitlan. Even though Montezuma appears to be a ruthless ruler, he has been kind to Nanautzin, he admires honesty, and he has great faith in the prediction that Quetzalcoatl will return. Montezuma's faith in the promise of this great and good god indicates the Aztec ruler's devotion to his religion.

From the favorable signs that appear in the year One Reed, Montezuma draws great confidence, but a time comes when the signs change. Montezuma is no longer the almost divine figure that Nanautzin has observed. Instead, the Great Speaker can no longer make up his own mind, which has become so divided that one part is contrary to the other part. Montezuma, like Ahab in *Moby Dick*, becomes obsessed. When he learns of the white men who have arrived at Chalco, the Great Speaker concludes that Quetzalcoatl's prediction is about to come true. Although the priests, the soothsayers, the noblemen, and the warriors warn Montezuma that these mysterious men are not Quetzalcoatl and his court, the Great Speaker is not to be shaken in his belief. Because Montezuma has alienated many of the neighboring tribes, he is hated; it is, therefore, easy for Cortés and his troops to enlist the aid of the alienated tribes, including the people of Tlazcala, in the march against Tenochtitlan.

Instead of trying to defend his city, Montezuma makes offerings to Cortés, whom he believes to be the gentle god Quetzalcoatl. It becomes an easy matter for Cortés to enter the realm of Montezuma and then, with the help of the alienated tribes, wreak havoc not only on the Great Speaker but also on the people of Tenochtitlan.

The narrative structure of *The Sun, He Dies* is strong, and the development of the character of Montezuma makes believable the idea that Tenochtitlan falls not because of the tactical superiority of Cortés but because of Montezuma's religious beliefs and obsessions. In addition to the recounting of history, the novel is a collection of tales that are an integral part of the beliefs of the Aztec nation. The Ugly One who becomes the Chief Orator for Montezuma II, although he comes full circle from being a lonely figure in Tlaxcala to being the figure left alone, is far wiser than the ignorant woodcutter Nanautzin who wanders into the forest owned by the Great Speaker. Nevertheless, the once powerful Aztec nation is destroyed and Nanautzin can only sing of what has been.

"What has been" is pertinent to many of Highwater's novels. Based on oral and recorded history, *Anpao*, *Journey to the Sky*, and *The Sun, He Dies*, for example, convey truths of three important American Indian cultures. The Indian respect for and allegiance to the forces of nature determined their actions. The significance of religion in the fall of Montezuma, in the ruins of Yucatan, and in the lives of Native Americans adds another dimension to recorded history.

THE GHOST HORSE CYCLE

Using his knowledge of Native American myth and his own techniques of storytelling, Highwater applied his enthusiasm for the retelling of history to his trilogy, collectively referred to as *The Ghost Horse Cycle*. In the first book, *Legend Days*, the story begins as a mythic chronicle of the character Amana, a young girl of the Blood tribe of the northern Plains, who lived in the late nineteenth century. Her people have contracted smallpox from the white traders and are dying in large numbers. Her sister, SoodaWa, sends Amana away; in a strange, dreamlike sequence, Amana is captured by the evil owls, rescued by the kindly foxes, and protected from harm by sleeping in a cave for a year. During that time, she receives a vision in which she becomes a man, a warrior, and hunts with other men. She is given a set of warrior's clothes by her spirit helper, which she must never reveal until the proper time. She returns to her village only to find two old women left, all the rest having died or fled.

Eventually Amana is reunited with her sister and her sister's husband, Far Away Son, who have been living with Big Belly, a chief of the Gros Ventres tribe. Amana marries Far Away Son, as is the custom among the Bloods—orphaned girls marry their sister's husbands. She tries to be a good wife, but secretly her vision makes her long to be a warrior. The story rehearses the agonizing plight of the northern Plains tribes as the extensive hunting of buffalo dwindled the supply of food, disease ravaged the population, and the whites' influence, such as whiskey, paralyzed Native American culture.

Legend Days—a book written as a myth and centered in recorded history—reads very much like other Highwater narratives, but *The Ghost Horse Cycle* trilogy is more personal than most Highwater works. Continuing with *Eyes of Darkness* and then with *I Wear the Morning Star*, it becomes evident that the myth only begins the story. Amana eventually weds a French trader named Jean-Pierre Bonneville and has a daughter, Jemina Bonneville, who in turn weds Jamie Ghost Horse, a Native American working as a Hollywood stuntman. They have two children, Reno and Sitko. The focus of the novels turns from the rather hazy myth of *Legend Days* to the concrete story of one family's efforts to survive the onslaught of the modern world in their lives.

Eyes of Darkness chronicles the marriage of Amana and Jean-Pierre, as well as Amana's introduction into white society, a transition that for her is never really successful. Her daughter Jemina's stormy marriage to Jamie Ghost Horse shows Native Americans confronting newly acquired economic realities, newly acquired problems such as alcoholism, and newly acquired stigmas, such as discrimination and racism.

I Wear the Morning Star focuses on Jemina's two children, Reno, who seeks to deny his American Indian heritage, and Sitko, who listens attentively to his grandmother's stories and longs for the old ways. Jemina is forced by circumstance and poverty to place the boys in an orphanage until she remarries a white man named Alexander Miller, and the boys return to her household only to aggravate further the number of underlying problems each is having. For the grandchildren of Amana, life has become too complex; they live in a world that is neither American Indian nor white, not knowing whether to follow the ways of the whites or to listen to the compelling stories of their grandmother. The need to adopt white customs and practices is apparent, but Sitko especially learns that Grandmother Amana offers something that the whites cannot: "[F]rom Grandmother Amana I learned how to dream myself into existence." Sitko becomes an artist and begins to explore his heritage through his art.

KILL HOLE

In *Kill Hole*, Highwater leads Sitko Ghost Horse, his artist-hero, through life experiences that appear as nightmarish sequences. They bring to light the idea that imagination is the only human identity of consequence. Sitko, an adopted child who has been renamed Seymour Miller by his father, suffers the indignities of this abusive parent who erases Sitko's North American Indian identity. Sitko's grandmother inspires the youth with her tribal stories, compelling him to seek his lost culture. Discovering art as his medium of expression, Sitko makes the visionary connection between his ancestral past of harmony with nature and the present marked by environmental calamities, a plague reminiscent of acquired immunodeficiency syndrome (AIDS), and a breakdown of human connections in a society that exhibits a hatred of art and a fear of the unknown.

In a Kafkaesque desert village, Sitko is tried for being an interloper; unless he can prove that he is a bona fide Indian, he will be put to death. Imprisoned, he comes in contact with a brutish dwarf who instills his hatred of the arts on the villagers he rules. Patu, Sitko's sympathetic supporter, overcomes her fear of art to nurture her compassion for him. Sitko survives prison by recounting his past and bringing truth and art together in picture stories. Highwater concludes his complicated story by affirming the power of artistic imagination over social antagonism. A number of commentators have noted that to some extent the tale represents Highwater's response to the assertions he is not Native American.

DARK LEGEND

Dark Legend provides Highwater a forum for introducing European concepts to non-European settings. The novel is based on the story of Richard Wagner's Ring cycle (1874; *Der Ring des Nibelungen*). It adapts the operatic story to mythic pre-Columbian America. The book teems with gods, goddesses, giants, and other supernatural beings. Magical maidens bathe in a gold-blessed river that loses its precious metal to Caru, a greedy dwarf. In short duration, the thief is captured and the gold is recovered, now forged into a ring and magic crown. Lord Kuwai and his consort Amaru remain worried; the recovered treasure no longer shines. Kuwai's avarice spreads disaster. His zeal for the treasure causes his son's death and estrangement from his only daughter. The valiant warrior Washi collects the gold, falls in love with the daughter, Idera, and returns the metal to the river. Earth becomes balanced again.

Virginia A. Duck
Updated by Craig Gilbert

OTHER MAJOR WORKS

NONFICTION: *Rock and Other Four Letter Words*, 1968 (as J. Marks); *Europe Under Twenty-five: A Young Person's Guide*, 1971; *Mick Jagger: The Singer, Not the Song*, 1973 (as J. Marks); *Fodor's Indian America*, 1975; *Indian America: A Cultural and Travel Guide*, 1975; *Song from the Earth: American Indian Painting*, 1976; *Ritual of the Wind: North American Indian Dances and Music*, 1977; *Dance: Rituals of Experience*, 1978; *Many Smokes, Many Moons: A Chronology of American Indian History Through Indian Art*, 1978; *The Sweet Grass Lives On: Fifty Contemporary North American Indian Artists*, 1980; *The Primal Mind: Vision and Reality in Indian America*, 1981; *Arts of the Indian Americas: Leaves from the Sacred Tree*, 1983; *Native Land: Sagas of the Indian Americas*, 1986; *Shadow Show: An Autobiographical Insinuation*, 1986; *Myth and Sexuality*, 1990; *The Language of Vision: Meditations on Myth and Metaphor*, 1994; *The Mythology of Transgression: Homosexuality as Metaphor*, 1997.

CHILDREN'S LITERATURE: *Moonsong Lullaby*, 1981; *Rama: A Legend*, 1994 (adaptation of *The Ramayana*); *Songs for the Seasons*, 1995 (Sandra Speidel, illustrator).

EDITED TEXT: *Words in the Blood: Contemporary Indian Literature of North and South America*, 1984.

BIBLIOGRAPHY

Churchill, Ward. *Fantasies of the Master Race: Literature, Cinema, and the Colonization of the American Indians*. Monroe, Maine: Common Courage Press, 1992. An intriguing exposé of the practice of pretending to be American Indian. Highwater receives ample attention in the book, and Churchill disputes Highwater's claim of North American Indian heritage.

Grimes, Ronald L. "To Hear the Eagles Cry: Contemporary Themes in Native American Spirituality." *American Indian Quarterly* 20 (June 22, 1996): 433-451. This lengthy multiparticipant discussion focuses on educating American Indians in religious precepts. Highwater serves as a source for several of the concepts discussed in the debate.

Katz, Jane, ed. *This Song Remembers: Self-Portraits of Native Americans in the Arts*. Boston: Houghton Mifflin, 1980. Katz's work includes essays from many different American Indian artists who are active in the visual arts, poetry, literature, and dance. Highwater's self-portrait centers on the importance of myth and Indian culture to his life and art.

Kutzer, M. Daphne, ed. *Writers of Multicultural Fiction for Young Adults: A Bio-Critical Sourcebook*. Westport, Conn.: Greenwood Press, 1996. Highwater is one of the writers of fiction for young adults included in this reference book; the fourteen-page entry about him features a biography, criticism, and a bibliography.

Shanley, Kathryn W. "The Indians America Loves to Love and Read: American Indian Identity and Cultural Appropriation." *American Indian Quarterly* 21, no. 4 (Fall, 1997). After recounting the controversy over Highwater's Indian heritage, Shanley addresses what she describes as the "primary issue" regarding the author: "His romanti-cized version of American Indian identity" and his assumption of "a place for himself as the primary spokesperson for Indians . . . with an arrogance that belies a disrespect for American Indian communities."

Stott, Jon C. "Narrative Expectations and Textual Misreadings: Jamake Highwater's *Anpao* Analyzed and Reanalyzed." *Studies in the Literary Imagination* 18, no. 2 (Fall, 1985): 93-105. Highwater's award-winning book *Anpao* is given a thorough critical analysis. Stott describes how his initial expectations of the book were based on his be-lief that Highwater was a "Native writer," and how these conceptions were challenged after revelations that Highwater was not of Blackfoot/Cherokee heritage.

PAUL HORGAN

Born: Buffalo, New York; August 1, 1903
Died: Middletown, Connecticut; March 8, 1995
Also known as: Paul George Vincent O'Shaughnessy Horgan

<small>PRINCIPAL LONG FICTION</small>
The Fault of Angels, 1933
No Quarter Given, 1935
Main Line West, 1936
A Lamp on the Plains, 1937
Far from Cibola, 1938
The Habit of Empire, 1938
The Common Heart, 1942
The Devil in the Desert: A Legend of Life and Death in the Rio Grande, 1952
The Saintmaker's Christmas Eve, 1955
Give Me Possession, 1957
A Distant Trumpet, 1960
Mountain Standard Time, 1962 (includes *Main Line West*, *Far from Cibola*, and
   The Common Heart)
Things as They Are, 1964
Memories of the Future, 1966
Everything to Live For, 1968
Whitewater, 1970
The Thin Mountain Air, 1977
Mexico Bay, 1982

<small>OTHER LITERARY FORMS</small>

Throughout his long and meritorious career, Paul Horgan was known as widely for his short fiction and nonfiction as for his novels. Most of his short fiction is found in three collections, but the best of his stories appear in *The Peach Stone: Stories from Four Decades* (1967). Like his fiction, Horgan's histories and biographies revolve around events and people of the American Southwest. His most prestigious history is *Great River: The Rio Grande in North American History* (1954), but *The Centuries of Santa Fe* (1956) and *Conquistadors in North American History* (1963) are also important works. His biographies, most notably *Lamy of Santa Fé: His Life and Times* (1975) and *Josiah Gregg and His Visions of the Early West* (1979), vividly chronicle the struggle of individuals and the clash of Spanish and American Indian cultures on the southwestern frontier. Horgan's work in drama includes the play *Yours, A. Lincoln* (pr. 1942) and the libretto to *A Tree on the Plains: A Music Play for Americans* (pb. 1943), an American folk opera with music by

Paul Horgan
(National Archives)

Ernst Bacon. His *Approaches to Writing* (1973) is composed of three long essays explaining his craft. Horgan's novel *A Distant Trumpet* was filmed in 1964; *Things as They Are* was filmed in 1970.

ACHIEVEMENTS

As a novelist as well as a distinguished writer of nonfiction, Paul Horgan devoted his career to the American Southwest. Although he is regarded as a regionalist, some critics have rightly pointed out that he uses regional figures and settings essentially as vehicles for universal themes, much as William Faulkner used regional materials. Horgan's work should not be identified with the popular, formulaic Western writing of such authors as Zane Grey, Louis L'Amour, and Max Brand; rather, he should be seen as a significant figure in the tradition of literary Western fiction that has attracted the attention of critics and readers since the early 1960's.

Recognition for Horgan's writing came in many forms. He won seventy-five hundred dollars in the Harper Prize Novel Contest for *The Fault of Angels* in 1933. He was awarded two Guggenheim fellowships (1945 and 1958) to work on his nonfiction. For *Great River*, Horgan won the Pulitzer Prize in history and the Bancroft Prize of Columbia University. In 1957, the Campion Award for eminent service to Catholic letters was presented to him. The Western Literature Association paid tribute to Horgan with its distinguished Achievement Award (1973), and the Western Writers of America cited him with their Silver Spur Award (1976). He was twice honored by the Texas Institute of Letters (1954 and 1971).

Just as important as these awards, and an indication of the wide range of Horgan's interests and abilities, are the ways in which he served his community and country. Horgan served as president of the board of the Santa Fe Opera (1958-1962) and the Roswell Museum (1946-1952). He became director of the Wesleyan Center for Advanced Studies in 1962 and remained so until 1967. President Lyndon B. Johnson made Horgan one of his first appointees to the Council of the National Endowment for the Humanities. In addition to being visiting scholar and writer-in-residence at a number of colleges and universities, Horgan served on the board of the Aspen Institute and the Book-of-the-Month Club.

Although some of his novels have sold in the millions and despite his long career, Horgan was not as well known as many of his contemporaries. Those who are familiar with his work, however, see him as a prescient figure, a writer whose concern with the complex, multicultural history of the Southwest anticipated the challenging revisionism of the 1970's and the 1980's, when scholars and fiction writers alike offered a new, critical look at the West.

BIOGRAPHY

Paul George Vincent O'Shaughnessy Horgan was born in Buffalo, New York, on August 1, 1903. He moved to Albuquerque, New Mexico, with his parents in 1915 and attended the New Mexico Military Institute in Roswell until 1921, when he left to be at home when his father was dying. After working for a year at the *Albuquerque Morning Journal*, he moved to the East Coast in 1923 to study at the Eastman School of Music in Rochester, New York. He returned to Roswell in 1926 and accepted the job of librarian at the New Mexico Military Institute. He remained in Roswell until 1942 and wrote his first five novels. Horgan spent World War II in Washington, D.C., as chief of the U.S. Army Information Branch of the Information and Education Division of the War Department, where he supervised all the information that was sent to American troops all over the world. Horgan returned to New Mexico after the war and worked on his nonfiction, but after 1960 he became associated with Wesleyan University in different capacities, living and writing on the Wesleyan campus. He died in Middletown, Connecticut, in March of 1995.

ANALYSIS

Paul Horgan's fiction is dominated on one level by a skillful, aesthetic evocation of the southwestern landscape and climate and a sensitive delineation of character. His novels are exceptionally well written, with sharp detail and imagery often matched by a lyrical tone perfectly suited to the basic goodness of his protagonists. Yet to dwell on this strong sense of place is to miss a basic theme in his works and to misjudge the appeal of his writing. The strength of Horgan's fiction lies in the reader's immediate and sympathetic identification with the protagonists. Curiosity is perhaps humankind's most distinguishing feature. This is true not only in an academic sense but in a personal way as well: To varying degrees, people take an interest in their ancestry and family histories. They want to know who they are and whence they come. It is both a peculiarity and a trademark of Horgan's fiction that this kind of knowing is its constant concern. The dramatic center in Horgan's books revolves around people learning the truth about themselves and their lives.

Horgan employs two main narrative strategies to accomplish his end. In books such as *Far from Cibola* and *A Distant Trumpet*, individuals must deal with an unexpected event upsetting the routine of everyday life and, as a result, are challenged to define their own lives more clearly. On the other hand, in novels such as *Things as They Are* and *Whitewater*, his protagonists conduct a more conscious search for an understanding of who they are and make a deliberate attempt to come to terms with their own pasts.

FAR FROM CIBOLA

Often in Horgan's fiction, discovering the truth about oneself occurs after some startling event disrupts the ordinary flow of life. Such is the case in *Far from Cibola*, which many critics regard as Horgan's best novel. This short work, set in and around a small town in New Mexico during the early years of the Great Depression, records what happens to a dozen of the local inhabitants during a day in which they are all briefly brought together as part of a large crowd protesting economic conditions. After the crowd threatens to turn into an unruly mob, the sheriff fires a warning shot above their heads into some trees and accidentally kills a teenager who had climbed up the tree to watch the excitement. The crowd disperses after the gunfire, and the remaining chapters describe what happens to the dozen characters the rest of the day. Although these figures span a broad band of the socio-economic spectrum of the New Mexican (and American) landscape of the 1930's, *Far from Cibola* is not simply another proletarian novel of that decade. Economic problems and hardships are uppermost in the minds of almost everyone in the story, but the fate of each character hinges on his or her ability to recognize and accept reality as it suddenly appears.

The opening chapter provides a good example of what happens to all the characters in the novel. It begins with serene, pastoral images: Mountains are shimmering in the morning haze, and smoke from breakfast fires rises straight into the clear April sky. In Ellen Rood's kitchen, there is a springlike feeling of peace and well-being. As she lays wood for her own stove, Ellen listens to the sounds of her two small children out in the farmyard. Her son, Donald, is chopping at some wood with an ax that is too big for his hands, and her daughter, Lena, is washing her face from a tin dish sitting on the edge of the well. Without warning, however, smoke rolls back into her eyes and sparks sting her arms when Ellen attempts to start the fire. At about the same time, Ellen realizes that her children are strangely quiet. When she investigates, she discovers a huge rattlesnake nearby; she quickly hacks it to death before it can harm her children. There are many scenes such as this one in *Far from Cibola*, in which people suddenly have an idyllic world overturned by a more sober, often harsher reality. How they react is a good measure of their character. Not everyone can prevail as Ellen does.

The incident in the courthouse provides a social context for what happens to the novel's individuals. Until the crowd becomes violent, everything is fairly calm and orderly. There may be hunger and economic desperation in the community, but people have not yet fully faced the fact that there are no hidden food supplies and the government cannot help them. The killing underscores this bleak reality, and society as a whole must deal with this truth, as Ellen had to face the rattlesnake outside her kitchen door.

A DISTANT TRUMPET

A Distant Trumpet, written more than two decades later, shows thematic concerns similar to those of *Far from Cibola*, but Horgan achieves them in a slightly different manner. The novel's primary setting is Fort Delivery, a frontier outpost near the Mexican border in the Arizona Territory during the late 1880's. Although there are a number of characters, the story centers on a young U.S. Army lieutenant named Matthew Hazard and an Apache scout called Joe Dummy. Deftly and incisively, Horgan dramatizes Hazard's and Joe Dummy's roles in helping to make peace with a rebellious band of American Indians who had escaped into Mexico, and the novel ends with Hazard, bitter and disillusioned, resigning from the Army when Joe Dummy is treated no better than the Indians he helped to defeat.

Rather than using startling and often violent images, as in *Far from Cibola*, Horgan makes extensive use of flashbacks to the American Civil War period and earlier as a useful device for pulling down and digging out illusion and sham and seeing the truth clearly. That Matthew Hazard is Horgan's vehicle for showing the necessity not only of recognizing but also of maintaining self-knowledge is brought out in a very short section titled "Scenes from Early Times." Consisting of a series of short questions and answers between Hazard and an unknown person, the conversation reveals the earliest and most important knowledge Matthew can recall: that he was his father's child. Indeed, it is no accident that this book often reads like a biography. To be one's father's child in *A Distant Trumpet* means being able to acknowledge the less well-known aspects of self as well as the more openly accepted parts. Tragedy occurs when individuals cannot or will not see that darker side.

One of the more striking scenes in the novel occurs when Matthew, on his way to Fort Delivery for the first time, meets White Horn. Sergeant Blickner, who has come to take Matthew to the fort, refuses to take an Indian along in his wagon, and Matthew must give him a direct order to do so. Even after this, Blickner baits White Horn on the way back and calls him Joe Dummy, a nickname picked up later by soldiers at the fort. In previous sections, however, White Horn's courageous and often heroic life has been described at length, so that he has become an individual to the reader. Thus, readers share the narrator's feeling of outrage and indignation that no one at the fort can see Joe Dummy as anything but another "grimy" Indian. Horgan laments bitterly the failure of these people to see clearly and suggests that they will be lost until they somehow discover the truth about themselves and their social structure. In this sense, Fort Delivery becomes an ironic name for an individual's self-imprisonment. Horgan's flashbacks in *A Distant Trumpet* force his readers to look beyond appearance and not accept the false and commonplace, in much the same way the rattlesnake and courthouse incident in *Far from Cibola* made people confront the unpleasant realities in their lives. *A Distant Trumpet* poignantly reveals what happens when individuals (and society) are unable to see worlds other than their own.

THINGS AS THEY ARE

In *Things as They Are*, perhaps the most autobiographical of all of his works, Horgan approaches the question of knowing oneself more directly. The novel is narrated by Richard, an adult writer who recounts certain events in his early childhood to help him understand the way he is now. Horgan continues Richard's story in two later novels: *Everything to Live For* and *The Thin Mountain Air*. *Things as They Are*, then, is a bildungsroman, a story of growth and awakening, and through this format, Richard articulates his need to understand himself and others more clearly.

Like most stories about growing up, the boy Richard undergoes a variety of experiences that the adult Richard must then interpret if he is to make some sense of his life. Although he describes a close family life and happy summer trips to the mountains, Richard also discloses certain important conflicts and tensions for the young boy: an uncle who commits suicide, an autocratic grandfather, a well-meaning but overly protective mother, a father who is not quite strong enough. The novel's structure in its simplest terms is a delicate balancing act between Richard's honestly depicting these family tensions and then explaining both what they meant to him and how they resulted in his seeing things as they are.

WHITEWATER

Things as They Are may be regarded as a prelude to *Whitewater*, which is also about a young man, Phillipson Durham, growing up. Set in the West Texas town of Belvedere during the years 1948-1949, the novel describes what happens to Phillipson and two high school classmates (Billy Breedlove and Marilee Underwood) during his senior year. Within this framework, the novel is essentially one long flashback by a much older Phillipson, who has written it, as the last chapter makes clear, for much the same reason Richard told his story in *Things as They Are*. Phillipson is probing for clues in his past that will allow him to understand the events of his senior year and what has happened to him since. Phillipson's search is less successful than Richard's and his conclusions more tentative.

Phillipson's quest for self-knowledge is marked by three central images in the novel: Lake Whitewater, Victoria Cochran's house, and the town's water tower. Lake Whitewater is a large, human-made lake formed when Whitewater Dam went into operation. What intrigues Phillipson is that deep under the lake's surface lies an abandoned town complete with houses, yards, and street lamps. Billy informs Phillipson that when the lake is calm, the town can still be seen. The lake and submerged town thus become a metaphor for Phillipson's own lost knowledge about himself. Like the town, his past is still there, waiting to be viewed and understood if only he can see it clearly. Linked with this image is Crystal Wells, the home of Victoria Cochran, an elderly widow who befriends Phillipson and becomes his mentor. At Crystal Wells, Phillipson escapes the dreary provincialism of Belvedere and explores his own ideas and beliefs. It becomes an intellectual oasis where he can begin to define his own life.

Opposed to this image is that of Belvedere's water tower, which Horgan unmistakably identifies with unthinking and impulsive behavior. Caught up in the excitement of springtime and the end of his senior year, Billy Breedlove climbs to the top of the tower to paint the words "Beat Orpha City" on its side. He loses his footing, however, and falls ninety feet to the ground below. Billy's death and Marilee's subsequent suicide are warnings to Phillipson that impulse and feeling by themselves threaten understanding and growth. Phillipson overcomes his grief at Crystal Wells and recognizes that his own education is only beginning. As the last section of *Whitewater* suggests, however, Phillipson years later is still growing, still trying to understand those events and himself, quite aware that there are things that he cannot and perhaps will never know completely. Nevertheless, as Richard does in *Things as They Are*, Phillipson focuses on maintaining moments of wakeful insight.

In understanding Horgan's novels, it is important to recognize that the protagonists are driven by a need to know themselves and their pasts. Given this theme, Horgan uses two main narrative techniques. On one hand, as in *Far from Cibola* and *A Distant Trumpet*, his characters are confronted with events that suddenly disrupt their lives and their normal sense of things. In novels such as *Things as They Are* and *Whitewater*, on the other hand, his protagonists deliberately set about exploring their pasts to learn about themselves. Horgan's message is the same in both cases: Individuals must pursue the truth about themselves, no matter what the cost. Anything else is escapism, a kind of vicarious participation in life.

Terry L. Hansen

OTHER MAJOR WORKS

SHORT FICTION: *The Return of the Weed*, 1936; *Figures in a Landscape*, 1940; *The Peach Stone: Stories from Four Decades*, 1967.

PLAYS: *Yours, A. Lincoln*, pr. 1942; *A Tree on the Plains: A Music Play for Americans*, pb. 1943 (libretto; music by Ernst Bacon).

POETRY: *Lamb of God*, 1927; *Songs After Lincoln*, 1965; *The Clerihews of Paul Horgan*, 1985.

NONFICTION: *New Mexico's Own Chronicle*, 1937 (with Maurice G. Fulton); *Great River: The Rio Grande in North American History*, 1954; *The Centuries of Santa Fe*, 1956; *Rome Eternal*, 1959; *A Citizen of New Salem*, 1961; *Conquistadors in North American History*, 1963; *Peter Hurd: A Portrait Sketch from Life*, 1965; *The Heroic Triad: Essays in the Social Energies of Three Southwestern Cultures*, 1970; *Encounters with Stravinsky: A Personal Record*, 1972; *Approaches to Writing*, 1973; *Lamy of Santa Fé: His Life and Times*, 1975; *Josiah Gregg and His Visions of the Early West*, 1979; *Of America East and West: Selections from the Writings of Paul Horgan*, 1984; *A Certain Climate: Essays on History, Arts, and Letters*, 1988; *A Writer's Eye: Field Notes and Watercolors*, 1988; *Tracings: A Book of Partial Portraits*, 1993; *Henriette Wyeth: The Artifice of Blue Light*, 1994.

CHILDREN'S LITERATURE: *Men of Arms*, 1931.

BIBLIOGRAPHY
Erisman, Fred. "Western Regional Writers and the Uses of Place." *Journal of the West* 19 (1980): 36-44. Reprinted in *The American Literary West*, edited by Richard W. Etulain. Manhattan, Kans.: Sunflower University Press, 1980. Placing Horgan in the company of Willa Cather, John Steinbeck, and John Graves, this article presents Horgan's writings as among those who meet the challenge of Ralph Waldo Emerson for artists to use the most American of materials—the experience of the West.

Gish, Robert. *Nueva Granada: Paul Horgan and the Southwest*. College Station: Texas A&M University Press, 1995. Contains a lengthy and previously unpublished interview with Horgan, as well as selected essays and articles about his life and Southwestern writings. Gish demonstrates how Horgan's work transcends Western regionalism and how it recognizes a "new West" of geographic, ethnic, and cultural diversity.

_____. *Paul Horgan*. Boston: Twayne, 1983. Gish argues that Horgan's writing is not merely regionalist, but moves from East to West and back again; he covers Horgan as novelist, short-story writer, historian, and essayist. Includes a chronology, notes and references, a selected, annotated bibliography, and an index.

_____. "Paul Horgan." In *A Literary History of the American West*. Fort Worth: Texas Christian University Press, 1987. Horgan receives a chapter in this important book of literary scholarship that assesses his place in American literary history as a writer of Southwest regionalism. Includes a selected bibliography of primary and secondary sources.

Labrie, Ross. "Paul Horgan (1903-1995)." In *The Catholic Imagination in American Literature*. Columbia: University of Missouri Press, 1997. Labrie analyzes representative works by Horgan and other Catholic writers and poets to describe how these works express each writer's particular interpretation of Catholic teaching.

McInerny, Ralph. "Paul Horgan." In *Some Catholic Writers*. South Bend, Ind.: St. Augustine's Press, 2007. This collection of brief articles about American and European writers whose work was in some way influenced by Catholicism includes an article on Horgan.

Pilkington, William T. "Paul Horgan." In *My Blood's Country: Studies in Southwestern Literature*. Fort Worth: Texas Christian University Press, 1973. Although Horgan was a prolific writer in a variety of forms, Pilkington argues that his best work reveals an understanding of human desires and disappointments as expressed in the concrete details of lived experience. Besides Christian values, Horgan's writing expresses features of Ralph Waldo Emerson's transcendental philosophy.

BARBARA KINGSOLVER

Born: Annapolis, Maryland; April 8, 1955

PRINCIPAL LONG FICTION
The Bean Trees, 1988
Animal Dreams, 1990
Pigs in Heaven, 1993
The Poisonwood Bible, 1998
Prodigal Summer, 2000
Lacuna, 2009

OTHER LITERARY FORMS

Barbara Kingsolver, known primarily for her long fiction, also has written travel articles, book reviews, essays, and poetry. Her nonfiction book *Holding the Line: Women in the Great Arizona Mine Strike of 1983* (1989) presents a compelling picture of the plight of miners in southern Arizona's copper-mining company towns. The form of her poetry collection *Another America/Otra America* (1992)—with Kingsolver's poetry and its Spanish translations printed on facing pages—invites cultural awareness. *Homeland, and Other Stories* (1989), a short-story collection, contains previously published and new work, most of which depicts the vagaries and pressures of different mother/daughter relationships. Some of the stories encompass fathers, brothers, and husbands as well, but all explore how family, past and present, affects the identity and perspective of the main character or the narrator in each story.

Kingsolver's essays include those in *High Tide in Tucson: Essays from Now or Never* (1995), which present her thoughts on parenting, home ownership, cultural habits, travel, writing, and other topics. Following the national upheaval surrounding the September 11, 2001, terrorist attacks, Kingsolver was asked to edit previous essays and add new material to a volume that she would call *Last Stand: America's Virgin Lands* (2002). The book includes photographs by Annie Griffiths Belt and text by Kingsolver celebrating America's remaining wilderness. In *Small Wonder* (2002), Kingsolver explores what it means to be a patriotic American and responsible citizen of the world. The essays reiterate her pacifist philosophy and her open-hearted embrace of the American tradition of dissent and active involvement in environmental, domestic, and political issues. Her love of the United States is clear in these works, as is her insistence on the right and responsibility to express one's ideas.

Animal, Vegetable, Miracle: A Year of Food Life (2007), written with her daughter Camille Kingsolver and her husband, Steven L. Hopp, is an intimate look at how Kingsolver and her family made the transition from Arizona to southwestern Virginia. The family committed to growing most of what they would eat and to buying locally grown foods to supplement their diet. The book has recipes, contributed by Camille, and scientific and political information on programs and legislation related to food production, contributed by Steven. It offers stories both hysterical—the sex lives of turkeys—and sobering—the modest gains of farmers who have decided to go organic and the damage done to the land by large agribusinesses.

ACHIEVEMENTS

Barbara Kingsolver has won many writing awards. In 1986, the Arizona Press Club presented her with its feature-writing award. She received American Library Association awards in 1989 for *The Bean Trees* and in 1990 for *Homeland*. She also won the Edward Abbey Ecofiction Award (1990) for *Animal Dreams* and the prestigious PEN Western Fiction Award (1991). In 1993 and 1994, she received a *Los Angeles Times* Book Award and Mountain and Plains Booksellers Association Award for *Pigs in Heaven*. She also received an Enoch Pratt Library Youth Book Award for *The Bean Trees*. In 1995, she received an honorary doctorate from De Pauw University.

Other awards honor Kingsolver's writings on ecology. In 2003, she won the Earth Day Award from the Kentucky Environmental Quality Commission for her works on timely environmental issues. In 2002, she was honored by Physicians for Social Responsibility and received the Frank Waters Award for her writings on the Southwest. Also in 2002, she was on the PEN/USA advisory board to evaluate the work of contemporary American authors. True to her activist principles, she founded the Bellwether Prize, given in support of new authors writing literature of social change.

BIOGRAPHY

Barbara Kingsolver was born in Annapolis, Maryland, in 1955. Her childhood was spent mostly in eastern Kentucky's rural Nicholas County. She began writing before she entered high school. In 1977, she earned an undergraduate degree in biology, magna cum laude, from De Pauw University in Indiana. Work toward her master of science degree at the University of Arizona in Tucson (1981) included a creative writing class. After completing her master's degree she worked as a science writer for the University of Arizona and began to write feature articles on the side, which appeared in publications such as *Smithsonian*, *Harpers*, and *The New York Times*.

In 1985, Kingsolver married Joseph Hoffman. She soon began to write what would become her first novel, *The Bean Trees*, doing so in insomniac interludes when she was pregnant with her daughter, Camille. Kingsolver subsequently was divorced; she then married Hopp and settled in Tucson. Kingsolver has been a political activist all her adult life. Just after 2000, she and her family relocated to a farm in southwestern Virginia. Their move spawned her nonfiction book *Animal, Vegetable, Miracle*.

ANALYSIS

Barbara Kingsolver's long fiction is best characterized as a contemporary version of the bildungsroman, but with a feminist perspective. Her main characters (women) develop themselves and find their place in their community. Traditionally, books by women that incorporate a female's quest—such as exploring one's sexuality or finding meaningful work in the world—end in punishment for that girl or woman. Also, traditional bildungsromans show a struggle against those who wish to stifle a female's journey, as in *The Awakening* (1899) by Kate Chopin, or the novels emphasize the price a woman pays for fully developing herself as a person, as in Willa Cather's *O Pioneers!* (1913).

Kingsolver's work departs from the punitive mold. Tension emerges as her female characters seek synthesis, a coming together that will meld place, memory, and the present moment to help create personal identity. Kingsolver's narratives also orchestrate the play between inner and outer landscapes. In *The Bean Trees*, Taylor Greer moves across Kentucky and through Oklahoma, landing in Tucson with a baby who will change her emotional geography. On page 3 of *Animal Dreams*, the still-mysterious Cosima announces her destination as Grace, Arizona—the site of her early life, stage for the novel's action, and catalyst of self-knowledge.

Pigs in Heaven includes another flight by Taylor and Turtle. Ultimately, the novel depicts their trek to the deep Cherokee past, which threatens Taylor's role as a mother and unlocks Taylor's and Turtle's ties to their own histories and identities. *The Poisonwood Bible* evokes the Belgian Congo of the 1960's in rich detail, juxtaposing it with the southern American landscape of memory and the recent past of Nathan Price's wife and four daughters. In Kingsolver's works, patriarchy emerges referentially as part of a female consciousness. It is not the frame of reference, as it is in the traditional bildungsroman.

Kingsolver's women negotiate new places for themselves within their personal, domestic, and social spheres. They acquire self-understanding through social interaction and introspection; these things bring harmony within and without. Her main female characters weather negotiation with themselves and their environments. They display character flaws, lapses in judgment, anger, and personal fears as well as idealism, generous hearts, moral consciences, and affection. Her women reach equilibrium rather than glorious redemption. Their personal insights are fragile in the way that most real-life understandings are, remaining constant only until new discoveries or crises force the women to make adjustments.

Taylor, Cosima (Codi), and the Prices are women who passionately pursue relationships spawned by family identity. Coming into their own carries an intrinsic connection to family, community, and state. In all of Kingsolver's books, the personal is acutely political. Codi, of *Animal Dreams*, discovers her true origins as she works with older Latinas in Grace to end environmental contamination. Leah, in *The Poisonwood Bible*, redefines her cultural and religious allegiances as she takes up residence in the "liberated" Congo. Kingsolver's long fiction is overtly political, her short stories obliquely so. (Her short fiction often focuses on the domestic sphere of women's lives.) Her women live in the real world and her narratives include men only occasionally. Male perspectives surface primarily when they affect the female characters and move the plot forward. *The Poisonwood Bible*, in which the Price entourage is dragged off to Africa, seems an exception. However, even in this novel, the women tell the entire story of their father's and husband's misguided mission.

Kingsolver's fiction places relationships—between parents and children, spouses and families—in the foreground and sets them against the larger social milieu. She gives no credence to the opinion that art is apolitical. The inherent inequities and racism faced by Latinos and Latinas, American Indians, and Africans surface not as the chief lament of her main characters or as the narrative frame for their lives but as elements of their daily lives.

THE BEAN TREES

Marrietta Greer, the traveling woman of *The Bean Trees*, sees herself as part of life in Pittman County, Kentucky—but she also has flair. She leaves town five years after high school graduation in a "'55 Volkswagen bug with no windows to speak of, and no back seat and no starter." She heads west in search of a new name and place, believing that mysterious signs will appear to help her along. She takes her name from Taylorville, Illinois, where she runs out of gas.

Deciding to go west until the car stops running, she reaches the "Great Plain," as she calls it, and finds herself in a broken-down car in Oklahoma. She appreciates the irony of landing in Cherokee territory: Her maternal grandfather had provided the one-eighth Cherokee blood required for her to qualify for tribal membership, and the idea of moving to the Cherokee Nation had become a family joke—their last hope if they face destitution. Before Taylor can leave a Cherokee bar in Oklahoma, a pleading American Indian woman deposits a child in Taylor's car and leaves the girl behind. Taylor names the silent child Turtle because she attaches herself to Taylor anywhere she can get a grip and holds on as fiercely as a biting mud turtle. It is clear that Turtle has been fiercely abused.

Chapter 2 introduces Lou Ann Ruiz, pregnant, living in Arizona, and struggling in a failing marriage with Angel. Taylor arrives in Arizona in chapter 3 and, through the auspices of Mattie (a woman who runs Jesus Is Lord Used Tires), Taylor and Lou Ann form a supportive and zany household. The two friends become involved in Mattie's clandestine work with Central American refugees.

The Bean Trees reorients readers toward daily experience, juxtaposing the ordinary life of picnics, car repairs, and the kitchen with, for example, the chilling account of Estevan and Esperanza's daughter being snatched by the Guatemalan government. Kingsolver's relatively uneducated but compassionate people live mundane lives, but it is precisely their lives that reveal the human side of political injustice. The novel braids the stories of ordinary women following their consciences, and it gives the lie to the idea that massive amounts of money and large organizations are needed to eradicate inhumanity.

The novel ends with a typical array of Kingsolver anomalies. Turtle is illegally but justly adopted, and family has been redefined as readers accept the safe place that Taylor and Lou Ann now inhabit. The politics of safe houses and churches aiding immigrants escaping crushing cruelty seems noble despite its clandestine nature.

ANIMAL DREAMS

In *Animal Dreams*, Codi Noline returns to Grace, Arizona, to care for Homer, her physician father, who has Alzheimer's disease. The narrative alternates between an omniscient speaker for the sections on Homer and a first-person speaker for the sections on Codi. This style emphasizes the postmodern effect of disjointed perspectives. Kingsolver, however, uses memory to create links between the sections and characters that override the break in form.

Codi discovers her personal tie to the nine Gracela sisters who founded the town of Grace. She also comes to terms with a baby she had buried when she was fifteen years old. Communally, she connects with the older women of the Stitch and Bitch Club, who alert her to the Black Mountain Mining Company's toxic presence in Grace. Together they challenge and defeat the corporate polluter. Letters from Nicaragua weave the theme of human rights throughout *Animal Dreams*.

As usual in Kingsolver's fiction, the scenes take place in domestic and familiar public places—kitchens, attics, front yards, schools, and trains—where personal circumstances allow a focus on larger social and political issues. There are no pat answers. An ordinary woman seeking justice dies, but the Stitch and Bitch ladies triumph. Codi moves toward a full life. All Souls' Day and the Corn Dance rituals unite the past and present and provide time for Codi to seek and find answers. *Animal Dreams* articulates the complicated intersection of private and public identities and offers hope.

PIGS IN HEAVEN

Pigs in Heaven revisits the lives of Taylor and Turtle, who are on a road trip visiting Hoover Dam when Turtle glimpses a near-fatal fall that leads to a spectacular rescue. Turtle's actions make her and Taylor celebrities, and their notoriety brings the Cherokee Nation into the story. Soon, Taylor is trying to keep Turtle from being "repossessed" by Cherokee lawyer Annawake Fourkiller. Taylor maintains telephone contact with her mother, Alice, and lives hand-to-mouth while avoiding Fourkiller.

To expedite matters, Alice travels to Oklahoma to reestablish her ties with a Cherokee cousin. She falls in love with an American Indian named Cash Stillwater. Telephone calls and negotiations result in Taylor and Turtle meeting with Annawake, Cash, Alice, and the Child Welfare Services. In a bizarre twist, Cash turns out to be Turtle's grandfather and proposes to Alice. The solution of joint custody and Alice and Cash's determination to be married unite everyone with their pasts, both deep and recent.

The chapters of *Pigs in Heaven* establish irregular intervals between Taylor and Turtle's adventures and accounts of Taylor's mother, who is beginning her own road trip to get away from her second husband as the novel starts. Taylor runs until she must return to

Oklahoma, and Alice travels to Cherokee land to reunite with her cousin. Throughout the novel, Kingsolver relies on the threads of Cherokee blood, Alice and Taylor's telephone calls, and the history of the Cherokee Nation to bind the plot lines. The novel's depictions of a ritual Cherokee stomp dance as well as the U.S. government's mistreatment of the Cherokees shows the reader how the past carries forward as both repetition and renewal.

THE POISONWOOD BIBLE

In *The Poisonwood Bible*, the ill-fated Price girls follow two men, a husband and their father, to the Belgian Congo just as fighting for liberation breaks out in earnest. Five separate journeys to find the self, within the framework of the family's African journey, are created simultaneously. The book is an ambitious undertaking, as Kingsolver creates the voices of six-year-old Ruth May, twelve-year-old twins Leah and Ada, and fifteen-year-old Rachel Price. She then follows them to adulthood (all but Ruth May, who dies of malaria), through the tumult of Congolese revolution and U.S. manipulation.

The surviving sisters fare better than their parents. Leah Price marries the university-educated Congolese rebel who was her teacher and remains in the country. Her thoughts outline the Congo's grinding poverty and the sheer energy it takes to survive in a society preyed upon by a colonial power and then by capitalist interests. Ada becomes a doctor, and Rachel runs a hotel for the Europeans who remain in Africa to foment unrest. Ironically, Rachel, the most self-centered and resentful daughter, comes closest to emulating her father despite her financial success.

Nathan Price sinks into madness and wanders wildly for years. Kingsolver provides an intimate portrait of his stupidity; his attempted exploitation of the Congolese stands as a metaphor for the plundering of the Congo. Rich details of landscape and tribal culture, including the traditional philosophy that shapes Congolese life, surface through the disparate voices of the Price girls. The tragedy of the Price family's lives, the ruin of Congolese tribal structure, and the breakdown of national order form concentric circles in the novel. The failure of private communication within the Price family and between the Prices and their African neighbors both prefigures and contributes to the failure and destruction of an ancient society in a ruthlessly short time.

Karen L. Arnold

OTHER MAJOR WORKS

SHORT FICTION: *Homeland, and Other Stories*, 1989.

POETRY: *Another America/Otra America*, 1992.

NONFICTION: *Holding the Line: Women in the Great Arizona Mine Strike of 1983*, 1989; *High Tide in Tucson: Essays from Now or Never*, 1995; *Last Stand: America's Virgin Lands*, 2002 (photographs by Annie Griffiths Belt); *Small Wonder*, 2002; *Animal, Vegetable, Miracle: A Year of Food Life*, 2007 (with Steven L. Hopp and Camille Kingsolver).

EDITED TEXT: *The Best American Short Stories, 2001*, 2001.

BIBLIOGRAPHY

Aay, Henry. "Environmental Themes in Ecofiction: *In the Center of the Nation* and *Animal Dreams.*" *Journal of Cultural Geography* 14 (Spring, 1994): 65-85. Aay's comparative study of Kingsolver's novel *Animal Dreams* and *In the Center of the Nation* (1991) by Dan O'Brien is one of the few scholarly discussions of Kingsolver's work.

DeMarr, Mary Jean. *Barbara Kingsolver: A Critical Companion.* Westport, Conn.: Greenwood Press, 1999. DeMarr not only examines Kingsolver's first four novels but also discusses her background as a feminist, a humanist, and a journalist. A good overview of Kingsolver's wide-ranging literary and political work.

Epstein, Robin. "Barbara Kingsolver." *The Progressive*, February, 1996. An informative interview with Kingsolver, who says most readers do not think that her writing is overly political. She adds that she has a responsibility to discuss her beliefs with readers.

Kingsolver, Barbara. Interview by Lisa See. *Publishers Weekly*, August 31, 1990. Kingsolver, in this interview with novelist Lisa See, discusses her early literary influences and her research and writing methods.

Ryan, Maureen. "Barbara Kingsolver's Lowfat Fiction." *Journal of American Culture* 18, no. 4 (Winter, 1995): 77-123. Ryan compares Kingsolver's first three novels with her short-story collection *Homeland, and Other Stories* in this extensive study.

Snodgrass, Mary Ellen. *Barbara Kingsolver: A Literary Companion.* Jefferson, N.C.: MacFarland, 2004. Alphabetical entries include analyses of characters, dates, historical figures and events, allusions, literary motifs, and themes from Kingsolver's writings. Excellent resource for any study of Kingsolver.

Wagner-Martin, Linda. *Barbara Kingsolver's "The Poisonwood Bible": A Reader's Guide.* New York: Continuum, 2001. Concise guide to Kingsolver's most popular novel, *The Poisonwood Bible*. Part of the Continuum Contemporaries series.

Wright, Charlotte M. "Barbara Kingsolver." In *Updating the Literary West*, edited by scholars of the Western Literature Association. Fort Worth: Texas Christian University Press, 1997. Informative essays reconsider the subjects of Western literature, taking into account a newly emerging canon that includes children's literature, ethnicity and race, environmental writing, gender issues, and more. Kingsolver's novels are discussed in the context of this changing genre.

ELIZABETH MADOX ROBERTS

Born: Perryville, Kentucky; October 30, 1881
Died: Orlando, Florida; March 13, 1941

PRINCIPAL LONG FICTION
The Time of Man, 1926
My Heart and My Flesh, 1927
Jingling in the Wind, 1928
The Great Meadow, 1930
A Buried Treasure, 1931
He Sent Forth a Raven, 1935
Black Is My Truelove's Hair, 1938

OTHER LITERARY FORMS

Before Elizabeth Madox Roberts was a novelist, she wrote poetry, including children's verse—facts that explain much about her work as a novelist—and she continued to produce some poetry throughout her career. Her first collection of verse, privately printed in 1915, was *In the Great Steep's Garden*, a pamphlet consisting of a few short poems accompanying photographs. A second collection of poetry, *Under the Tree*, appeared in 1922, published by Huebsch, which soon became the Viking Press and the publisher of Roberts's subsequent work. A revised edition of *Under the Tree* appeared in 1930, and a third collection of Roberts's poetry, *Song in the Meadow*, came out in 1940.

In addition, Roberts wrote short stories, which, like her poetry, found a ready market in leading magazines of the day. Her short fiction was collected in *The Haunted Mirror* (1932) and *Not by Strange Gods* (1941).

ACHIEVEMENTS

Elizabeth Madox Roberts's reputation as a writer furnishes an interesting case study in literary fashions and critical evaluation. Few novelists have begun their careers to such popular and critical acclaim as Roberts achieved with *The Time of Man* in 1926, acclaim that was renewed and confirmed by *The Great Meadow* four years later. With the 1935 publication of *He Sent Forth a Raven*, however, Roberts's literary reputation went into a precipitous decline. By her death in 1941, it had struck bottom. Since then, there have been intermittent attempts, including several book-length studies, to resurrect her reputation, frequently with highly inflated praise. Claims that she is among the half dozen or so great American novelists of the twentieth century do her as much disservice as does the vague "regionalist" label that her special pleaders decry.

Perhaps as a result of her early success and her relative isolation in Kentucky, Roberts seems likewise to have overestimated her powers: With talents along the lines of a May

Elizabeth Madox Roberts
(National Archives)

Sarton, Roberts was apparently encouraged to think of herself as another William Faulkner, with a little Herman Melville and Thomas Mann thrown in for good measure. Her style, so often termed "poetic," achieves some fine effects indeed, but at immense cost to the narrative flow of her novels. Her style is allied to her narrative focus, almost invariably the novel's female protagonist, whose perceptions and sentiments are spun out at length while the reader waits for something to happen. Little does happen, except that the heroines take long walks. The effect is somewhat reminiscent of an agrarian Virginia Woolf. Perhaps the reader is treated to such a subjective focus because Roberts's protagonists, however different, are to some extent alter egos of their author, whose own comments blend imperceptibly into their observations.

The results of all this are slow-moving and sometimes flimsy plots, dimly realized characters (except usually for the protagonist), loss of authorial perspective, and tedium. As if these results were not unhappy enough, Roberts also had trouble dealing with ideas and with the overall plans for her novels.

Despite all these limitations and failings, Roberts deserves a revival. Most readers will find her lighter novels, *A Buried Treasure* and *Black Is My Truelove's Hair*, still entertaining, and *The Great Meadow* possesses some epic qualities. All of Roberts's novels involve significant themes, and all deal incidentally with significant social issues, such as economic conditions, racism, and sexism. In particular, both feminists and antifeminists will find much of interest in Roberts's depiction of her female protagonists, in her treatment of male-female relationships, and in Roberts's own biography.

BIOGRAPHY

Elizabeth Madox Roberts's life was marked by a few salient facts. Descended from early settlers of Kentucky, she was the second of eight children born to Mary Elizabeth Brent and Simpson Roberts, Confederate veteran, teacher, grocer, and occasional surveyor-engineer. Roberts lived most of her life in Springfield, a small county-seat town on the southwestern edge of the Kentucky bluegrass region. She attended high school in Covington, Kentucky (1896-1900) and college at the University of Chicago (1917-1921), where she received the David Blair McLaughlin Prize for prose and the Fiske Poetry Prize, served as president of the poetry club, and became a member of Phi Beta Kappa before graduating with a doctorate in English. She began college at the age of thirty-one because limited finances and ill health delayed her. She suffered from poor health much of her life.

From 1910 to 1916, Roberts made various stays with a brother and a sister in Colorado, in part to recuperate from what was possibly tuberculosis. At the height of her literary career, she experienced severe headaches and a skin rash, both possibly nervous in origin. During her last years, when she wintered in Florida for her health, she suffered severely from Hodgkin's disease (cancer of the lymphatic system), the eventual cause of her death.

Because of her ill health and perhaps her own disposition, Roberts led a quiet personal life, at times almost reclusive. She never married, though she always enjoyed a circle of friends, including friends from her Chicago years whom she later wrote and sometimes visited. In a sense, she never left the family circle, building her own house onto her parents' Springfield home when she came into money from her writing. She also enjoyed contacts and visits with her brothers and sisters. At heart, she was a solitary, introspective individual who guarded her privacy, growing a hedge around her backyard garden. Besides reading and writing, her favorite activities included listening to music, gardening, sunbathing, and taking long walks into secluded areas of the countryside (from which she returned to make voluminous notes).

These conditions of Roberts's life exercised strong influences, both positive and negative, on her writing career. Her family's proud pioneer heritage not only stimulated her imagination but also encouraged her to paint an idyllic picture of Kentucky's past and present. The sleepy farming region around Springfield was also a rich source of material—indeed, her prime source—but at the same time it effectively isolated her from literary circles that might have served to encourage, temper, and appreciate her efforts. These functions were served briefly by her stay at the University of Chicago. Her heady experience of Chicago, where literary circles flourished both inside and outside the university, filled her with ideas and propelled her into sustained literary production, but perhaps this hothouse experience also encouraged her to overreach herself as a writer.

The effects of Roberts's circumscribed personal life can also be detected in her fiction, particularly in her efforts to depict character and to describe male-female relationships, possibly also in her habitual narrative focus. To a great extent, Roberts's fiction provides an ironic counterpoint to her personal life. In most of her novels, the main narrative interest is her heroines' search for identity, worked out through the rituals of courting and mating: Her heroines suffer their shipwrecks but eventually find safe harbor in marriage. The men in their lives are either grandfatherly, brutish, bucolic, or childishly vengeful; the heroines get advice from the grandfatherly ones, are hurt by the brutish ones, and marry either the bucolic or childishly vengeful ones. Fathers are frequently possessive, obstructing their daughters' paths to marriage; one can only wonder about Roberts's relationship with her father, who refused her money for college and then had her underfoot for the rest of his life. To Roberts's credit, it must be said that in her novels, men, however unpromising, are absolutely vital to the scheme of things.

On the other hand, too, if Roberts's personal life had been less circumscribed, she might not have taken up writing at all. Writing became her means of achieving identity— and against stronger odds than any of her heroines had to face. However sickly and easily demoralized Roberts might seem, she had a vein of iron in her character that also came out in her heroines and in her themes. Even Roberts's ill health furnished her with potent material. Her heroines frequently develop by means of long illnesses and convalescence, from which they emerge born again, like a butterfly from its pupa. It was perhaps toward such a rebirth that Roberts was aiming in her writing.

ANALYSIS

Although commentators on Elizabeth Madox Roberts like to describe her main theme in such terms as "the ordering of chaos" or "the triumph of spirit over matter," one need not be so high-minded and vague. A hardheaded Kentucky version of her major theme would be more specific: ownership of the land. This theme reflects an old, revered attitude in Kentucky, where in some parts even today one can be shot for trespassing. The theme also reflects an old, revered American (even Anglo-Saxon) attitude, a pioneer urge to settle and possess, if necessary by violence—an urge that today achieves its debased avatar in the mass media and advertising.

In its gentler, more settled aspects, however, Roberts's theme embodies a Jeffersonian, agrarian vision of American democracy, the American Dream of independence through ownership of the land. The theme eventually embodies a more universal vision, a vision of harmony with the land, a realization, serenely accepted, that those who possess the land are also possessed by it. Unhappily, whether expressed by Roberts or by other American writers whose characters want to own chicken farms or raise rabbits, the theme is a poignant reminder that many Americans have in actuality been vagabonds, whether the pioneer variety or today's rootless variety. In this sense, then, the theme embodies an idyllic but unrealized American Dream; it was apparently Roberts's conviction, however, that this dream came very close to being realized in Kentucky.

In developing her theme, Roberts reveals the influence of her favorite philosopher, George Berkeley, the eighteenth century bishop who denied the existence of matter, holding that "things" exist only as "ideas" or "spirits" in the minds of God and people. Such a philosophy would seem, at first, to preclude any relationship with the land; on the contrary, it points to a divine immanence, to the spiritual nature of all things, including the land. The philosophy also implies the worth of "subjective" truth, justifying Roberts's narrative focus on the lengthy observations of her protagonists. As a result of this focus, her novels are full of loving descriptions of the land, the flora and fauna, and the weather. Held constantly before the reader, the land forms an immense backdrop or tableau against which human action is played out, a background so overwhelming at times that the characters seem to emerge out of it and then sink back into it.

Because of their closeness to the land, many of Roberts's characters exhibit a sameness: Mostly simple farmers, their lives governed by the imperatives of the seasons, crops, animals, they identify with the soil in their talk and in their impulses. Rather inarticulate, they have a blood-knowledge of the earth that requires little discussion. The continuity of their lives with the land is also reflected in their impulses to create life, to mate and procreate. To Roberts, these characters represent an ideal, a settled state, though to her readers they might seem too bucolic to be interesting.

The state of health represented by such characters is what Roberts's protagonists aspire to and her maladjusted characters lack. Like the bucolic characters, Roberts's protagonists seek to mate and procreate. The protagonists do not achieve their aims easily, though, having to reenact the archetypal struggle of their pioneer ancestors before they reach a settled state. When misfortune frustrates their desires, they get back in touch with the earth through the simple therapies of raising chickens, growing a garden, sunbathing, or taking rides in the country. Some end up marrying farmers. Such is the ultimate salvation of Theodosia, the highbred protagonist of *My Heart and My Flesh*, whose alienation from the land is an index of her initial maladjustment. Other unhappy characters in Roberts's novels are similarly out of touch with the land, such as Stoner Drake in *He Sent Forth a Raven* and the evil Langtry in *Black Is My Truelove's Hair*.

These patterns of behavior exhibited by her characters are the prime means through which Roberts develops her theme, with examples of each pattern generally to be found in each of her novels. To some extent, however, each novel emphasizes a particular aspect of her theme, with *He Sent Forth a Raven* being Roberts's most ambitious effort to pull all her characteristic motifs together in a single work.

THE GREAT MEADOW

Although *The Great Meadow* was Roberts's fourth novel, it was apparently the first conceived. This is appropriate, since thematically *The Great Meadow* comes first among her novels. Set around the time of the American Revolution, it celebrates the early settlement of Kentucky, that other Eden, that paradise, that promised land. The epic qualities of this novel have led some commentators to compare it to Homer's *Odyssey* (c. 725 B.C.E.; English translation, 1614), though it could more appropriately be compared to Vergil's *Aeneid* (c. 29-19 B.C.E.; English translation, 1553). Like Latium, Kentucky has to be wrested from the "aborigines." The novel even has its epic heroine with a noble name, Diony, and noble progenitors, sturdy Pennsylvania Methodists and Quakers on her mother's side and Virginia Tidewater gentry on her father's. Diony is, in truth, the founder of "a new race," though before she marries and sets out for Kentucky, she has to get her father's permission (in typical fashion for Roberts's possessive fathers, he at first denies her).

After a slow start in Albemarle County, Virginia, the novel follows Diony, her husband, and a small party of settlers as they trek across the rugged Appalachians to Harrod's Fort, where they proceed to fight off Native Americans and establish farms. The growth of their settlement corresponds to Diony's growth as a person, largely a development of awareness. A convinced Berkeleian who frequently quotes from the philosopher's works, she receives a real challenge to her beliefs when she is banged in the head with a tomahawk, but the tomahawk incident and the scalping of her mother-in-law are only smaller parts of the overall challenge represented by the alien wilderness. In the beginning, Diony had imagined God as a benevolent deity creating "a world out of chaos," but since everything that exists is a thought of God's, God must also have created the wilderness, where wolves howl and savages prowl. Unlike Daniel Boone—or for that matter the Native Americans—Diony cannot feel at home in the wilderness; instead, she must remake the wilderness into her vision of home, a vision of a settled, orderly, agrarian society where the land is "owned."

Although Diony clings stubbornly to her vision of order, the wilderness does make her more tolerant of disorder. Even before she leaves for Kentucky, she has a "wilderness marriage . . . without law" (performed by a Methodist minister). Later, her experiences of hardship and deprivation at Harrod's Fort lead her to observe that "men wanted law to live by" but that women and babies "followed a hidden law"—that is, a law based on concrete, immediate human needs. This frontier tradition of making do the best one can, without too much scrupling about moral and legal niceties, serves Diony well at the end of the novel. Her husband, Berk Jarvis, goes into the wilderness to seek revenge against the Native American, Blackfox, who has his mother's scalp. When Berk does not return in a year or so, he is presumed dead, and Diony marries Evan Muir, who had helped provide for her after Berk left. Then, three years after he left, Berk shows up. Faced with two husbands and a child by each, Diony exercises the frontier woman's option: She sends Evan away, takes Berk back, and then goes to bed for a good, sound sleep.

The same spirit of make-do morality also characterizes the settlers' relations with the Native Americans. Diony's mother, Polly, influenced by Quaker thought, not only opposes the slaveholding favored by the Tidewater gentry but also opposes taking land from the American Indians. At the dinner table where the men are enthusiastically discussing "the promise land" of Kentucky, Polly angrily announces that Kentucky "belongs to the Indians" and that white trespassers there will get "skulped." Quiet reigns while the men contemplate images of "battle, fire . . . rapine, plunder." These thoughts, however, dampen their enthusiasm only momentarily. Striking the table for emphasis, they argue that Kentucky, "a good country," belongs to those strong enough to take and hold it—that is, "the Long Knives." Later, the last term is revised to "civilized man." Apparently, the latter argument is the one Roberts favors, since the rest of her novel eulogizes the settlers' taking of Kentucky. For example, as Diony's party breaks through Cumberland Gap, Roberts describes them as marching forward, "without bigotry and without psalm-singing," to take "a new world for themselves . . . by the power of their courage, their order, and their endurance." Thus is a time-honored Kentucky tradition established.

If *The Great Meadow* celebrates the vision of this other Eden, *A Buried Treasure* and *Black Is My Truelove's Hair* celebrate the realization of the vision. Like all of Roberts's novels except *The Great Meadow*, they are set in early twentieth century Kentucky, roughly contemporaneous with the period of their composition. Both novels were expanded from shorter pieces and show the effects of padding and lengthening, but at the same time they are Roberts's most entertaining novels and exhibit, in its purest form, her theme of living on the land. Generally light and pleasant works, they depict a pastoral scene where the land is the source of happiness and renewal.

A BURIED TREASURE

A Buried Treasure differs from other novels in its comic tone and in its older protagonist, Philadelphia Blair. Philly's farmer husband, Andy, finds a pot of old gold and silver coins under a stump on their land, and the rest of the novel concerns their efforts to announce their find and at the same time protect it from thieves. The flimsy plot is complicated somewhat by Philly's machinations to slip away her cousin's daughter, Imogene (whose possessive father, Sam Cundy, will not let her wed), and marry her to Giles Wilson. In addition, a subplot, introducing experimentation with point of view and synchronous time, treats seventeen-year-old Ben Shepherd's search for his ancestors' graves. To a great extent, the whole novel is an extended pun on the meanings of "buried treasure."

Ben Shepherd finds the graves of his ancestors, who naturally go all the way back to the pioneer settlers of Kentucky. Imogene marries her beau, a jolly young farmer who wears horseshoes. Philly becomes more aware of her deep love for Andy, particularly when he loans the widow Hester Trigg (who gives him cherry pie) two pearls that he got from the treasure pot and normally wears in a small sack tied around his lower abdomen. Both Philly and Andy become more aware of their love for the land, from whence the treasure pot came, put there perhaps by some ancestor. Despite an evil old hen that eats her own eggs, and the threat of two itinerant house painters who are thieves, the novel ends happily in a communal ring dance out in the pasture under the moonlit sky of the summer solstice.

BLACK IS MY TRUELOVE'S HAIR

Compared to *A Buried Treasure*, *Black Is My Truelove's Hair* is somewhat less satisfactory. Its title drawn from an Appalachian ballad containing the line "I love the ground whereon he stands," *Black Is My Truelove's Hair* concerns a young woman, Dena Janes, who "loved too much" and whose first lover, the black-hearted Langtry, is untrue. A truck driver who brags that he has no home, Langtry takes Dena on the road, refuses to marry her, treats her brutally, and threatens to kill her if she ever loves another man. After six days, Dena flees home, walking most of the way. Beginning at this point (the affair with Langtry is told through brief flashbacks), the novel treats Dena's gradual rehabilitation in the rural community and her eventual engagement to marry the miller's son, Cam Elliot. Although received at first with leering remarks and invitations, Dena is not given the Hester Prynne treatment. Even on her way home from the Langtry affair, the distraught Dena maintains she has "a right to a life that makes good sense." Apparently the people of the community agree.

Dena restores herself with the help of time, a sympathetic sister, routine chores of gardening and tending animals, sunbathing, and the advice of the local oracle, the apple-grower Journeyman, who observes that Dena is like one of his overburdened apple trees, "destroyed by its own abundance." As Dena recovers, the passage of time is marked by great to-dos over a strayed gander and a lost thimble; these comic commotions are supposed to be highly symbolic, but to the reader they may seem merely silly. The reader is also likely to find the ending anticlimactic. The fearsome Langtry shows up, gun in hand, but when he chases Dena into Journeyman's moonlit orchard and views her abundance, he shoots to miss. The story is resolved when Journeyman appears, destroys the gun, and buries it in the earth, leaving Dena free to go her own way.

THE TIME OF MAN

While *The Great Meadow* and the pastoral novels emphasize the positive aspects of Roberts's theme, *The Time of Man* and her other novels emphasize negative aspects. Dealing with poor tenant farmers who move from place to place, *The Time of Man* shows the plight of people who live on the land but do not own it. They have, in effect, been reduced to beasts of burden. Laboring mainly for others, they receive only enough from their labors to ensure their continuing usefulness, their subsistence. Their inability to escape from this cycle probably means that their children will continue it.

Although Roberts's subject raises weighty social issues, suggesting a novel along the lines of John Steinbeck's *The Grapes of Wrath* (1939), *The Time of Man* is not a novel of social protest. Instead, with Roberts's narrative focus on the mind of her protagonist, *The Time of Man* is more a bildungsroman, tracing the development of Ellen Chesser from a girl of fourteen to a woman in her mid-thirties.

The reader follows Ellen as she bounds about the woods and fields, joins a group of other teenagers, gets a boyfriend, loses her boyfriend, withdraws into her hurt, meets another man, marries him, has four children, is estranged from her husband when he is unfaithful, experiences the death of her fifth child, and is reconciled with her husband. In short, whatever her social status, Ellen's experience of life over a generation is typical of most people's; in this sense, then, her experience is representative of "the time of man"—experiences of beauty and love, disappointment and tragedy, all within the context of passing time. Her ability to hold her experiences within this context is the key to her appreciation of beauty and love and her endurance of disappointment and tragedy. This ability derives from her closeness to the land, her sense of the seasons and participation in the rhythms of the earth: her jaunts through the woods, her work in the fields and garden, her courtship and marriage, her children.

Ellen illustrates what the Native Americans knew—that one can live in harmony with the land without owning it. To this extent, the several moves she makes from farm to farm, first with her parents and then with her husband, are almost irrelevant. Still, Ellen is aware of the inequities and injustices of the landowner-tenant system, a carryover from slave plantations, with some landowners continuing to act as if they own their tenants. She is incensed when her husband, while she and the children starve, identifies with, even takes pride in, the richness and show of their arrogant landlord. Both she and her husband carry around a vision of having their own farm someday, in "some better country." Perhaps they are headed toward this vision when, at the end of the novel, after her husband has been wrongly accused of barnburning and run out of the country, they are on the road again.

Roberts's first novel, *The Time of Man* is judged by some critics to be her best. Her exposition of her heroine's mind and development is a consummate job, and the novel does include some recognition of social problems in "the great meadow" of Kentucky; many readers, however, will feel that Roberts dwells too long on Ellen's early years, so that the first part of the novel drags.

JINGLING IN THE WIND

Roberts's other novels could all be called "novels of maladjustment," since they all show, in one manner or another, people who are out of touch with the land. Of these, *Jingling in the Wind*, which includes Roberts's only depiction of an urban setting, presents the most extreme case. There is much that Roberts finds artificial, even bizarre, in the city, such as neon advertisements that usurp the stars. In short, *Jingling in the Wind*, sometimes described as a satiric fantasy, is an outright attack on many trends of modern civilization. The loose plot concerns a couple of rainmakers, Jeremy and Tulip, who give up their unnatural profession in order to marry and have children. Usually considered Roberts's worst novel, *Jingling in the Wind* is interesting for its contribution to her grand theme.

MY HEART AND MY FLESH

Another novel of maladjustment is *My Heart and My Flesh*, centering on Theodosia Bell, a neurasthenic product of the wealthy landowning class. In this Faulknerian work exhibiting the results of southern decadence, the protagonist gradually loses everything that has insulated her from contact with the land—her wealth, her boyfriends, her home, her grandfather and sottish father, even her feelings of racial superiority (she discovers she is a half sister to three mixed-race people in town). As a child, Theodosia is so out of place in the countryside that a pack of hounds attack her. As an adult, when disillusionment, poverty, and sickness have brought her down to earth, she moves in with the pack, even eats their food. Later she finds health and happiness by teaching in a country school, living in her pupils' homes, and marrying a farmer. Thus, the pattern of rebirth through contact with the land is perfectly illustrated by Theodosia.

HE SENT FORTH A RAVEN

Conversely, a negative example is provided by Stoner Drake, the monomaniacal old man in *He Sent Forth a Raven*. The title's biblical reference to Noah, who trusted in God, provides a lucid contrast to Drake's blasphemous behavior. When his second wife dies, Drake vows never to set foot on God's green earth again. His anger hardening into inflexible principle, he keeps his word, never venturing from the house and managing his farm from a rooftop observatory, summoning workers and family members with blasts on a hunting horn or conch shell. The blasts symbolize not only his pathetic defiance of God but also his alienation from other people and the land. To Drake, of course, they symbolize command, and in his house he is an absolute dictator.

Drake's rancorous behavior is self-punishing, but it also takes a toll on the people around him. For example, he prevents his daughter, Martha, from entertaining suitors. When one finally ventures a polite visit as a guest, Drake confronts him and Martha with loud, vile charges of fornication. The young man leaves, and Martha, thunderstruck, falls into fever and delirium, temporarily losing her hearing; when after some weeks it returns, the first things she hears are "the loud horn and the screaming of the swine." She thereafter reconciles herself to being a spinster and to banking the fires at night (so the house will not catch fire and her father burn up with it).

Standing in contrast to Drake is his granddaughter, Jocelle, the novel's heroine, who takes a lesson from her aunt's fate. Growing up in the house with Drake and Martha, Jocelle manages to live a relatively normal life because she is free to roam the fields, sometimes even beyond the range of the horn. Like all of Roberts's female protagonists, Jocelle does suffer her traumas, but she is strong enough to bounce back. For example, when Drake's nephew, Walter, rapes her, Drake renews his ridiculous vow, but Jocelle eventually recovers from her shock. At the end of the novel, she is happily married and a mother, her husband the manager of the farm, while Drake sits before the fireplace and hardens into brittle senility, unable to remember the reason for his vow.

Harold Branam

OTHER MAJOR WORKS

SHORT FICTION: *The Haunted Mirror*, 1932; *Not by Strange Gods*, 1941.

POETRY: *In the Great Steep's Garden*, 1915; *Under the Tree*, 1922, 1930; *Song in the Meadow*, 1940.

BIBLIOGRAPHY

Campbell, Harry Modean, and Ruel E. Foster. *Elizabeth Madox Roberts: American Novelist*. Norman: University of Oklahoma Press, 1956. A biographical and critical study containing analyses of Roberts's novels and short stories.

McDowell, Frederick P. W. *Elizabeth Madox Roberts*. New York: Twayne, 1963. A basic introduction to Roberts's life and work, featuring analyses of her novels and short stories. Includes a bibliography and an index.

Nicolaisen, Peter. "Rural Poverty and the Heroics of Farming: Elizabeth Madox Roberts's *The Time of Man* and Ellen Glasgow's *Barren Ground*." In *Reading Southern Poverty Between the Wars, 1918-1939*, edited by Richard Godden and Martin Crawford. Athens: University of Georgia Press, 2006. Collection of essays in which contributors maintain that many southern writers, social scientists, and activists who professed to be progressive actually upheld the traditional economic and social systems that maintained poverty. The essay on Roberts discusses how her novel, *The Time of Man*, fits the contributors' claims.

Perry, Carolyn, and Mary Louise Weaks, eds. *The History of Southern Women's Literature*. Baton Rouge: Louisiana State University Press, 2002. Roberts is one of the authors included in this examination of southern women writers. Part 3, "Renaissance in the South, 1900-1960," contains an essay on Roberts's work.

Rovit, Earl H. *Herald to Chaos: The Novels of Elizabeth Madox Roberts*. Lexington: University Press of Kentucky, 1960. Rovit provides a thorough analysis of Robert's style. He discusses Roberts's presentation of heroic characters engaged in epic struggles against the forces of nature, her critical neglect, and her role in American literature.

Simpson, Lewis P. "History and the Will of the Artist: Elizabeth Madox Roberts." In *The Fable of the Southern Writer*. Baton Rouge: Louisiana State University Press, 1994. This analysis of Roberts's work and her relationship to the South is one of eleven essays in Simpson's examination of southern writers. Includes a bibliography and an index.

_____. "The Sexuality of History." *Southern Review* 20 (October, 1984): 785-802. In this special issue of memoirs, reminiscences, and essays on Roberts, Simpson discusses her as a particularly modern writer whose struggle to repudiate the philosophy of idealism is the major theme of her work. He compares Roberts to William Faulkner in their awareness of the inwardness of history.

Spivey, Herman E. "The Mind and Creative Habits of Elizabeth Madox Roberts." In *All These To Teach*, edited by Robert A. Bryan, Alton C. Morris, A. A. Murphree, and

Aubrey L. Williams. Gainesville: University of Florida Press, 1965. Spivey argues that although Roberts's achievements were greater than realized by her contemporaries, her handicaps as an artist were more than she was able to overcome. He claims that Roberts is too much concerned with people in general and too little with particular individuals, that there is not enough external action in her work, and that her unmastered technical experiments prevent reader understanding.

Tate, Linda. "Elizabeth Madox Roberts: A Bibliographical Essay." *Resources for American Literary Study* 18 (1992): 22-43. A summary and critique of previous criticism of Roberts's work. Tate argues that Roberts's role in the Southern Renaissance has not been sufficiently explored and claims that the highest untapped appeal of her work is feminist criticism.

_____. *A Southern Weave of Women: Fiction of the Contemporary South*. Athens: University of Georgia Press, 1994. This examination of southern women's fiction published in the late twentieth century discusses Roberts's novels as background for the work of the later writers.

LESLIE MARMON SILKO

Born: Albuquerque, New Mexico; March 5, 1948
Also known as: Leslie Marmon

PRINCIPAL LONG FICTION
Ceremony, 1977
Almanac of the Dead, 1991
Gardens in the Dunes, 1999

OTHER LITERARY FORMS

Leslie Marmon Silko's first published book is a collection of poems called *Laguna Woman: Poems* (1974). Her earliest published works were short stories, published in magazines, most of which were later included in *Storyteller* (1981). This book defies genre classification by including short fiction, poetry, retellings of traditional stories, and family photographs, all linked by passages of commentary and memoir. Her interest in images interacting with words led Silko to produce a film in 1980 with Dennis Carr titled *Estoyehmuut and the Gunnadeyah* (Arrowboy and the Destroyers). In shooting the film in Laguna, New Mexico, using pueblo residents and elders instead of professional actors, Silko documented a time and place that no longer exist.

Silko's nonfiction works include *The Delicacy and Strength of Lace: Letters Between Leslie Marmon Silko and James Wright* (1986; edited by Ann Wright), and *Yellow Woman and a Beauty of the Spirit: Essays on Native American Life Today* (1996), a collection of essays. In *Sacred Water: Narratives and Pictures* (1993), she self-published her essay on water interwoven with her Polaroid photographs. The first edition was hand sewn and glued by Silko; a subsequent edition was conventionally bound.

ACHIEVEMENTS

The publication of Leslie Marmon Silko's first novel, *Ceremony*, along with N. Scott Momaday's winning of the 1969 Pulitzer Prize for *House Made of Dawn*, marked the beginning of a surge in publishing by Native American authors—the Native American renaissance of the late 1960's and early 1970's. Yet just as her works defy genre classification, Silko transcends the category of Native American writer. Her earlier works draw heavily on her own experiences and the traditional stories of Laguna Pueblo; later works move beyond the pueblo while maintaining a strong connection with the Southwest and with traditional and autobiographical materials. Her first two novels, *Ceremony* and *Almanac of the Dead*, are experimental in form, testing the limits of the novel as a genre and format. Indeed, Silko once said that she loves working in the novel form because its flexibility imposes so few limitations on the writer. Her third novel, *Gardens in the Dunes*, adheres more closely to conventional novel form, but like the previous two, it is highly political.

Silko's books, particularly *Ceremony* and *Storyteller,* are widely taught in colleges and universities; her short fiction and poetry are widely anthologized. Her works have been translated into Italian and German and are popular internationally, both in translation and in the original English.

Silko's works in fiction, nonfiction, and poetry earned her a National Endowment for the Arts Discover Grant (1971), *The Chicago Review* Poetry Award (1974), the Pushcart Prize for Poetry (1977), a MacArthur Prize Fellowship (1981), the *Boston Globe* prize for nonfiction (1986), a New Mexico Endowment for the Humanities "Living Cultural Treasure" Award (1988), and a Lila Wallace-Reader's Digest Fund Writers Award (1991). Her story "Lullaby" was selected as one of twenty best short stories of 1975.

BIOGRAPHY

Leslie Marmon Silko was born to Leland (Lee) Howard Marmon and Mary Virginia Leslie in 1948. Her extended mixed-heritage family (Laguna, Mexican, white) had a rich history of tribal leadership and a rich tradition of storytelling. Growing up at Laguna Pueblo, Silko rode horses, hunted, and was free to explore the land of her ancestors, land that was inextricably tied to the traditional stories told by her aunts and grandmother.

In 1964, Silko entered the University of New Mexico. In 1966, she married Richard Chapman and gave birth to Robert William Chapman. During her sophomore year, she took a creative writing class. Despite the success of a short story written for that class, "The Man to Send Rainclouds," which was published first in *New Mexico Quarterly* and then in Kenneth Rosen's anthology of Native American writing as the title piece, Silko did not yet see herself primarily as a writer. After receiving her bachelor of arts degree in 1969, she entered the University of New Mexico law school in the American Indian Law Fellowship program. During the same year, she separated from and eventually divorced Chapman.

In 1971, Silko left law school. Convinced that the American justice system was inherently unjust, and believing that her own role was to call attention to this injustice by telling stories, she entered graduate school in English at New Mexico. She soon left to teach at Navajo Community College. During the same year, she married John Silko (whom she would also later divorce) and gave birth to her second child, Cazimir Silko.

Leaving the Southwest for the first time, Silko moved with her husband and children to Ketchikan, Alaska, in 1973. The impact of the Alaskan landscape and climate can be seen in her short story "Storyteller," written during this time, and it resurfaces in *Almanac of the Dead.* She also began writing *Ceremony* while in Alaska, re-creating her beloved southwestern landscape.

Silko returned to Laguna for a short time before moving to Tucson in 1978, where she taught at the University of Arizona. She eventually settled on a ranch outside Tucson, enjoying the physical labor of ranch life. In 1981, the year in which *Storyteller* was published, Silko was awarded the MacArthur Prize Fellowship. Sometimes called the genius award, the MacArthur Prize provided five years of financial support, allowing her, for the first time, to devote all of her efforts to writing. While writing *Almanac of the Dead*, she became incensed about Arizona politics, leading her to paint a mural of a snake with political graffiti on the outside wall of her Stone Avenue office. Though later owners painted over the mural, it was well received by the people of the neighborhood and was important both in helping Silko (who describes herself as a "frustrated painter") to overcome writer's block and to develop further her technique of combining images with words. After the publication of *Almanac of the Dead* in 1991, Silko's desire for independence from the publishing world and her experiments with photography (in part inspired by her father, a professional photographer) led her to self-publish *Sacred Water: Narratives and Pictures*.

ANALYSIS

Leslie Marmon Silko once stated that she tries to write a very different book every time. Indeed, her novels are as different from one another as they are from her books in other genres. Despite such diversity, however, Silko's novels share certain common traits. All draw heavily on her personal experiences, but they are not conventionally autobiographical. Although only *Ceremony* deals exclusively with Native American themes and characters, Native American themes and characters are central in the other novels as well.

Silko was so attuned to the political situation in northern Mexico that, in *Almanac of the Dead*, published two years before the Zapatista uprising in Chiapas, her description of an uprising in northern Mexico seems prophetic. Silko's work makes use of her eclectic reading on topics as diverse as the Gnostic gospels and orchid collecting.

Silko uses very little dialogue, yet her characters are richly drawn through the use of an omniscient narrator who reveals their inner thoughts and reactions. Her descriptions are vivid and detailed. Though predominantly serious, all of Silko's novels display her wry, ironic sense of humor. An important recurring theme in all of Silko's novels is the conflict between the "destroyers," those whose disregard for the land leads them to exploit it and its people for profit, and those who are in touch with and respect the land. Although those in touch with the land are usually the indigenous people who have not separated themselves from nature, indigenous people can be destroyers, and whites can be in touch with the land.

CEREMONY

In *Ceremony*, Tayo, a young veteran of mixed Laguna and white ancestry, returns from World War II with what would now be called post-traumatic stress disorder. When the U.S. Veterans Administration (V.A.) hospital sends him home to the pueblo uncured, his family asks the tribal healer, old Ku'oosh, to perform the traditional ceremony for reincorporating warriors into the community. The ceremony is only partially successful; Tayo is still deeply disturbed, blaming himself for his cousin and friend Rocky's death and turning to alcohol along with a group of friends who are also veterans. After a fight with his friend

Emo, Tayo is sent back to the V.A. hospital, but his treatment is no more successful than it was the first time.

Betonie, a Navajo medicine man who uses unconventional methods, is more successful. He conducts a Navajo healing ceremony for Tayo that sets him on the road to recovery. When Tayo leaves, Betonie says that to complete the ceremony Tayo must recover the spotted cattle that Tayo and his Uncle Josiah had planned to raise but that had presumably wandered off in Tayo's absence after Josiah died. Tayo discovers that the cattle were stolen by white ranchers and realizes that he had believed the lie that only Indians and Mexicans stole because whites did not need to steal. With the help of Ts'eh, a mysterious woman who turns out to be the spirit of the sacred mountain, Tayo takes the cattle home.

Meanwhile, Emo has become one of the destroyers, a participant in witchery, and he convinces the rest of the group to cooperate in his plan to kill Tayo. Warned by Ts'eh, Tayo is able to resist the witchery. He returns home and tells his story to the elders in the kiva, who recognize Ts'eh as the spirit who brings rain and healing to their drought-stricken land. Tayo's separation from his community, in part caused by the war but also caused by his rejection as an illegitimate "half-breed," was symptomatic of a larger rift in the community. His healing demonstrates that things must change, that the new must be incorporated into the old, and that the "half-breed" can act as a mediator between the old traditions and the new world. Much of *Ceremony* is told in flashbacks. Traditional Laguna stories are woven throughout, set off from the text. The language is lyrical, and the message is of healing and conciliation.

ALMANAC OF THE DEAD

When Silko read from this novel at the time of its publication, she announced, "This book attempts to crush linear time." It succeeds by repeatedly shifting time frames. Silko interweaves an enormous cast of characters involved in multiple subplots. They tell the story, in an indeterminate time in the not-too-distant future, of a spontaneous uprising across the Americas of dispossessed indigenous peoples who move throughout the novel toward an apocalyptic convergence on Tucson.

Lecha and Zeta are twins, mixed-blood Yaquis, who have been given pieces of an old Mayan book (the almanac of the title). Unlike the Mayan codices, this book has stayed in the hands of the people. As they work to transcribe the pieces, they discover that the Mayans foretold the coming of the white European invaders—and foretold their demise as well. Seese, a young white woman whose baby has been kidnapped, consults Lecha, who is a psychic, and stays to work for her. Sterling, an old man who is exiled for revealing tribal secrets, also comes to work at the twins' ranch.

Other characters include Allegria, a mercenary architect, and her husband, Menardo, who live near Mexico City; the Tucson branch of the Blue family, mafiosi who dominate the Tucson real estate market; the Indian twin brothers Tacho and Wacah, who embody the mysterious power of twins and lead the people north toward Tucson; and Marxist Mexican revolutionaries Angelita (La Escapia) and El Feo. Their stories intertwine as they converge on Tucson, where the Barefoot Hopi warns that the familiar way of life on earth will end unless the destroyers change their ways and respect the earth. "Eco-warriors" to the north threaten a suicide bombing of a dam. The novel ends as all are poised on the brink of revolution.

GARDENS IN THE DUNES

In an unpublished interview, Silko described her third novel as "full of flowers and light." Set in the time immediately following the stock market crash of 1893, *Gardens in the Dunes* tells the story of Indigo and Sister Salt. The young sisters are the last of the Sand Lizards, a fictional tribe based loosely on the Colorado River tribes that were wiped out around the beginning of the twentieth century. After a Ghost Dance they are attending is raided by the police, the girls are separated from their mother as they flee. Later, their grandmother dies and Indigo is captured by the police. She is sent to boarding school in Riverside.

There Indigo is befriended by Hattie and Edward, a wealthy couple who live near the school. Before marrying Edward, Hattie attended Harvard University until her unconventional thesis proposal on the Gnostic gospels was rejected. Edward is a professional plant collector who sells rare specimens to wealthy buyers. They take Indigo along on their European trip during the school's summer break. Indigo sees the Jesus of the European churches as another manifestation of Wovoka, the prophet of the Ghost Dance. Edward's scheme to steal citron cuttings fails; Hattie, disgusted by his greed, divorces him and vows to help Indigo find her family.

Meanwhile, Sister Salt is befriended by Big Candy, who fathers her baby, the "little black grandfather." When Big Candy's preoccupation with wealth causes him to neglect Sister Salt and the baby, she and the Chemehuevi twins leave to farm land that the twins acquired from an aunt. The sisters are reunited, returning to the old gardens. Indigo plants the seeds and bulbs she collected on her journey, mixing the impractical but beautiful flowers with the traditional food crops. As in earlier works, Silko emphasizes the need to live in harmony with the land, the dangers of capitalism, and the need to use the new along with the old.

Robin Payne Cohen

OTHER MAJOR WORKS

SHORT FICTION: *Yellow Woman*, 1993.

PLAY: *Lullaby*, pr. 1976 (with Frank Chin).

POETRY: *Laguna Woman: Poems*, 1974.

NONFICTION: *The Delicacy and Strength of Lace: Letters Between Leslie Marmon Silko and James Wright*, 1986; *Sacred Water: Narratives and Pictures*, 1993; *Yellow*

Woman and a Beauty of the Spirit: Essays on Native American Life Today, 1996; *Conversations with Leslie Marmon Silko*, 2000 (Ellen L. Arnold, editor).

MISCELLANEOUS: *Storyteller*, 1981 (includes poetry and prose).

BIBLIOGRAPHY

Allen, Paula Gunn. "The Feminine Landscape of Leslie Marmon Silko's *Ceremony*." In *Studies in American Indian Literature: Critical Essays and Course Design*. New York: Modern Language Association of America, 1983. Interprets Silko's *Ceremony* from a feminist perspective and sees it as divided into two kinds of characters: earth spirits in harmony with the earth and spirit destroyers. Allen maintains that this is a novel of feminine life forces and the mechanistic death force of witchery; the women are equitable with the land, the life force, a thesis that is central to Native American culture. Allen analyzes the main characters and the causes for Tayo's illness from a Jungian perspective; she discusses Silko's poetry and the storyteller tradition that underpins her fiction. Includes a brief and helpful bibliography of Silko's work and of criticism about her fiction.

Barnett, Louise K., and James L. Thorson, eds. *Leslie Marmon Silko: A Collection of Critical Essays*. Albuquerque: University of New Mexico Press, 1999. These essays cover the entire range of Silko's work through *Almanac of the Dead*, offering biographical information on Silko as well as an extensive bibliography of primary and secondary sources complete with a helpful bibliographical essay.

Chavkin, Allan, ed. *Leslie Marmon Silko's "Ceremony": A Casebook*. New York: Oxford University Press, 2002. Collection of essays offers readings of Silko's novel from a variety of theoretical perspectives and provides background information on Native American culture. Includes an interview with Silko.

Fitz, Brewster E. *Silko: Writing Storyteller and Medicine Woman*. Norman: University of Oklahoma Press, 2004. Fitz analyzes *Almanac of the Dead* and several of Silko's short stories, focusing on the relationship between the written word and oral storytelling tradition of Silko's family and Laguna culture.

Krupat, Arnold. "The Dialogic of Silko's *Storyteller*." In *Narrative Chance: Postmodern Discourse on Native American Indian Literature*, edited by Gerald Vizenor. Albuquerque: University of New Mexico Press, 1989. Discusses *Storyteller* from the point of view of the work of literary theorist Mikhail Bakhtin.

Larson, Charles R. *American Indian Fiction*. Albuquerque: University of New Mexico Press, 1978. Views Silko as an author who is very aware of her cultural and ethnic identity and as a writer of "authentic" Native American novels. Provides an in-depth analysis of *Ceremony*, summarizes the plot, and discusses the experimental structure of the novel. Relates the story in *Ceremony* to the Grandmother Spider motif and myth. Discusses the poems included in *Ceremony*, asserting that they act as a second persona in the novel, as a medicine man.

Nelson, Robert M. *Leslie Marmon Silko's "Ceremony": The Recovery of Tradition*. New York: Peter Lang, 2008. Nelson focuses on the Navajo and other Native American texts that form the backbone of Silko's novel, describing how she adapts and relates these texts to her narrative.

Owens, Louis. "The Very Essence of Our Lives: Leslie Silko's Webs of Identity." In *Other Destinies: Understanding the American Indian Novel*. Norman: University of Oklahoma Press, 1992. Owens examines Native American novels written between 1854 and the 1990's, focusing on the common themes of self-discovery and cultural recovery. He analyzes *Ceremony* as a search for identity through memory and returning home.

Salyer, Gregory. *Leslie Marmon Silko*. New York: Twayne, 1997. A critical study of Silko's work, describing how her fiction has been influenced by her Laguna background and by Native American stories. Includes a bibliography and an index.

Teuton, Sean Kicummah. "Learning to Feel: Tribal Experience in Leslie Marmon Silko's *Ceremony*." In *Red Land, Red Power: Grounding Knowledge in the American Indian Novel*. Durham, N.C.: Duke University Press, 2008. Teuton's analysis of *Ceremony* is included in his study of Native American literature in the late 1960's and 1970's. Examines how these books used historical memory and oral tradition to create a more "enabling knowledge" of the lives and possibilities of American Indians.

Wiget, Andrew. *Native American Literature*. Boston: Twayne, 1985. Wiget offers an analytical overview of *Ceremony* and compares the novel to N. Scott Momaday's *House Made of Dawn*. He maintains that *Ceremony* explores the death of, or threats to, traditional Native American values and ways and sets the human struggle against mythic Native American legends. Includes a brief but useful bibliography.

WILLIAM GILMORE SIMMS

Born: Charleston, South Carolina; April 17, 1806
Died: Charleston, South Carolina; June 11, 1870

OTHER LITERARY FORMS

William Gilmore Simms wrote extensively in all major literary genres. He began as a poet and achieved his first widespread fame in the northern United States with his long poetic work *Atalantis: A Story of the Sea* (1832). Although he continued to write and publish his verse throughout his lifetime and, indeed, felt himself to be a good poet, his reputation has never rested on his poetic abilities. Still, his poetry is not without interest, for Simms often reveals a sharp eye for natural detail in his descriptions, especially of the southern landscape. His accomplishments as a writer of short fiction only began to be appreciated in the late twentieth century.

Simms's emphasis on realism can be seen in such works as "The Hireling and the Slave," and his wonderful command of folk humor can be found in such literary "tall tales" as "Bald-Head Bill Bauldy" and "How Sharp Snaffles Got His Capital and Wife." Longer stories such as "Paddy McGann" contain further elements of the tall tale and folklore. Simms was not a good dramatist; he wrote a number of aborted plays and, in the case of *Pelayo*, adapted a failed drama into novel form. His best play is considered to be *Michael Bonham: Or, The Fall of Bexar, a Tale of Texas* (pb. 1852), which deals with the Texas war for independence.

In his nonfiction works, Simms often turned to the history of the South. Of his four major biographies, two—*The Life of Francis Marion* (1844) and *The Life of Nathanael Greene* (1849)—grew out of his abiding interest in the Revolutionary War in the South; both men also appeared as characters in his novels. His historical writings include *The History of South Carolina* (1840), a general history of the state, beginning with its settlement; *South-Carolina in the Revolutionary War* (1853), which concentrated on that part of the state's history that he so often used in his fiction; and his contemporary account of the Civil War, *Sack and Destruction of the City of Columbia, S.C.* (1865), an inspired example of reporting.

Although Simms was not always accurate or unbiased, he was a surprisingly good historian. He collected sources throughout his life and made use of private recollections and memories. His work provides a storehouse of information often overlooked by more standard historical works. Simms's combination of the factual and the imaginative in his historical romances is one of his strongest and most appealing traits.

ACHIEVEMENTS

Although during his lifetime William Gilmore Simms's popularity as a novelist ranked second only to that of James Fenimore Cooper, his reputation steadily diminished after his death, so that by the beginning of the twentieth century he was little more than a footnote in literary histories. With the University of South Carolina Press publications of *The Letters of William Gilmore Simms* (1952-1956; five volumes, Mary C. Simms Oliphant, editor) and the first volumes of *The Centennial Edition of the Writings of William Gilmore Simms* (1969-1975; sixteen volumes, John C. Guilds and James B. Meriwether, editors), however, there has been a growing interest in his work. Still, Simms's contributions to the development of American literature in the first half of the nineteenth century have been much underrated. Put simply, Simms was the most important antebellum southern man of letters. He created a body of work that is awesome in size and scope. More than eighty separate volumes were published during his life, and ongoing research is uncovering more of his writings hidden in forgotten periodicals or under various pseudonyms.

When, in 1832, Simms first traveled to New York City, he was determined to establish himself as a writer of national importance. He made the necessary publishing connections and paid homage to the leading Northern literary figures. The publication of his poetic work *Atalantis* in that year was enthusiastically received, but it and his short novel *Martin Faber*, published the following year, were still apprenticeship pieces that followed patterns set down by others. With *Guy Rivers*, *The Yemassee*, and *The Partisan*, Simms not only staked out his own literary territory but also publicly placed himself in competition on a national level. Simms was an ardent supporter of the idea that America must produce its own unique brand of writing, inspired by its own land and people and experiences. Simms's own interest lay in the South, but, as he explained in the preface to *The Wigwam and the Cabin* (1845), by mastering sectional material, the writer could still be of national importance, since no single writer could adequately depict the United States as a whole.

It was in his commitment to the South that Simms achieved his greatness. He saw the South as a land of exciting potential. He loved its rawness as well as its manners, its violence as well as its vitality. Its heritage was rich, he felt, but largely unknown to people both inside and outside the region. Thus Simms, with his passion for history and folklore, set out to reveal this past to southerners and northerners alike, to correct the historical picture he found so lacking. In his romances, he helped to define the popular image of the South from precolonial times up to the American Civil War. Northerners, Simms maintained, had no right to feel superior to their southern brethren, but southerners had all too often been remiss in preserving and appreciating their own heritage.

As the political disputes between North and South intensified, Simms became a protector of a way of life he felt was being threatened. In this time of trouble, he maintained that the past held lessons for the present: The courageous spirit of the pioneer and the partisan soldier could still inspire, the inherent nobility of the manor-born ladies and gentlemen could still instruct. Thus, Simms's tales of an earlier era, marked by characters of indomitable strength, could be seen as examples for his own time.

The sheer quantity of Simms's work remains staggering and his overall achievement approaches the heroic. Although he sometimes bemoaned the lack of appreciation and support he received in the South, most of his contemporaries, despite occasional carping, freely awarded him the laurels of leadership. A less courageous and confident person would never have faced the challenges that Simms invited. Before the war, he sought, through his own example, to impart a sense of dignity to the southern artist. For the five years he lived after the war, he struggled to rekindle the pride of a defeated people, in the middle of his own great personal tragedy. As a critic and an editor, as a poet and a writer of fiction, he worked at first with energy and enthusiasm, later out of a kind of desperation against the inevitable, but he never stinted in his devotion to art and to a world that came to lie in ruins around him.

BIOGRAPHY

William Gilmore Simms was born in Charleston, South Carolina, on April 17, 1806, the second son and only surviving child of William Gilmore and Harriet Ann Augusta Singleton Simms. Simms's father came from Ireland after the American Revolution and established a successful mercantile business in Charleston. His mother's family, the Singletons, had lived in the port city for generations. Her grandfather, Thomas Singleton, was one of the Charleston citizens arrested by the British authorities during their occupation and, despite his advanced age, sent in exile to St. Augustine; her father, John Singleton, had fought as a soldier on the side of the patriots.

Simms's mother died in 1808, and shortly thereafter, his father, grief-stricken at the loss of his wife, left Charleston to journey westward, placing his only child in the care of his late wife's mother, Mrs. Gates (she had remarried in 1800 after the death of John Singleton in 1799). The elder Simms went on to lead what must have seemed an incredibly exciting life to his impressionable son; the boy heard tales of his father's fighting under Andrew Jackson in the Indian Wars in Florida and later at the Battle of New Orleans in the War of 1812 before settling in Mississippi, then the edge of the frontier. Thus, Simms the boy grew up surrounded by legends and dreams of almost mythical characters—the Revolutionary War heroes on the Singleton side of the family, and the pioneer-soldier he saw in his own father. Both romantic threads would run throughout Simms's writings. In addition, growing up in historic Charleston allowed him to visit sites of revolutionary incidents in and near the city. His unflagging interest in history (especially that of South Carolina but also of foreign lands) provided a foundation for his wilder imagination, and his writings would always contain a solid understructure of fact.

Although tradition has held that Simms grew up in genteel poverty in Charleston, feeling ostracized by that aristocratic city's more prominent citizens, his father had, in fact, left him substantial property holdings, and Simms was recognized early for his achievements. Still, it is equally clear that Simms was sensitive to slight—partly because of boyhood loneliness after the loss of his immediate family—and his enormous artistic energy no doubt fed on this partial uncertainty.

In 1812, at the age of six, Simms began school in Charleston. He entered the College of Charleston when he was ten, and at twelve he began work in a local apothecary shop. He was already writing poetry and drama. By the age of sixteen, he had published verse in a Charleston newspaper; at age seventeen he was editing a juvenile periodical, the first of many editorships he would undertake in his lifetime. The next year, 1824 to 1825, Simms spent with his father in Mississippi. Together they ranged into the wilderness, where Simms met and carefully observed the types of frontiersmen (rascals and rogues among them) and American Indians that would people his romances.

When Simms returned to Charleston in 1825, he set about establishing himself as a writer. His first volume of verse, *Monody on the Death of Gen. Charles Cotesworth Pinckney* (1825), made him a prominent local talent. In 1826, he married Anna Malcolm Giles. The next year Simms was admitted to the bar and published his second and third volumes of poetry. In 1828, he became editor of the *Southern Literary Gazette*; in 1829, his fourth volume of verse appeared, and his fifth followed in 1830. Also in 1830, he became copartner in Charleston's *City Gazette*. In this role he figured as a leading opponent to the Nullification Controversy, which was dividing South Carolina into two very fractious parties. Simms's opposition brought him into serious disfavor with many important citizens, and it was an experience that he would remember with a mixture of anger and regret.

The year 1832 was a decisive one for Simms. His wife, Anna, died in February. Overtaxed by emotional and professional demands, Simms gave up his legal practice (never a foremost interest), sold the *City Gazette*, and journeyed to New York City, determined to make his way in earnest as a literary man. In New York, he formed what was to be a lifelong friendship with James Lawson. Simms would use Lawson's home as his northern base until the Civil War finally intervened; Lawson would be among the first to help Simms in the dark days after the war as well. With Lawson's encouragement and advice, Simms published his sixth volume of poetry, *Atalantis*, in 1832. When it proved extremely popular with the Northern audience, Simms followed it with his first novel, *Martin Faber*, and his first collection of short fiction, *The Book of My Lady*, both in 1833. With the publication of *Guy Rivers* in 1834 and of *The Partisan* and *The Yemassee* in 1835, Simms had announced his literary directions, as these three books were the first of his border, revolutionary, and colonial romances, respectively.

The next twenty or so years were generally good ones for Simms. In 1836, he married Chevillette Eliza Roach, the daughter of a prominent land owner in South Carolina. As part of his marriage inheritance, Simms obtained Woodlands plantation, which became his most prized retreat, an emblem of all he saw best in the southern way of life. The demands of his lifestyle made it necessary that Simms publish as much and as often as possible, but because of the laxity of copyright laws he often received far less than he was due for what he did write. Simms would travel to New York about once a year to confer with his publishers (for a time new works by Simms came out annually) and to visit old friends. He enjoyed his growing reputation as spokesman for the South. Although he was always interested in politics and acted as an informal adviser to a number of political leaders in South Carolina, he served only one term in government, as a member of the South Carolina House of Representatives from 1844 to 1846. His most notable literary position during this time was as editor of the *Southern Quarterly Review* from 1849 to 1854.

Beginning in the 1850's, Simms became a leading voice in the call for the South's secession from the Union and in the defense of slavery. He is too often remembered for the attitudes struck in these pronouncements, so at odds with modern understanding, at the expense of his more important creative works. As a public figure, Simms attracted the opprobrium aimed at the South as war became inevitable. His 1856 lecture tour of the North on the role of the South in the American Revolution had to be cut short when Simms enraged his audiences with his vigorous and even pugnacious arguments against the Union stand. He welcomed the final break and was confident of Southern victory, but as the war progressed, he came to see the specter of defeat.

The last years of Simms's life were tragic. In 1862, Woodlands was partially burned but was rebuilt through the subscriptions of appreciative South Carolinians. In 1863, his second wife died, a devastating blow to Simms, who had also lost nine of his children. In 1865, Woodlands was again set ablaze, this time by stragglers from General Sherman's army. Simms lost in this conflagration his private library of ten thousand volumes, considered to be the finest in the South at the time.

During the five years remaining to him after the war, Simms worked as never before, as editor of two newspapers—the *Columbia Phoenix* and the *Daily South Carolinian*—and as the author of still more poems, addresses, short fiction, and serialized novels. Despite his own almost inconceivable losses, Simms did what he could to bring about the resurrection of the South. When he died on June 11, 1870, a world and a way of life had clearly passed with him.

ANALYSIS

As early as 1835, in the preface to *The Yemassee*, William Gilmore Simms attempted to define his goals as a writer. He distinguished his full-length fiction as romances rather than novels. Following definitions already in vogue, Simms described the novel as picturing ordinary people in everyday situations, both domestic and common. These works he traced to Samuel Richardson and Henry Fielding. The romance, on the other hand, he saw as the modern-day equivalent to the ancient epic, drawing its inspiration and power from both drama and poetry. The romance (as practiced by writers such as Sir Walter Scott, Edward Bulwer-Lytton, and James Fenimore Cooper) was of "loftier origins" than the novel. Its characters were individuals caught up in extraordinary, uncertain, even improbable events. As Simms saw it, the writer of a romance was not as bound by strict logic as was the novelist; indeed, the romancer's ingenuity in plotting was often a strong point in the work. As critics have pointed out, a number of Simms's supposed literary sins—stock characters, absurd resolutions, inflated dialogue—resulted from the Romantic tradition in which he worked rather than from a lack of art or skill.

REALISM

To categorize Simms simply as a writer of romances is, however, somewhat misleading, and later studies emphasized the strong sense of realism that is found in his work. During his lifetime, Simms was regularly accused of exceeding the bounds of propriety. He answered these objections on numerous occasions. In his "Advertisement" to *Mellichampe*, for example, he insisted that his purpose was to "adhere as closely as possible, to the features and the attributes of real life." Thus, although he endeavored to invest his stories with noble characters involved in stirring adventures, he wished to write neither "a fairy tale, [n]or a tale in which none but the colors of the rose and rainbow shall predominate."

This sense of realism, which must have seemed uncouth in Simms's own time, has come to be recognized as one of his strongest traits. He was clearly influenced by the "realism" of the legends and frontier tales of his youth and in the writings of the southern and southwestern humorists. Augustus Baldwin Longstreet's *Georgia Scenes* was published in 1835, the same year as *The Yemassee* and *The Partisan*. (Simms would himself write several brilliant tall tales such as "Bald-Head Bill Bauldy" and "How Sharp Snaffles Got His Capital and Wife.") Simms's sense of realism did not apply only to "low" characters and their exploits, however, as has often been implied. Simms would modify the nobility, the wisdom, even the courage of his "model characters," his aristocrats, if the story warranted it. His heroes could learn, could fail, could grow; and his villains were often surprisingly complex, capable of unexpected decency and courageous deeds.

Underlying all of Simms's romances was a strong awareness of history, of what had actually happened at the time and place about which he wrote. Simms felt free to bend fact to the demands of art, but not to misrepresent the essential truth of the situation. The *facts* of history, he said, standing by themselves, carried little weight, but the artist—the creative writer—by giving *shape* to the facts, could give them life and meaning. Thus, it is the writer who is the true historian, and it was as an "artist-historian" that Simms wrote most of his romances.

As all commentators on Simms like to point out (and as Simms himself was aware), he usually wrote too rapidly and carelessly. He simply produced too much for the good of his own reputation. His faults are often glaring, but they are usually the result of haste and little or no revision. Simms could write with clarity and precision, but he could also sacrifice both for blood and thunder. Simms was a storyteller, and his books, for all their length, keep a steady pace. When he turned his hand to psychological interpretations of characters, when he tried to "analyze the heart," he often did so with the concomitant loss of energy and drive. In his best works, however, he was able to combine complexity of character with a compelling story.

REVOLUTIONARY WAR NOVELS

Simms wrote eight romances dealing with the Revolutionary War in the South, and as a group they represent his best work. The novels cover the period from 1775, when the first open warfare began, to 1783, when the British abandoned Charleston and the soldiers returned home to a new and difficult way of life. The internal chronology of the novels does not correspond to the sequence of their composition. *Joscelyn: A Tale of the Revolution*, which was meant to be the "opening scene" in Simms's "grand drama" of the South's seven-year war of Revolution, was one of the very last works he wrote, and the only one of the eight never to appear in book form during his lifetime. It appears as volume 16 of *The Centennial Edition of the Writings of William Gilmore Simms*. *Joscelyn* is set around the Georgia-South Carolina border and describes the early conflicts between those who joined in the growing freedom movement and those who remained loyal to the crown. It also shows that people on both sides of the issue could be motivated by cruelty as well as courage, by selfishness as well as honor.

THE PARTISAN, MELLICHAMPE, *and* KATHARINE WALTON

Simms conceived of the three novels *The Partisan*, *Mellichampe*, and *Katharine Walton* as a trilogy, with developing characters and overlapping plots, although each was also meant to stand as an independent work. These books cover the events of 1780, following the fall of Charleston to the British. *The Partisan* is a big, sprawling book that Simms later described as a "ground-plan," a setting of the stage for the works to come. It introduces numerous characters, both historical—Francis Marion, Lord Cornwallis, Sir Banastre Tarleton, Horatio Gates, Baron de Kalb—and fictional—Major Robert Singleton, Colonel Richard Walton and daughter Katharine, Lieutenant Porgy—who return in later works in the series. *The Partisan*'s story lines include the development of Marion's guerrilla forces in the swamps of South Carolina, the growth of love between Singleton and Katharine Walton, and the agony of Colonel Walton's decision to align himself with the rebel cause. The novel closes with a detailed description and analysis of the Battle of Camden (August, 1780), wherein Gates and the Southern Continental Army were soundly defeated by Cornwallis.

Mellichampe is set in the fall of 1780. It put less emphasis on the large historical picture and was more clearly intended as a work of fiction, although here again the facts of the war are not forgotten. In *Mellichampe*, Simms expands his description of Marion's role in the war, develops several minor characters found in *The Partisan*, and illustrates the "excesses of patriotism" and the necessity of honor in times of conflict. The third book of this trilogy, *Katharine Walton*, again takes up the story of Colonel Walton, his daughter, and Robert Singleton. It is set largely in Charleston during the last months of 1780 and describes the social life and attempts at rebellion in the captured city at this very trying time.

THE SCOUT

The next in the series is *The Scout*, which moves into the central region of South Carolina. It is, in some ways, the most "romantic" and melodramatic of the novels. Its plot of feuding brothers and mysterious outriders is heavy with conventions, but in its description of the marauding outlaw bands that terrorized the backcountry and in its discussion of Nathanael Greene's siege of the British fort at Ninety-Six (upstate South Carolina) in the summer of 1781, *The Scout* is an impressive and absorbing story.

The Forayers and *Eutaw*, which were first conceived as one book, follow the retreat of the British from Ninety-Six to Charleston and present the events leading to the climactic battle at Eutaw Springs, South Carolina, in September, 1781, which effectively ended British rule in the state, although the battle itself was a draw.

WOODCRAFT

The last of the Revolutionary War novels is *Woodcraft*, which begins in December, 1782, after the British evacuation. Its theme is the readjustment of soldiers to domestic life, and its main character is Lieutenant Porgy, the wastrel aristocrat soldier whom many feel to be Simms's most successful character. Porgy appears in five of the eight novels, but his most important role is in *Woodcraft*. Basically a comic character (Porgy is often compared to William Shakespeare's Falstaff, although such comparisons rarely go beyond surface descriptions), this fat soldier confronts the challenges of peace after the adventures of war. Born of the landed gentry, Porgy is known to have wasted his inheritance as a young man, and despite his courage and wit, he is not one of Simms's noble heroes. He is, however, among the most likable and (with reservations) the most admirable of Simms's characters, and it is his mood of reconciliation (after one final battle) and acceptance that presides over this last book. Some critics hold *Woodcraft* to be Simms's best work (although *The Forayers* and *Eutaw* might be better choices), and it certainly shows Simms at his most relaxed and amiable.

GUY RIVERS

Commonly listed under the category of Simms's border romances are *Guy Rivers*, *Richard Hurdis*, *Border Beagles*, *Beauchampe*, *Helen Halsey*, *Charlemont*, "Voltmeier: Or, The Mountain Men," and "The Cub of the Panther." These works lack the specific historical overview of the Revolutionary War novels—they are closer to Simms's own time and are not as likely to be built around identifiable events—but they do give excellent descriptions of the frontier of the Old South—the customs, speech patterns, and lifestyle of settlers, outlaws, and adventurers. The first of these, *Guy Rivers*, was Simms's first full-length novel as well. Set in the mountainous region of Georgia, where gold was being mined in the early nineteenth century, the story centers on the conflict between Guy Rivers, a notorious outlaw (though once a respected lawyer) and Ralph Colleton, a young South Carolinian whose own frustrations with love and family have led him to the frontier. There he meets Mark Forrester, a native of the region who helps Ralph in his "natural" education. Colleton foreshadows such later Simms heroes as Robert Singleton, Ernest Mellichampe, and Willie Sinclair (in *The Forayers* and *Eutaw*), while Forrester anticipates Thumbscrew Witherspoon in *Mellichampe* and Supple Jack Bannister in *The Scout*, woodsmen who teach the young aristocrats the need for clear thinking and honorable actions. Rivers is the melodramatic villain of the type that would chew the scenery and threaten feminine virtue in a number of Simms's works: Barsfield in *Mellichampe*, Edward Conway in *The Scout*, Captain Inglehardt in *The Forayers* and *Eutaw*.

RICHARD HURDIS

Richard Hurdis, the second of the border novels, is perhaps the best of them. Set in Alabama, the story is loosely based on the outrages of John Murrell and his outlaw gang, which roamed throughout Alabama and Mississippi. Simms apparently had met witnesses to or even participants in some of this gang's doings while visiting his father in Mississippi as a boy. The plot is somewhat similar to that of *The Scout*. In each novel, two brothers—one virtuous and one criminally inclined—find themselves at odds; both books are concerned with the attempts to bring outlaw bands to justice. In a sense, *Border Beagles* is a continuation of *Richard Hurdis*; a tale of bandits on the Mississippi frontier, it is generally considered a less effective story than its predecessor.

BEAUCHAMPE

Beauchampe was Simms's retelling of the notorious Beauchampe-Sharpe Kentucky tragedy, a murder case in which Beauchampe killed Warham Sharpe, the seducer of Margaret Cooper, whom Beauchampe had married. In 1856, Simms returned to this story in *Charlemont*, which detailed the events leading up to the tragedy in *Beauchampe*. Thus, *Beauchampe*, although published first, was, in Simms's words, the "sequel" to *Charlemont*. Simms's last two border romances were both published in magazines in 1869. "Voltmeier" was published again in 1969 as volume 1 of *The Centennial Edition of the Writings of William Gilmore Simms*. "Voltmeier" and "The Cub of the Panther" were drawn from Simms's personal observations and experiences during trips into the mountainous regions of North Carolina, and they contain some of his best writing.

THE YEMASSEE *and* THE CASSIQUE OF KIAWAH

Simms dealt with the settling of South Carolina in the early eighteenth century in two important works, *The Yemassee* and *The Cassique of Kiawah*. *The Yemassee* was Simms's most popular novel and, because of its American Indian theme, was immediately compared to the works of Cooper. The novel described the 1715 Yemassee Indian War against the colonists. Simms's tale concentrates on two main characters: Governor Charles Craven (a historical figure), who takes the disguise of Gabriel Harrison for much of the book, and Sanutee, the chief of the Yemassee. Simms illustrates Sanutee's problem with sympathy and understanding—the Native American had originally welcomed the settlers and then found himself and his tribe threatened by them—but the novel finally argues in favor of the whites and the advanced civilization they bring with them.

Despite *The Yemassee*'s popularity—it is still the work for which Simms is best remembered—the novel is not as impressive as *The Cassique of Kiawah*, a much later and more mature work, which deals with similar material but has received little critical attention. It has been argued that Simms's picture of the American Indian was more realistic than Cooper's. He avoided the idea of the "noble savage," but often imbued his Native Americans with traits of courage and dignity. In addition to these two novels, Simms used colonial and American Indian material in several of his shorter works found in *Carl Werner* (1838) and *The Wigwam and the Cabin*.

PELAYO, COUNT JULIAN, THE DAMSEL OF DARIEN, *and* VASCONSELOS

Simms's interest in European history, especially in Spanish history, dated back to his childhood and formed the basis for four foreign romances. *Pelayo* had been conceived when Simms was seventeen as a drama on the conquest of Spain by the Moors. The play was never performed, and the material later grew into a novel. *Count Julian* was the sequel to *Pelayo*, but its publication was delayed for a number of years because its manuscript was lost for a time. *The Damsel of Darien* was inspired by the adventures of explorer Vasco Núñez de Balboa, while *Vasconselos* concerned itself with Hernando de Soto's explorations in the New World. Most critics and readers would agree that these works are among Simms's weakest.

MARTIN FABER *and* CONFESSION

Simms's first novel, *Martin Faber*, recounts the first-person confessions of the title character, who has seduced and murdered one girl and married another, whom he then begins to suspect of adultery. Faber tells his story in prison, just before his execution. The book is a short and emotional work, and it was quickly linked to William Godwin's *Things as They Are: Or, The Adventures of Caleb Williams* (1794), although its antecedents could also be found in numerous gothic romances.

Simms returned to this type of story in *Confession*, which, in his introduction, Simms linked to Godwin. *Confession* was the reworking of an idea Simms had played with as a younger writer. He explained that he had forgotten the work before he found the manuscript by accident years later. As he reread it, he was "led away" by the psychological aspects of the tale. *Confession* tells of Edward Clifford, a young lawyer who is consumed by jealousy of his wife. Convinced of the worst, Clifford kills the entirely virtuous woman; when he later discovers the truth, he condemns himself to a life of wandering and self-recrimination. The similarities to Shakespeare's *Othello, the Moor of Venice* (pr. 1604) are obvious, although Simms maintained that the materials were "gathered from fact."

The same interests in crime, guilt, and retribution are found throughout his other works—he was always intrigued by the psychological complexities of sinners and criminals—and it could be argued that *Beauchampe* and *Charlemont* might better be placed in this group than among the border tales. These psychological novels, however, are not the works for which Simms is remembered. Although his constantly inquiring imagination was stirred by these situations, he was the master of scope and action rather than the kind of close analysis these topics demanded. The twists and entanglements of plot that could be overridden in his more sweeping works became all too obvious when related at a slower, more concentrated pace.

In his lasting works, Simms's long undervalued contribution to America's literary heritage is clearly evident. His was the voice of the South—the maker of its romances, the singer of its legends, the keeper of its history, and the defender of its traditions. More than any other writer, he embodied his time and place: its grandeur, its courage, and its wrongheadedness.

Edwin T. Arnold III

OTHER MAJOR WORKS

SHORT FICTION: *The Book of My Lady*, 1833; *Carl Werner*, 1838; *The Wigwam and the Cabin*, 1845; *Southward Ho!*, 1854.

PLAY: *Michael Bonham: Or, The Fall of Bexar, a Tale of Texas*, pb. 1852.

POETRY: *Monody on the Death of Gen. Charles Cotesworth Pinckney*, 1825; *Early Lays*, 1827; *Lyrical, and Other Poems*, 1827; *The Vision of Cortes*, 1829; *The Tri-Color*, 1830; *Atalantis: A Story of the Sea*, 1832; *Areytos: Or, Songs of the South*, 1846; *Poems Descriptive, Dramatic, Legendary, and Contemplative*, 1853.

NONFICTION: *The History of South Carolina*, 1840; *The Geography of South Carolina*, 1843; *The Life of Francis Marion*, 1844; *Views and Reviews in American Literature, History, and Fiction*, 1845; *The Life of Captain John Smith*, 1846; *The Life of Chevalier Bayard*, 1847; *The Life of Nathanael Greene*, 1849; *South-Carolina in the Revolutionary War*, 1853; *Sack and Destruction of the City of Columbia, S.C.*, 1865; *The Letters of William Gilmore Simms*, 1952-1956 (5 volumes; Mary C. Simms Oliphant, editor).

MISCELLANEOUS: *The Centennial Edition of the Writings of William Gilmore Simms*, 1969-1975 (16 volumes; John C. Guilds and James B. Meriwether, editors).

BIBLIOGRAPHY

Busick, Sean R. *A Sober Desire for History: William Gilmore Simms as Historian*. Columbia: University of South Carolina Press, 2005. Busick argues that Simms is best understood as a historian, and he describes Simms's efforts to record and comprehend American history and to preserve the past. Among other topics, he addresses Simms's ideas about the relation of fiction to history.

Frye, Steven. "Metahistory and American Progressivism: Cultural Dialogics in Simms's *The Yemassee*." In *Historiography and Narrative Design in the American Romance: A Study of Four Authors*. Lewiston, N.Y.: Edwin Mellen Press, 2001. Frye analyzes romances by Simms and three other nineteenth century American writers, describing how these novels employ various techniques and models for writing history.

Guilds, John Caldwell. *Simms: A Literary Life*. Fayetteville: University of Arkansas Press, 1992. Guilds has attempted to rescue Simms from obscurity, editing several twentieth century editions of Simms's novels, as well as collections of essays about the southern author. In this account of Simms's life and writing, Guilds maintains that Simms's historical fiction provides an "epic study" of the United States and should be recognized as the work of a major writer.

_____, ed. *"Long Years of Neglect": The Work and Reputation of William Gilmore Simms*. Fayetteville: University of Arkansas Press, 1988. The twelve essays in this collection address Simms as novelist, poet, historical philosopher, humorist, lecturer, and literary critic.

Guilds, John Caldwell, and Caroline Collins, eds. *William Gilmore Simms and the American Frontier*. Athens: University of Georgia Press, 1997. Collection of essays analyzing the frontier motif in Simms's works, including the novels *Guy Rivers* and *Border Beagles.*

Johanyak, Debra. "William Gilmore Simms: Deviant Paradigms of Southern Womanhood?" *Mississippi Quarterly* 46 (Fall, 1993): 573-588. Discusses the portrayal of women in Simms's fiction. Johanyak claims that just as intellectual, independent, or masculinized women are repeatedly destroyed by seducers in Simms's work, readers are encouraged to view them as deviant and as contributing to their own downfall.

Mayfield, John. "'The Soul of a Man': William Gilmore Simms and the Myths of Southern Manhood." *Journal of the Early Republic* 15 (Fall, 1995): 477-500. An examination of southern men in Simms's fiction. Mayfield argues that both as literary figures and as paradigms, Simms's characters are failures, being stereotypes with little to offer.

Watson, Charles S. *From Nationalism to Secessionism: The Changing Fiction of William Gilmore Simms.* Westport, Conn.: Greenwood Press, 1993. Watson closely analyzes Simms's work to demonstrate his changing political opinions. From 1825 until 1848, Simms was a nationalist, creating patriotic romances; however, as the United States edged closer to Civil War, he became a secessionist, as evidenced by his later works.

Wimsatt, Mary Ann. *The Major Fiction of William Gilmore Simms: Cultural Traditions and Literary Forms.* Baton Rouge: Louisiana State University Press, 1989. Focusing on Simms's novels, Wimsatt provides one of the most useful discussions of Simms's work, reevaluating many of the misconceptions and dismissive attitudes about his fiction. She makes use of biographical as well as historical information, and she discusses Simms's novels within the context of twentieth century critical formulations about the romance genre.

ROBERT PENN WARREN

Born: Guthrie, Kentucky; April 24, 1905
Died: West Wardsboro, near Stratton, Vermont; September 15, 1989

OTHER LITERARY FORMS

Robert Penn Warren wrote successfully in so many genres that Charles Bohner called him "the pentathlon champion of American literature." In addition to his novels, he published short stories, numerous volumes of poetry, and a considerable amount of nonfiction. Warren's fiction and his poetry often consider the same philosophical themes: the meaning of history, the loss of innocence and the recognition of evil in the fallen world, and the difficulty of finding a moral balance in a world in which traditional Christian values seem to be faltering. For example, in his book-length poem *Brother to Dragons: A Tale in Verse and Voices* (1953), Warren begins with a historical event—a brutal murder of a slave by Thomas Jefferson's nephew, Lilburne Lewis—and creates a philosophical examination of people's fallen nature. Warren does something very similar in his novel *World Enough and Time*. The story is based on a murder that occurred in 1825, but the novel, like the poem, becomes an examination of people's fall from innocence and the difficulty of establishing moral ideals in a fallen world.

Warren's concerns over history and morality are also evident in his earliest, nonfiction works. In his first book, a biography, *John Brown: The Making of a Martyr* (1929), Warren contends that Brown did not tread the path of morality quite so righteously as Ralph Waldo Emerson had thought he had; in his fallen condition, Brown mistook his own egotism for pure idealism. Warren's neo-orthodox insistence on people's fallen nature and his skepticism about the possibilities of pure idealism, both of which are reflected in his novels, led him to accept the traditionalist attitudes of the southern intellectuals who made up the Fugitive Group, and he contributed to the agrarian manifesto *I'll Take My Stand*

(1930). Warren did, however, espouse a more liberal attitude toward racial matters in his later nonfiction works *Segregation: The Inner Conflict in the South* (1956) and *Who Speaks for the Negro?* (1965).

Warren's social criticism ultimately proved less influential than his literary criticism. His *Selected Essays* (1958) contains perceptive studies of Samuel Taylor Coleridge's *The Rime of the Ancient Mariner* (1798), Joseph Conrad's *Nostromo* (1904), William Faulkner, Ernest Hemingway, and Katherine Anne Porter. These essays are important not only for what they say about these authors but also for what they reveal about Warren's own work. Even more important than these essays, however, was Warren's collaboration with Cleanth Brooks. Their textbooks, *Understanding Fiction* (1943) and *Understanding Poetry* (1938), helped to change substantially the way literature was taught in the United States.

Warren continued to publish literary criticism at intervals throughout his life; indeed, *New and Selected Essays* appeared in the year of his death, 1989. With a poetry-writing career that spanned fifty years, however, he was at least equally well known as a craftsman in that genre. His poems have been widely anthologized, and he is recognized as one of the foremost American poets of the twentieth century.

ACHIEVEMENTS

For most readers, Robert Penn Warren's name is probably most associated with his novel *All the King's Men*, for which he won both the Pulitzer Prize for fiction and the National Book Award. He also won the Robert Meltzer Award from the Screen Writers Guild for the play based on that novel. Warren's short story "Blackberry Winter" also has been highly acclaimed and widely anthologized. Other readers think of Warren primarily as a poet, and with good reason; he won the Pulitzer Prize for poetry twice, first for *Promises: Poems, 1954-1956* (1957), which also won the Edna St. Vincent Millay Prize and the National Book Award for poetry, and a second time for *Now and Then: Poems, 1976-1978* (1978). *Selected Poems: New and Old, 1923-1966* (1966) won the Bollingen Prize from Yale University, and *Audubon: A Vision* (1969) won the Van Wyck Brooks Award and the National Medal for Literature. Warren was elected to the American Philosophical Society in 1952 and to the American Academy of Arts and Sciences in 1959. He was named first poet laureate of the United States in 1986.

BIOGRAPHY

Robert Penn Warren's background and experience had a tremendous impact on the thematic concerns of his fiction. He demonstrated the need, common to so many southern writers, to cope with the burden of the past. He also wrote out of a scholar's familiarity with and devotion to certain prominent literary artists, past and present, particularly the Elizabethan and Jacobean dramatists Conrad, Faulkner, and T. S. Eliot. Warren's academic studies, pursued in a long career as an English professor, may have had a great deal to do with the structure of his works and their typically tragic mode. His recurring subject, however, was the peculiar experience of the South; a love-hate relationship with a dying heritage runs throughout his work.

Born to Robert Franklin and Anna Ruth Penn Warren on April 24, 1905, in the tiny Kentucky town of Guthrie, Warren grew up in an almost classic southern situation. His father, a banker and businessman struggling to support a large family, did not initially fire the young Warren's imagination as his grandfather did. The emotional bond between Warren and his maternal grandfather, Gabriel Thomas Penn, ripened during long summers spent on his grandfather's tobacco farm. Here, Warren experienced the pastoral charms of agrarian life, soaked up the nostalgic glow of the American Civil War from his grandfather, and absorbed the rhetoric and humor that permeates the southern storytelling.

Gabriel had been a cavalryman during the Civil War, and he spent many an afternoon with his grandson reliving the legendary time. It is not surprising that the boy looked upon the Civil War as America's great epic, as imbued with nobility and tragedy as Homer's *Iliad* (c. 750 B.C.E.; English translation, 1611) He was not blind, however, to the irony and ambiguity of his grandfather as representative of the values of the aristocratic horse soldier. Warren commemorated his realization that the romantic image of the Confederate cavalryman had its darker side in the poem "Court Martial" in *Promises: Poems, 1954-1956*, which is about his grandfather's hanging of bushwhackers without benefit of legal trial. Because this poem was written much later, however, it is possible that the ambiguous view of the grandfather was partially constructed from a more mature understanding. The event, however, was a true one that evidently made a deep impression on the young Warren. In any case, Warren was absorbing background for a number of later novels, such as *Wilderness: A Tale of the Civil War* and *Band of Angels*. In neither of these does he write as an apologist for the Old South, but he does expose the moral shortcomings of Northerners, much as he does in his early biography of John Brown.

Warren also was absorbing the local tales of tobacco war, when the growers of dark-fired tobacco banded together to boycott the tobacco company that regulated prices. Warren's first novel, *Night Rider*, was written from childhood memories of such local stories. Warren's brother, Thomas, who became a grain dealer, knew all the farmers of the region and was adept at repeating such tales.

The young Warren loved nature; collected butterflies, snakes, rocks, and leaves; and aspired to paint animals (an interest reflected in his poem about John Audubon). Later, he hunted with his brother and learned taxidermy. These experiences were more important, perhaps, to the content of his poetry than to his fiction. In spite of his persistent affinity for nature, he usually recognized in his fiction its essential amorality: "The blank cup of nature," he calls it in *World Enough and Time*.

In spite of the contribution to his early imaginative development by his grandfather and his agrarian milieu, the influence of Warren's father was subtle and pervasive, perhaps more significant in the long run to the human relationships explored in his novels. Ambiguous father-son relationships appear over and over in such novels as *All the King's Men*, *The Cave*, *At Heaven's Gate*, and *A Place to Come To*. None is modeled on Warren's actual relationship to his own father, but they reflect a combination of admiration, guilt, and mystery that suggests some deep personal involvement in the issues they raise.

Warren often admitted to an odd sense of guilt about "stealing his father's life." Robert Franklin Warren had wanted to be a lawyer and a poet but had become a businessman instead, because of financial responsibilities not only to his own family but also to a family of half brothers and sisters left without a provider when his father died. One of Warren's favorite reminiscences was about finding a book with some poems written by his father in it and carrying it with delight to him. His father summarily confiscated the book, and his son never saw it again. Warren thought perhaps his father had been embarrassed or pained at this reminder of a goal long since set aside. According to Warren, his father never regretted the obligations that dictated the terms of his life. Indeed, he took joy in them. Warren speaks with an admiration bordering on awe of the seemingly effortless rectitude of his father and of the ideal relationship between his father and mother.

As the result of an accident when he was fifteen years old, Warren lost his sight in one eye and was thus prevented from pursuing a career as a naval officer, as he had planned. Warren went, instead, to Vanderbilt University and came under the influence of John Crowe Ransom and the Fugitives, a group of academics and townspeople who met regularly to discuss philosophy and poetry. Ransom soon recognized Warren's unusual ability and encouraged him to write poetry.

Warren graduated summa cum laude from Vanderbilt in 1926 and pursued a master of arts degree at the University of California, Berkeley. While there, he became an ardent student of Elizabethan and Jacobean drama, which perhaps struck a responsive chord in an imagination already steeped in the violence and melodrama of southern history. He started to work on a doctorate at Yale University but left as a Rhodes scholar for Oxford, England, where he received a bachelor of letters degree in 1930.

During this period, Warren wrote his first book, *John Brown*. To some extent, this book grew out of an impulse shared with a number of his Vanderbilt friends and other writers of the Southern Renaissance. They were concerned about the exclusively Northern bias of most historians dealing with events leading up to and during the Civil War and its aftermath. Certainly, Warren presents a jaundiced view of the radical abolitionist. Brown seems to have provided a nucleus for Warren's meditations about the effects of power and the misuses of altruism that were to be explored in a number of later novels, especially *Night Rider* and *All the King's Men*. He also wrote his first fiction while at Oxford, a short story called "Prime Leaf," about the impact of the Kentucky tobacco war on an old man, his son, and his grandson. The old man has a role similar to that of the elder Todd in *Night Rider*, the wise man who bows out of the organization when it resorts to vigilante tactics.

Warren taught at a number of universities, including Louisiana State, where he lived in the legendary ambience of the southern demagogue Huey Long, whose presence lies behind the fictional Willie Stark of *All the King's Men*. Warren later said that he knew nothing about the real Long, but the mythical Long was on everyone's lips. Even casual conversations often dwelled on questions of power and ethics, of means and ends, and of "historical costs." In an essay titled *"All the King's Men*: The Matrix of Experience," in John Lewis Longley's *Robert Penn Warren: A Collection of Critical Essays* (1965), Warren writes,

> Melodrama was the breath of life. There had been melodrama in the life I had known in Tennessee, but with a difference; in Tennessee the melodrama seemed to be different from the stuff of life, something superimposed upon life, but in Louisiana people lived melodrama, seemed to live, in fact, for it, for this strange combination of philosophy, humor and violence. Life was a tale that you happened to be living—and that "Huey" happened to be living before your eyes.

These remarks demonstrate that Warren was not primarily a historical novelist; rather, he was a classicist, fascinated with the universal patterns in particular experience. He thus discouraged close comparisons between Willie Stark and Long, pointing out that he wrote the first version of the story as a verse drama in Italy, as he watched Benito Mussolini consolidate his power.

In Warren's writing career, the years from 1943 to 1950—though a dry period for poetry—were productive ones for fiction and literary criticism. In addition to *All the King's Men*, he produced *At Heaven's Gate*, about the unscrupulous liaison between government and industry, and *World Enough and Time*, about a nineteenth century murder case. When Warren was poetry consultant for the Library of Congress in 1944-1945, Katherine Anne Porter, who was fiction consultant that year, threw on his desk the confession of Jeroboam Beauchamp, hanged for murder in Kentucky in 1826. Porter announced cryptically that she was giving him a novel. This was, indeed, the germ for his most complex novel, *World Enough and Time*.

Warren's dry period in poetry eventually ended after he divorced his first wife, Emma Brescia, married the writer Eleanor Clark, and fathered two children. He began writing excellent poetry and produced several more novels. A long association with Yale University began in 1950.

In 1986 Warren was named the first poet laureate of the United States, a post he held for two years. He died of cancer in 1989 at his summer home near Stratton, Vermont.

ANALYSIS

Often, what Robert Penn Warren said about other writers provides important insight into his own works. This is especially true of Warren's perceptive essay "The Great Mirage: Conrad and *Nostromo*" (in *Selected Essays*), in which he discusses the enigmatic speech of Stein in Conrad's *Lord Jim* (1900):

> A man that is born falls into a dream like a man who falls into the sea. If he tries to climb out into the air as inexperienced people endeavor to do, he drowns—*nicht wahr*? . . . No! I tell you! The way is to the destructive element submit yourself, and with the exertions of your hands and feet in the water make the deep, deep sea keep you up.

Warren interprets the dream here as "man's necessity to justify himself and his actions into moral significance of some order, to find sanctions." The destructiveness of the dream arises from humans' nature as egotistical animals with savage impulses, not completely adapted to the dream sea of ideas. The one who learns to swim instead of drowning in the unnatural sea of ideas is he who realizes that the values he creates are illusion, but that "the illusion is necessary, is infinitely precious, is the mark of his human achievement, and is, in the end, his only truth." Warren calls *Nostromo* "a study in the definition and necessity of illusion." This phrase could also describe most of Warren's works of fiction.

Warren's classification of thematic elements in Conrad's stories could also be applied to his own. Warren writes that Conrad is concerned with the person who lacks imagination but clings to fidelity and duty (like the old captain in *Youth*, 1902), the sinner against human solidarity and the human mission (like Kurtz in *Heart of Darkness*, 1902, and Decoud in *Nostromo*), and the redeemed individual (Jim in *Lord Jim* and Dr. Monygham in *Nostromo*). Warren says that Conrad is most interested in the latter—"the crisis of this story comes when the hero recognizes the terms on which he may be saved, the moment, to take Morton Zabel's phrase, of the 'terror of the awakening.'"

One might note that in Warren's novel *At Heaven's Gate*, Jerry's dirt-farmer father fits the pattern of natural rectitude, while Slim Sarrett, the nihilistic, cynical artist, is certainly the sinner against human solidarity. No one seems to be redeemed in *At Heaven's Gate*, though Jerry might have a chance in a hypothetical future, since he has acquired considerable self-knowledge. Mr. Munn in *Night Rider* has also stripped away his own illusions, but he dies, like William Shakespeare's Macbeth, without redemption. In other novels of this period, however, Jack Burden in *All the King's Men*, and perhaps even the murderer in *World Enough and Time*, achieve some kind of absolution. Warren and Conrad share this deep obsession with the need for redemption, and though the sentiment is religious and may be expressed in Christian imagery, it is consistently humanistic in emphasis. The world they both recognize is a naturalistic one, but people must live in two worlds, the world of facts and the world of ideas, which they create themselves. Warren's notion of submission to the realm of ideas is analogous, perhaps, to Hemingway's code of the hunter, the fisherman, the bullfighter, or the soldier, which provides existential meaning in a meaningless world.

Warren's early novels, particularly *Night Rider, All the King's Men*, and *World Enough and Time*, which critics generally agree are his best, trace a pattern of increasing complexity in the theme of people's vacillation between the fantasy of dreams and the reality of facts. After *World Enough and Time*, which is almost too densely packed and convoluted in theme, Warren relaxed his insistence that everything must be said on the subject of illusion and reality in one novel. Later works, such as *Meet Me in the Green Glen* and *Wilderness*, though not conspicuously different in theme, concentrate on a particular manifestation of the problem—on the nature of love in *Meet Me in the Green Glen*, and on the nature of altruism in *Wilderness*.

Actually, Warren's examination of the apposition between the world of ideas and the world of facts begins in his first book, *John Brown*. Warren portrays the militant abolitionist as not so much obsessed with freeing slaves as with starring in his own myth. Brown is encouraged in this role by the unqualified praise of Ralph Waldo Emerson, whom Warren believed to be a writer of empty words, with little perception of the real world; Warren quotes Emerson as saying of Brown, "He is a man to make friends wherever on earth courage and integrity are esteemed—the rarest of heroes, a pure idealist, with no by-ends of his own." Warren did not for a moment believe that Brown was a "pure idealist"; moreover, Warren had a continuing distrust of "pure idealists," whoever they might be. In his fiction, Warren was inclined to show abstract idealists as lacking in self-knowledge, capable of self-righteous violence because they refuse to acknowledge their own irrational impulses. The best example of this personality-type in Warren's fiction is Adam Stanton, in *All the King's Men*, who assassinates Willie because Willie, the man of fact, seduced Adam's sister.

John Brown, however, as one who uses exalted ideas to inflate his own self-image, is more akin to Warren's Professor Ball, Dr. MacDonald, and Mr. Munn of *Night Rider*; Bogan Murdock, the industrialist, and Slim Sarett, of *At Heaven's Gate*; and Wilkie Barron, the manipulative false friend of Jeremiah Beaumont, in *World Enough and Time*. Willie, though categorized by Jack as the "man of fact," in contrast to Adam, the "man of idea," has his own idealistic dream of the people's hospital, free to anyone who needs it. Whether that dream was truly altruistic, however, or tinged by the secret need for a personal monument to his existence, is ambiguous.

NIGHT RIDER

Warren thus suggests that the self is itself part of the dream sea of ideas. Warren's protagonists are often initially passive persons whose emptiness is filled by other more dynamic personalities. Having acquired a somewhat fictitious self under such influence, they proceed to act in the real world as though that dream were true—often with tragic results. Thus, Mr. Munn seems an innocuous, ordinary young lawyer when he first appears in *Night Rider*, but he is drawn irresistibly to his more dynamic friend, Mr. Christian, who has a legitimate concern for the plight of the tobacco growers at the mercy of the price-controlling tobacco company. Munn learns to savor his new role as labor leader. He is ripe, then, for indoctrination by more conniving, professional agitators, Professor Ball and Dr. MacDonald, who preach a secret society that will scrape the fields of uncooperative growers and punish backsliders who dare to violate the embargo.

What begins as a lawful strike by the downtrodden majority becomes lawless action by a vigilante group that destroys crops, burns warehouses, and commits murder. In the case of Munn, the crisis of this psychic change in direction comes when he realizes that his assigned task to assassinate the tobacco farmer Bunk Trevelyon, whom he once defended in court on a murder charge, is not only his "duty" to the group; it also satisfies something very personal in himself that he has not yet recognized. Trevelyon had committed the murder of which he was once accused, and the African American who was hanged for that murder was innocent. Trevelyon thus becomes the symbol for Munn's half-conscious cooperation in framing the African American, or, to use another favorite term of Warren, Munn's original sin. In this ritual of retribution, the shared myth of community justice fuses with Munn's private myth of killing the shadow self, an act of both self-condemnation and deliberate concealment of a secret crime.

After this private confrontation and ritual killing of his shadow self, Munn makes no more moral objections to anything Ball and MacDonald want to do. The three lead a concerted assault on the company warehouses, which results in a number of casualties. One person who dies is young Benton Todd, who had been an ardent admirer of Munn. Moreover, Todd hoped to marry Mr. Christian's daughter, Lucille, who has been having a secret affair with Munn. If Trevelyon symbolizes the murderous shadow self that Munn has hated to acknowledge, Benton Todd suggests the lost idealism, the better dream that Munn has betrayed.

Munn's subsequent flight to the West to escape prosecution for a murder he did not commit might have resulted in redemption, but it does not. The pattern of redemption is presented to him obliquely by the story of Proudfit, the impoverished farmer who is sheltering Munn. Proudfit tells of his own checkered career in the West, as a buffalo hunter and hide-tanner, with companions as rough and wild as himself. Eventually, however, he lives in peace among American Indians. When he becomes ill, the Native Americans care for him, using all their resources of natural healing and religious ritual. In his fever, he eventually has a vision of Kentucky, where he was reared, and a young woman waiting beside a stream. His strength then begins to return, so he leaves the Native American friends and goes back to find the very woman he saw in his vision, now his wife, and the very hill he saw, which is now his farm.

Proudfit's story is both an engrossing dialect narrative and a unique version of the underlying myth of death and resurrection. Proudfit's humble redemption contrasts with the myth of sin and damnation implied in Munn's career. Both Proudfit and Munn have a period of withdrawal (Proudfit, among the American Indians; Munn, on Proudfit's remote farm), time to rethink their past lives and future goals. This experience is analogous, perhaps, to the withdrawal and contemplation that the mythic hero undergoes before he returns to his homeland as a new man. Munn, however, is not transformed. He does become mildly obsessed with the innocent African American who died in Trevelyon's stead, but he cannot even remember the man's name. Perhaps his inability to name the scapegoat is intended to suggest Munn's distance from the redemption offered by Christ's sacrifice. This does not mean that Warren was advocating Christianity; he was admitting, at least, a moral vacuum where traditional values have been eliminated in a society concerned primarily with power and wealth.

ALL THE KING'S MEN

The polarity of idea and fact receives more explicit development in *All the King's Men*. Again, an essentially passive person, Jack Burden, feeds emotionally on a more dynamic personality, Willie Stark. Jack calls himself—somewhat cynically—an idealist, but his idealism consists mostly of a fastidious preference for not getting his hands dirty with some of Willie's more questionable political maneuvers. Willie is good-naturedly tolerant of Jack's moral preferences, since he has Tiny Duffy to do his dirty work.

Jack considers himself a good judge of character and motives, but when a cherished image about the purity and goodness of his old girlfriend, Anne Stanton, is proven to be false, he is devastated and lost in self-doubt. Anne, who is quite a passive, unfulfilled person herself, has become Willie's mistress. Jack's first impulse is to flee, to escape, to drown, to fall into what he calls the Great Sleep. From this symbolic death, Burden is born again into a bleak but emotionally insulating belief in the Great Twitch—an understanding of the world as completely amoral and mechanistic, wherein no one has any responsibility for what happens. Here, indeed, Jack has stepped out of the fantasy of dreams into the reality of facts.

Jack can now consent to let Willie use the information he has uncovered concerning Judge Irwin's long-forgotten political crime. Jack soon discovers how brutal the world of fact can be, when Judge Irwin's suicide reveals that the judge was actually Jack's own father. Hardly recovered from this blow, Jack recognizes a measure of responsibility for the deaths of Willie and his best friend, Adam, who is shot by Willie's bodyguard after the assassination. Through his passivity and noninvolvement, Jack had virtually handed over Anne to his more dynamic boss, and thus set the stage for assassination.

The novel is a fascinating study of symbiotic relationships, of which the most striking is that between Willie, the practical politician, and Adam, the puritanical idealist and perfectionist. Warren also suggests a politically symbiotic relationship between the demagogue and the people he represents. In social terms, the world of *All the King's Men* is more complex than that of *Night Rider*. Munn's career is essentially that of the tragic hero, the good but not exclusively good man who is corrupted by power. Willie, however, is sustained not only by his own drive for power but also by the concerted will of his constituency, who feel themselves to be socially and politically helpless. He is probably more significant as an antidote to their depression than as an answer to their physical needs. Even though Willie wants to change the world of facts for their benefit—build roads, bridges, a free hospital—it is for his psychological impact, exemplifying the triumph of the common person over the privileged elite, that he is beloved. Thus, even the man of facts floats in the symbolic sea of ideas.

WORLD ENOUGH AND TIME

If the relationship between dream and reality is complicated in *All the King's Men*, in *World Enough and Time* it becomes intricately complex. Seldom have human aspirations been so relentlessly exposed, one after another, as frail illusions. Though it might be termed a historical novel because it is based loosely on an actual event, or a philosophical novel because it comments repeatedly on the abstract meaning of human behavior and aspiration, *World Enough and Time* is better termed a psychological novel, or more precisely, perhaps, an examination of the psychological motivations for philosophizing. It is certainly not, like Andrew Marvell's poem "To His Coy Mistress," to which the title ironically alludes, a neat argument for seizing pleasures while one may. It is not a neat argument for any philosophical position, but it illuminates the sequential confusion of a reasonably thoughtful, well-meaning person trying to identify himself and justify his actions.

Jeremiah Beaumont, the orphaned son of an unsuccessful Kentucky farmer in the early nineteenth century, becomes the loved protégé of Colonel Cassius Fort, a well-known lawyer and statesman of the region. Jerry's exalted view of Colonel Fort receives a cruel blow from his dashing friend Wilkie Barron, a popular man-about-town and dabbler in politics. Wilkie tells Jerry of a beautiful woman he once loved in vain, who was seduced by an older man who had come to console her when her father died. When the young woman, Rachel Jordan, had a stillborn child, the older man abandoned her. The knave who wronged her was the unimpeachable Colonel Fort.

The persuasive Wilkie succeeds in promoting in a somewhat passive Jerry a romantic vision of wronged womanhood. From this point on, Jerry creates his own drama of love and revenge, though Wilkie continues to manipulate him in ways he never understands until near the end of his life. Jerry repudiates Colonel Fort, his surrogate father, and woos and eventually wins the lovely Rachel, who is in a neurotic state of depression, not because of the supposed perfidy of Colonel Fort but because of her baby's death. Jerry, blind to the real source of her despondency, hounds her into commanding him to defend her honor. Fort refuses a duel with Jerry, however, and the honorable vengeance seems destined to fizzle. Rachel is again pregnant, and Jerry is fitting into the comfortable role of country squire. An unknown messenger brings to Rachel a slanderous handbill in which Colonel Fort, presumably denying to his political opponents his affair with Rachel, claims that Rachel had slept with a slave. Fort had gallantly claimed paternity of the child as a chivalric gesture. This shocking document, which is actually a forgery written by Wilkie, precipitates Rachel's labor, and Jerry's child is also born dead. Jerry, in remorse, kills Fort—not openly in a duel, as he had planned, but secretly, letting it appear to be a political assassination.

Jerry's trial is a bewildering process where deceit and truth become inextricably mixed. Wilkie appears, however, and reveals Jerry's vow to kill Fort, the reaction Wilkie had himself orchestrated even before Jerry had met the wronged lady. All is lost, and Jerry is sentenced to hang. Rachel comes and stays with him in his basement jail cell, where they indulge in a passionate interlude—a veritable frenzy of love in the face of imminent death.

The unpredictable Wilkie appears at the last minute, after the lovers have unsuccessfully tried to commit suicide by drinking laudanum. Wilkie rescues them and sends them west to live in the desolate island refuge of a notorious bandit. This is a return to nature, but a nature devoid of its original innocence, incapable of healing the scars of "civilization." Jerry sinks into a bestial pattern and Rachel into insanity, eventually killing herself. Jerry, who finds out that the slanderous handbill came from Wilkie, is himself murdered as he seeks to find his way back to the hangman, resigned now to the most austere prize of all— neither love nor honor, but simply knowledge.

The flight to the West seems an almost gratuitous extension of suffering, especially since the real Jereboam Beauchamp, who murdered Colonel Solomon Sharp in 1825, did hang for his crime. The real trial and death of Beauchamp and his wife, Ann Cook, were only slightly less miserable, however, than Warren's fictional account.

Warren's extension to allow further demoralization of the lovers does help to explore all possible approaches to the problem of reconciling the ideal and the real. At first, Jerry believes that the idea must redeem the world: The mental context defines the object. Unfortunately, this route leads to an idealism divorced from action and allows a further evil to develop in the world—the death of his child. Then he believes that the world will redeem the idea—that is, the act of killing Fort will vindicate the idea of honor. In his flight to the West, he commits a third error, the opposite to his first: to deny the idea completely and embrace the physical world—"to seek communion only in the blank cup of nature."

Perhaps this tortured journey through innocence and experience should arrive at some reconciliation of opposites, but, if so, that too seems more dream than reality. "There must be a way whereby the word becomes flesh," muses Jerry in his last days. Even so, "I no longer seek to justify. I seek only to suffer." If this is not a particularly lucid analysis of philosophical possibilities, it may nevertheless be true psychologically to the mental and moral confusion in which people live. Perhaps it is intended to represent the "terror of the awakening" that Warren finds in Conrad's *Lord Jim* when the "hero recognizes the terms on which he may be saved."

In his later novels, Warren continued to deal with the tension between the ideal and the real. The central mystery is usually the self, which the protagonist does not know except through a painful dialectic between exalted idea and gross fact. The protagonist also suffers from an inability to identify his real father or the real home where he belongs. Jack Burden and Jeremiah Beaumont both have several surrogate fathers, but they are responsible for the deaths of those to whom they owe the greatest filial loyalty. In *At Heaven's Gate*, Jerry Calhoun rejects his real father, the man of natural rectitude and love, and gives his devotion to Bogan Murdock, who, in Conrad's phrase, is hollow at the core.

A PLACE TO COME TO

Even in Warren's last novel, *A Place to Come To*, the protagonist's first act is to despise his father and flee from his homeland; his last is to return to his hometown and make peace with the gentle stepfather he had never wanted to meet and the deaf father who had humiliated him as a child. As Warren wrote in "The Ballad of Billie Potts," the son must always return to the father, who often represents the flawed and fallen world that is our heritage.

WILDERNESS

The struggle between the ideal and the real in Warren's later novels is most explicit in *Wilderness*, about an idealistic young Jew from Bavaria who comes to the United States to fight for the freedom of the slaves. When his father, a political prisoner in Berlin, dies, Adam Rosenzweig realizes that he has "lived only in the dream of his father's life, the father's manhood, the father's heroism." The trip to America is a way to star in his own heroic story. Adam's career in America is a progress in disillusionment; the telltale symbol of the compromising world of physical fact is his clubfoot, which he has desperately sought to hide in a specially constructed boot. If *World Enough and Time* is Warren's most complex treatment of idealism, *Wilderness* is his most direct treatment of this recurring subject, uncluttered by secondary themes or plots. Some critics prefer it for that reason, though it lacks the depth and humanity of Warren's earlier epic treatment of romantic idealism.

MEET ME IN THE GREEN GLEN

Meet Me in the Green Glen is a pastoral novel about the nature of love. The love of a homeless young Italian immigrant for a dowdy country wife begins with carnal passion devoid of any attempt to idealize sexual attraction. The ironically named Angelo has distinct similarities to Conrad's "natural man," Nostromo, who lives in the physical world with little thought of any other. In fact, Angelo protects himself from any really serious bond with Cassie, the frustrated wife of a paralyzed man, casting her in the more tawdry dream of "scarlet woman" with gifts of a tight red dress and cosmetics. Only at the last, when she pleads for his life in court by confessing to the murder of her husband, of which Angelo is accused, does he recognize a love that transcends the merely physical. Just as Adam in *Wilderness* becomes more human when he admits the strength of flawed reality, so Angelo becomes more human when he recognizes the strength of dreams. In spite of Cassie's confession, Angelo is condemned to die. Cassie, unable to save her lover, drifts off in the dream sea of ideas, forgetting the sordid elements of their affair and only retaining the dream that transcends the body's need.

In these and other episodes in his fiction, Warren showed his fascination with what he called, in his Conrad essay, "the Great Mirage." It is a dark vision that sees all human values as illusions, yet insists—with the passion that fueled six decades of creative work—that such illusions are necessary, and that humanity must continue to invent itself.

Katherine Snipes

OTHER MAJOR WORKS

SHORT FICTION: *Blackberry Winter*, 1946; *The Circus in the Attic, and Other Stories*, 1947.

PLAYS: *Proud Flesh*, pr. 1947; *All the King's Men*, pr. 1958 (adaptation of his novel).

POETRY: *Thirty-six Poems*, 1935; *Eleven Poems on the Same Theme*, 1942; *Selected Poems, 1923-1943*, 1944; *Brother to Dragons: A Tale in Verse and Voices*, 1953; *Promises: Poems, 1954-1956*, 1957; *You, Emperors, and Others: Poems, 1957-1960*, 1960; *Selected Poems: New and Old, 1923-1966*, 1966; *Incarnations: Poems, 1966-1968*, 1968; *Audubon: A Vision*, 1969; *Or Else—Poem/Poems, 1968-1974*, 1974; *Selected Poems 1923-1975*, 1976; *Now and Then: Poems, 1976-1978*, 1978; *Brother to Dragons: A New Version*, 1979; *Ballad of a Sweet Dream of Peace*, 1980 (with Bill Komodore); *Being Here: Poetry, 1977-1980*, 1980; *Rumor Verified: Poems, 1979-1980*, 1981; *Chief Joseph of the Nez Percé*, 1983; *New and Selected Poems, 1923-1985*, 1985; *The Collected Poems of Robert Penn Warren*, 1998 (John Burt, editor).

NONFICTION: *John Brown: The Making of a Martyr*, 1929; *Modern Rhetoric*, 1949 (with Cleanth Brooks); *Segregation: The Inner Conflict in the South*, 1956; *Selected Essays*, 1958; *The Legacy of the Civil War: Meditations on the Centennial*, 1961; *Who Speaks for the Negro?*, 1965; *Democracy and Poetry*, 1975; *Portrait of a Father*, 1988; *New and Selected Essays*, 1989; *Cleanth Brooks and Robert Penn Warren: A Literary Correspondence*, 1998 (James A. Grimshaw, Jr., editor); *Selected Letters of Robert Penn Warren*, 2000-2001 (2 volumes; William Bedford Clark, editor).

EDITED TEXTS: *An Approach to Literature*, 1936 (with Brooks and John Thibault Purser); *Understanding Poetry: An Anthology for College Students*, 1938 (with Brooks); *Understanding Fiction*, 1943 (with Brooks); *Faulkner: A Collection of Critical Essays*, 1966; *Randall Jarrell, 1914-1965*, 1967 (with Robert Lowell and Peter Taylor); *American Literature: The Makers and the Making*, 1973 (with R. W. B. Lewis).

BIBLIOGRAPHY

Blotner, Joseph. *Robert Penn Warren: A Biography*. New York: Random House, 1997. Blotner began this work while Warren was still alive and had the good fortune to have the cooperation not only of his subject but also of the larger Warren family. This book is straightforward and chronological, and it makes a good beginning for a study of Warren.

Bohner, Charles. *Robert Penn Warren*. 1962. Rev. ed. Boston: Twayne, 1981. This lucid survey encompasses details of Warren's literary career and an analysis of his major themes. It also provides a study of the development of Warren's art as evidenced in his novels and short fiction, his poetry (through *Being Here: Poetry 1977-1980*), and his major essays. Includes a detailed chronology and a valuable select bibliography.

Burt, John. *Robert Penn Warren and American Idealism*. New Haven, Conn.: Yale University Press, 1988. Burt describes his book as traversing "regions" of Warren's work:

the elegies, the narrative poems, and three major novels—*Night Rider, All the King's Men*, and *World Enough and Time*. What unifies these works, Burt maintains, is Warren's ambivalence about experience, an ambivalence endemic to American idealism.

Clark, William Bedford, ed. *Critical Essays on Robert Penn Warren*. Boston: G. K. Hall, 1981. A comprehensive collection of criticism by leading literary scholars of Warren's major work as novelist, poet, biographer, and essayist. Among the contributors are Harold Bloom, Malcolm Cowley, Carlos Baker, John Crowe Ransom, and Randall Jarrell. The collection includes a valuable 1969 interview with Warren by Richard Sale.

Ferriss, Lucy. *Sleeping with the Boss: Female Subjectivity and Narrative Pattern in Robert Penn Warren*. Baton Rouge: Louisiana State University Press, 1997. A feminist analysis, focusing on Warren's novels. Ferriss argues that although Warren wrote in a traditional masculine style, his narratives contained a "female voice" with the potential to change a plot's direction.

Gray, Richard, ed. *Robert Penn Warren: A Collection of Critical Essays*. Englewood Cliffs, N.J.: Prentice-Hall, 1980. Many of the essays in this collection date from the 1960's, and about two-thirds of them deal with Warren's novels. Represented in the volume are a number of recognized Warren specialists, among them James Justus, Leonard Casper, and Victor Strandberg. A competent and comprehensive essay prefaces the volume, which contains a short bibliography helpful to general students.

Grimshaw, James A. *Understanding Robert Penn Warren*. Columbia: University of South Carolina Press, 2001. An introduction to and commentary on Warren's novels and other works. Chapter 2 focuses on the early fiction, from 1939 to 1955, while chapter 3 examines the later fiction, from 1955 to 1977. Includes notes, a bibliography, and an index.

Guttenberg, Barnett. *Web of Being: The Novels of Robert Penn Warren*. Nashville: Vanderbilt University Press, 1975. Examines Warren's nine novels from *Night Rider* through *Meet Me in the Green Glen*, with emphasis on their existential element. Advances the premise that through all the novels the individual struggles to attain the true being of selfhood through self-awareness.

Hendricks, Randy. *Lonelier than God: Robert Penn Warren and the Southern Exile*. Athens: University of Georgia Press, 2000. Hendricks examines the theme of exile in Warren's work, maintaining this subject is crucial to understanding Warren's theories of language, ideas about race, and his regionalism.

Justus, James H. *The Achievement of Robert Penn Warren*. Baton Rouge: Louisiana State University Press, 1981. A cogent study. Justus argues that Warren's work largely derives from the cultural circumstances of time and place in his career. The book is divided into four sections examining Warren's themes, poetry, nonfiction prose, and novels.

Madden, David, ed. *The Legacy of Robert Penn Warren*. Baton Rouge: Louisiana State

University Press, 2000. A collection of critical and biographical essays on Warren's life and work, including discussions of *All the King's Men*, his poetry, and Warren as a mentor and a moral philosopher. Includes bibliographical references and an index.

Watkins, Floyd C., John T. Hiers, and Mary Louise Weaks, eds. *Talking with Robert Penn Warren*. Athens: University of Georgia Press, 1990. A collection of twenty-four interviews, extending from 1953 to 1985, in which Warren talks about his work with characteristic honesty, openness, folksiness, and wit from the joint perspective of writer, interpreter, and critic. The group of interviewers includes Ralph Ellison, Marshall Walker, Bill Moyers, Edwin Harold Newman, Floyd C. Watkins, and Eleanor Clark.

FRANK WATERS

Born: Colorado Springs, Colorado; July 25, 1902
Died: Arroyo Seco, near Taos, New Mexico; June 3, 1995
Also known as: Frank Joseph Waters

<small>PRINCIPAL LONG FICTION</small>
Fever Pitch, 1930 (also known as *The Lizard Woman*)
The Wild Earth's Nobility, 1935
Below Grass Roots, 1937
The Dust Within the Rock, 1940
People of the Valley, 1941
The Man Who Killed the Deer, 1942
River Lady, 1942 (with Houston Branch)
The Yogi of Cockroach Court, 1947
Diamond Head, 1948 (with Branch)
The Woman at Otowi Crossing, 1966
Pike's Peak: A Family Saga, 1971 (rewritten, one-volume novel based on *The Wild Earth's Nobility*, *Below Grass Roots*, and *The Dust Within the Rock*)
Flight from Fiesta, 1986

<small>OTHER LITERARY FORMS</small>

In addition to his long fiction, Frank Waters wrote a number of books that combine history, ethnography, mythology, and speculative essay. All of these are centered in the American Southwest, and all deal, in whole or in part, with American Indian subjects. Of these, *Book of the Hopi* (1963) comes closest to ethnography in the strict sense, being the actual Hopi versions of their mythology, ritual, and belief, which Waters recorded from the words of tribal spokesmen. *Masked Gods: Navaho and Pueblo Ceremonialism* (1950) covers analogous material in relation to the Navajo and Pueblo tribes, and contains substantial sections in which these traditional beliefs are compared to the teachings of the Far East (particularly Tibetan Buddhism) and with the findings of nuclear scientists.

Pumpkin Seed Point: Being Within the Hopi (1969) is a personal account of Waters's three-year residence among the Hopi, while he was compiling material for *Book of the Hopi*. *Mexico Mystique: The Coming Sixth World of Consciousness* (1975) treats the history, myth, and science (particularly calendrical) of Mexico. *Mountain Dialogues* (1981) is more eclectic in style, a series of essays ranging in subject matter from the relation of mind and matter to the bipolar symbolism reflected in the land around Waters's New Mexico home.

Waters's three biographies all deal with Western subjects: *Midas of the Rockies: The Story of Stratton and Cripple Creek* (1937) is the biography of Winfield Scott Stratton, and *To Possess the Land* (1973) is the biography of Arthur Rockford Manby. *The Earp Brothers of Tombstone* (1960) is based on the recollections of Virgil Earp's third and last wife, Allie Earp, and material from Waters's own research.

In 1946, Waters published *The Colorado* as part of the Rivers of America series (Farrar and Rinehart), and in 1964, an art monograph, *Leon Gaspard*. From 1950 to 1956, he was a regular contributor to the *Saturday Review* with reviews of books about the West. Numerous periodicals contain his essays on ethnography, history, and literary criticism, as well as a few short stories.

ACHIEVEMENTS

Frank Waters gave the American Southwest its finest and most complete literary rendering. In both his fiction and his nonfiction, he sought to give literary vitality to the spirit of place imbuing that section of the American continent and to show how this spirit variously affects the different peoples who live there, finding its expression in mythology, lifestyle, architecture, and ritual, all reflecting, in their different ways, the "vibratory quality of the land itself." Whether he portrays life by presenting the facts of history (as in his nonfiction) or in the symbols of his novels, or whether he writes about the mythological realm that occupies the zone between the two, his work captures the deep resonance of his locale and thus the significance of place to people's development.

Waters is probably best known for his work on and about American Indians, and he was one of the few writers whose work earned the respect of both the literary establishment and the American Indian communities. He was also one of the few writers who could work successfully both in ethnography and in prose fiction. His firsthand knowledge of the Indian tribes of the Southwest and his deep respect for their traditions and their connections to their locale made it possible for Waters to write about these matters without romanticism, and thus to reveal not only the rugged dignity of their lives but also the value of their wisdom.

Thus, *The Man Who Killed the Deer*, Waters's most popular novel, has long been recognized as a classic in the literature on the Native American, just as *Book of the Hopi* is a landmark in ethnography. In the late twentieth century, the relevance and quality of his other work resulted in a greater degree of recognition, made tangible by the republication of much of his fiction.

BIOGRAPHY

Frank Joseph Waters was born on July 25, 1902, and spent most of his childhood and youth in Colorado Springs. These years provided much of the material for his early novels *The Wild Earth's Nobility*, *Below Grass Roots*, and *The Dust Within the Rock* and consequently for their revised version, *Pike's Peak: A Family Saga*. Waters's grandfather became the model for Joseph Rogier, the main character of these books, and Waters's boyhood experience in the Cripple Creek mining camps provided much of the background.

His experiences as an engineering student at Colorado College (from 1922 to 1925) and as a day laborer in the Salt Creek oil fields are also incorporated into these early novels.

After his work at Salt Creek, Waters traveled to California, where he was employed by the telephone company in the border town of Calexico. It was there, among Chinese laborers, opium dens, and general degradation, that he came across Tai Ling, who became the protagonist of *The Yogi of Cockroach Court*. This novel was actually drafted before his Colorado novels, but technical problems prevented its completion until some years later.

The move to California marks a dividing line in Waters's treatment of his material. The personal experiences from before the move went into novels of a semiautobiographical nature. Those that drew their material from after the move were not autobiographical, though they continued to draw their characters from people Waters knew, their settings from places where he had lived, and even their incidents from actual events. (The ending of *The Yogi of Cockroach Court*, for example, was taken directly from newspaper accounts.)

Waters moved to the town of Mora in the Sangre de Cristo Mountains of New Mexico. There he wrote *The Dust Within the Rock* and planned *People of the Valley*, drawing again on his youth in Colorado. The latter novel takes its material from the Mora locale, an isolated valley that is inaccessible for most of the year and that was settled by Spanish-speaking peoples from Mexico. It was in Mora, too, that Waters witnessed the rituals of the Penitente cult, which he incorporated into the novel.

After leaving Mora, Waters moved to Taos. From there, in the late 1930's, he drew the material (again, based on actual events) for *The Man Who Killed the Deer* and later for two nonfiction works, *Masked Gods* and *Mountain Dialogues*. He continued to make Taos his home, returning there after the war and working as editor for *El crepusculo*, a local Spanish-English newspaper; he also worked from 1953 to 1956 as an information consultant at Los Alamos Scientific Laboratory. These latter two positions are reflected in *The Woman at Otowi Crossing*, though it is evident from *Masked Gods*, published sixteen years earlier, that Waters had long been concerned with the curious juxtaposition of atomic research facilities and Indian kivas in the Four Corners area.

In 1977, Waters was married to Barbara Hayes; thereafter, the couple divided their time between homes in Taos and in Tucson, Arizona. In his later years, Waters devoted his attention principally to the writing of nonfiction. He died on June 3, 1995.

ANALYSIS

The writing of Frank Waters is always concerned with the tensions that underlie human existence: male and female, reason and instinct, conscious and unconscious, progress and tradition, linear and nonlinear, matter and energy (or spirit). His fictional characters are involved in efforts to reconcile these tensions, either within themselves or in the world of events. The search for reconciliation is inseparable from what Waters called the spirit of place: Once one is able to embody the unconscious rhythms of one's locale, one may move more completely toward the reconciliation of these tensions.

In another sense, Waters attempted to give literary expression to this spirit of place. Viewed sociologically, his novels show how this spirit imbues the various racial types of the Southwest. The spirit of place is found in the blood, experienced as a "blood-power" from which one can never quite break free. Because of these instinctual or biological ramifications, the novels about "racial types" are not mere sociological studies but expressions of a spiritual search.

Waters said that the three novels *People of the Valley, The Man Who Killed the Deer*, and *The Yogi of Cockroach Court* express his interest in the racial types of the West: the Spanish or Mexican, the Native American, and the mestizos, or those of mixed race. *The Woman at Otowi Crossing*, which deals primarily with Caucasians, completes this study of racial types. *Pike's Peak* portrays the mingling of various racial types, but here Pikes Peak itself is portrayed as an active agent.

This late novel thus makes graphic what in the previous novels was a subtle but powerful undercurrent: In all of Waters's work, the earth itself plays a dominant role. It is the matrix that reconciles polarity. Fruitful and destructive by turns, benevolent or menacing, it resists people's efforts at domination or comprehension yet demands of them that continuing process of individuation that is inseparable from the reconciliation of polarity. The earth, the source of life, embodies a mystery that cannot be overcome but must be understood through faith. As the beginning and end of people's essential polarities (such as life and death, summer and winter), it is both a material fact and a rhythmic energy with which one must be in harmony.

Harmony, however, does not indicate a static equilibrium. Waters's novels end with reconciliation, yet the reconciliation leads to ongoing movement. As Waters points out in an explication of the Nahuatl hieroglyph "Ollin" (movement), the tension between dualities results in movement. This movement is found not only in the processes of the natural world but also inside the heart of people. This ancient Nahuatl concept is reflected in all of Waters's novels. The central reconciliation is in the human heart, as the characters attempt to find that harmony in movement that enables them to be part of the great pattern of Creation.

PEOPLE OF THE VALLEY

People of the Valley was Waters's first nonautobiographical novel to be published. The most obvious social polarity—progress and tradition—is the main impetus of the plot. The government is going to build a dam that will uproot all the people of the Beautiful Blue Valley. The name is significant: The color blue symbolizes the abiding faith of the people in their traditional ways and in the faithful fruitfulness of the valley itself. (This symbolic use of the color blue returns in other novels, most notably *The Man Who Killed the Deer*, where Dawn Lake, the center of the Pueblo religious life, is referred to as the Blue Eye of Faith.) In this period, when their faith is threatened, the people of the valley look to Maria, a local *bruja*, for her reaction and her strength, her wisdom and her faith.

Maria has been in the Beautiful Blue Valley for as long as anyone can remember and has become, in the minds of its inhabitants, synonymous with the valley itself. She knows its secrets and its cures and has lived through its periods of fruitfulness and flood. She is, then, an embodiment of the spirit of place; by turns, she is a goad and a comfort, a shrewd businesswoman and a prophet. As the story progresses (a chapter is devoted to each period of her life), it becomes clear why she is the repository of the implicit faith of the people: She is trusted because of her own implicit trust in the earth, in the essential trustworthiness of its rhythms, even of its floods. Because she accepts the earth in all of its many moods, she is the spokesperson for its wisdom. Like the earth, she can be sharp and repelling, or healing and comforting. Like the earth, she accepts all who come to her, whether as lovers, questioners, or even husbands. Within change, however, she abides in a faith that grows, year by year.

In addition, Maria makes the welfare of the earth—of the valley—synonymous with her own welfare. She has reconciled the duality of self and other by making her own wealth inseparable from that of the valley, and hence of its people. The clearest example of this comes from her early life, when, destitute, she survived by gathering discarded wheat-seed from the local fields. This seed she divided into superior and inferior. The latter she used for food; the former she kept until spring, when she would trade it for a double measure to be collected at the next harvest. This process she repeated yearly. Because she kept the best seed for replanting, the wealth of the valley's wheat increased; because she received a double measure at harvest, her own wealth increased as well. Her wealth, however, was never monetary; rather, it was in the natural yield of the earth, and in the faith that such a yield is sufficient for all purposes.

In the end, it is this faith that makes Maria significant. Faith, too, is the essence of the people of the valley, and of their traditions. Without such faith, life there is not possible. This faith, as she points out, is not a concept, but a baptism into life itself, into the rhythmic experience of harmony, which comes from giving oneself wholly to the spirit and energy of one's locale, the spirit of place. The significance of the dam is that it stops the flow of faith, which is likened to water. Faith refreshes life and gives it meaning; the dam causes stagnation, a break in natural rhythms. The example of Maria shows, however, that if one's faith is deep enough, it will not be disrupted by surface events. In the end, this faith is in the heart, and what one sees in the external world corresponds to one's inner nature.

THE MAN WHO KILLED THE DEER

The idea of faith carries over into Waters's next novel, *The Man Who Killed the Deer*. Whereas Maria had grown slowly into her faith and had never been torn from it, Martiniano must find a faith within the exacerbated polarities of his nature. The disruptions of progress had not come to Maria until she was an old woman; they come to Martiniano during his formative years. Because of this, his search is one of finding what he has lost, not simply deepening what he already knows.

Half Apache and half Pueblo, Martiniano's mixed blood indicates the duality of his nature, the spirit of independence and rebellion opposed to the spirit of acceptance and harmony. Sent away to a government school at an early age and thus deprived of his initiation into the kiva at the proper age, Martiniano must be taught to find harmony, not only with his world but also within himself, where the pole of masculine independence has not recognized the pole of the "female imperative."

The story of the novel is, on the surface, a simple one. Martiniano has killed a deer out of season, against regulations of the U.S. government as well as against those of the pueblo. The matter seems simple, but as the story unfolds, it becomes clear that the apparently simple event has many layers. It is not so much that Martiniano has broken the white person's law, but that his insistence on his own independence of action indicates an inner disharmony and a lack of wisdom. It indicates, finally, a lack of connection with the mystery of life itself. In place of this connection is a belief that a person can be free when alone, when cut off from society or the earth, from the source of faith, symbolized by the lake in the mountains above the pueblo, "The Blue Eye of Faith," the center of the pueblo's religious-ceremonial life.

The deer that Martiniano has killed becomes for him a totem, appearing to him in various places and guises to demonstrate that there is something in his situation that he cannot defeat by confrontation, something that he first must understand, to which he must submit. Eventually, the deer appears in his wife, Flowers Playing; as she grows with child, with the mystery of life, Martiniano begins to lose connection with her.

Martiniano learns, slowly, that even his own sense of manhood is held in bondage to the feminine part of his being and that until he reconciles this polarity, he will never feel fully alive. This is best symbolized by the description of the Deer Dance (in a passage found in both *The Man Who Killed the Deer* and *Masked Gods*). Flowers Playing is one of the Deer Mothers in the ceremony, the embodiment of the mystery of organic life. The Deer Dance symbolizes how the male force of independence and escape is held bondage, unwillingly but necessarily, by the female imperative, the rhythms of Earth that are deeper than the ego. The dance offers another vantage on the spirit of place, here appearing as the "blood power" from which people can never break free and on which they are dependent for the development of wisdom.

There is another sense in which Martiniano's action was not done in isolation: His killing of the deer has repercussions that are felt in the wider sphere of politics. It has made more difficult the pueblo's case for restoration of Dawn Lake. As the pueblo elders point out again and again, one person's action is like a pebble dropped into a pool; the ripples extend far beyond the action itself. The effort of the elders enables Martiniano to see that much wider whole, of which he is an integral part and without which he is an incomplete human being.

The pueblo elders embody a different way of knowing from that of the white race, which has control of the lake. The polarity is rational-linear opposing nonrational-nonlinear. The method of the elders is intuitive, and, while it does not deny the validity of rational methods (any more than the female imperative denies the validity of the male drive for independence), it does indicate a deeper level of wisdom. The elders know the eventual result of their legal disputes over Dawn Lake far before these results come over the telegraph, even when all indications (relayed, of course, over the telegraph) point to the futility of their case.

To the elders—as, it seems, to Waters himself—linear or rational knowledge is not as encompassing or effective as the more intuitive method of the Indians. The difference between these two methods of knowing is a duality to which Waters returns in later books, particularly *The Woman at Otowi Crossing*. It is interesting to note, in this context, that just as the pueblo elders correctly predicted that they would regain their Dawn Lake, so Waters himself, in his novel, predicted the actual political event; for just as in the novel the Native Americans regain rights to their lake, so, thirty years later, did they do so in fact, through a congressional decision in December of 1970.

THE YOGI OF COCKROACH COURT

Waters's next novel, *The Yogi of Cockroach Court*, takes the working of polarities one step further to juxtapose Eastern mysticism (particularly Buddhist) to life in a Mexican border town. Sociologically, Waters is here concerned with the mestizo culture. Barby is an example of this type. Orphaned as a child, he is brought up by Tai Ling, who runs a small shop, The Lamp Awake, beside the prostitute district, Cockroach Court. The name of the shop itself introduces the duality of light and dark, associated respectively with the clarity of the mind and the darkness of the senses. Tai Ling is repeatedly pictured meditating by his lamp, amid the swirl of a violent, dark world.

Barby and Guadalupe (Barby's lover, and another person of mixed race) cannot detach themselves from that dark world, which to Tai Ling is the result of blindness, the working out of karma. Their relationship is a tempestuous one, fueled by Barby's impotent desire for control. This impotence results from Barby's rootless feeling of inferiority, from his inner division. Where Barby is at the mercy of his internal division, Guadalupe is at the mercy of external ones. In the daytime, she is alive in the absorption in her own physical vitality; at night, she comes under the domination of Barby.

These complexities are interwoven with the life of Tai Ling, whose lamp illumines the darkness of the physical world in which he sits, even as his search for a way to transcend the play of polarities illumines the darkness of his mind. Inherent in Tai Ling's search for transcendence, however, is yet another polarity: The life of transcendence is itself polarized with life in a physical body. In this way, Tai Ling is still involved in duality, or karma, and in the end, just as Barby cannot dominate Guadalupe except in darkness, so Tai Ling cannot subdue the ongoing karma of the physical world until the darkness of death surrounds him.

Both Barby and Tai Ling bring about their own deaths by attempts to conquer the physical world. The difference between them is nevertheless a significant one: Barby dies while blinded by passion, aggression, and ignorance; Tai Ling, whose mind is clearer, finally sees and accepts his inner polarity, accepts his karma and his situation, and sees the folly of trying to transcend the world by separating oneself from it. Tai Ling, therefore, achieves a reconciliation, and though it comes at the moment of death, there is great hope in it, as Tai Ling finally comes to a unity with his world, comes to true knowledge.

Tai Ling's realization is not a rational one. He uses rationality to dissect his ego, but his realization is intuitive. He speaks of the difference between those who see that life's journey is a spiral and those whose vision is so limited that the curve of the spiral seems a straight line. To people of unconsidered action, whose vision is limited to the rational, horizontal plane, all seems linear, not cyclic. The person of contemplation, however, sees the nonlinear nature of things that underlies the linear but does not negate it. Thus, the treatment of two ways of knowing is here given an additional perspective.

THE WOMAN AT OTOWI CROSSING

The Woman at Otowi Crossing deals primarily with Anglos and thus completes the cycle of novels dealing with racial types. It also brings many of Waters's concerns into a contemporary focus. As in previous books, the action develops out of the tension between polarities. The developing, intuitive awareness of Helen Chalmers is juxtaposed to the development of the atomic bomb on the mesa above her. Both developments signal people's evolutionary potential, and both involve the unification of matter and energy.

Helen has come from a broken marriage to operate a small teahouse at the edge of Pueblo Indian land. Coincident with the beginning of the Los Alamos Research Laboratory—called The Project—she discovers a growth on her breast. Her assumption that it is cancerous, and the resultant immediacy of death, triggers in her a chain reaction of explosively expanding awareness, an explosion that radically alters her view of the world around her and her relationship with it.

The scene of Helen's discovery ends with Facundo, a member of the pueblo kiva, tossing pebbles against her window. The moment is significant, for in the kiva, the American Indians continue their attempt to understand and ensure the unity of matter with energy, or spirit. Facundo's response to Helen's condition is one of immediate comprehension, but his response is undramatic. He simply points to the sun, the source of life, empowered by the same unity of energy and matter that the people of the project seek to harness. Facundo's emphasis, however, is on the presence of that process, that reality, in each moment.

Thus, Helen's task becomes what will eventually become the task of everyone: to integrate her newfound knowledge with the tangible events of her life. The discovery of the bomb requires the same integration; the two discoveries together create a new world order in which one must learn to live. Again, the methods of the Native Americans point the way to reconciliation, for they have shown how the development of insight and the knowledge of the unity of matter and spirit can be integrated into, and are in fact a necessary part of, a stable, viable society.

Waters draws a number of additional parallels between the activities of the Pueblo kiva and those of the project. Both are shrouded in secrecy, and both have their selected initiates who take on new identities vis-à-vis the rest of their society. (Members of the kiva take on the identity of cosmic forces; project members take on new, common names: Niels Bohr becomes Nicholas Baker.) Both kiva and project exclude women, and in both there is an attempt to empower the mystery of life, to make use of the unity within the duality represented by matter and energy, matter and spirit. (These parallels echo Waters's speculations in *Masked Gods*, where he writes of the common search of all people, whether in a Tibetan monastery, an Indian kiva, or an atomic research laboratory.)

Along with these parallels, however, the book demonstrates obvious differences as well. Primary among these is that the rituals of the Pueblo are to ensure the ongoing life of all creatures, whereas the activity of the project is directed toward death. The method of the kiva, being intuitive and nonrational, includes and embraces polarity, whereas the method of the project, being rational, divides one entity from another. Even this polarity, however, can result in a reconciliation, not in the external world, necessarily, but within the individual heart. The scientists involved in creating the bomb are presented in warm, human terms. Gaylord, a young scientist and the lover of Helen's daughter, comes to a more intuitive, even mystical awareness as a result of his exposure to radiation.

PIKE'S PEAK

Pike's Peak is a kind of summing up of Waters's work. This may be understood literally, because the novel is a rewritten and shortened version of three early novels, the titles of which are retained as major divisions of the new novel. It may also be understood symbolically, because in its panoramic scope, *Pike's Peak* encompasses many of Waters's lifelong concerns.

Joseph Rogier, the protagonist, is largely a fictionalized version of Waters's grandfather; Waters himself, like the character March (grandson of Rogier and part Native American), spent much of his youth in the mining camps of Cripple Creek, went to college as an engineering student, and worked in the Salt Creek oil fields. The novel transcends the category of autobiographical fiction, however, because of Waters's use of symbolism, in particular that of Pikes Peak itself, which stands as both tangible fact and intangible symbol. A mystery to be understood, an ungraspable meaning that one feels impelled to grasp, it stands at the borderline between the conscious and the unconscious, at once numinous and tangible.

The peak both draws and repels Rogier, who seeks within it for its golden heart. The pull is irresistible, and in his effort to plumb the peak, Rogier slowly lets go of all his social responsibilities. His building firm deteriorates, his family becomes near destitute, and he loses the respect of the community and becomes an object of mockery. His search is an obsession, not for mere gold, and not for riches (though he is not above their temptation), but for the symbolic golden heart, within himself as it is within Pikes Peak, shining in the center of the dense granite, or in the center of the flesh.

The method of his search combines the rational and the irrational. The obsession is irrational, and at its service he places his considerable rational gifts and material wealth. Yet, despite his knowledge of engineering and geology, he cannot strike a significant vein, while those of lesser knowledge, and without his material resources, make seemingly lucky strikes, literally at the drop of a hat. Rogier's situation has parallels to that of Martiniano, for he, like Rogier, finds something in his search that he cannot conquer by rational means or external manipulation. Rogier's attempts to find gold—symbolic or literal—lead him increasingly deeper into darkness and isolation. Like the deer for Martiniano, the peak for Rogier becomes a sort of totem, appearing as a lure, as a guide, or as an obstacle—a truth he cannot grasp, but that is constantly within his sight.

The tragedy of Rogier is that his view of the world is linear. As a miner, he has literal and symbolic tunnel vision. By going straight ahead, mining a vertical shaft, he hopes to find the essence of the mystery symbolized by the mountain itself. Its apparent tangibility as real gold draws him irresistibly, but Rogier's linear viewpoint blinds him to the world around him, isolating him from the sympathies and understanding of his family. His search for truth takes place at the expense of human warmth and community, and he finds, as does Martiniano, that such obsessive pride—even if it seems to be a search for truth—is doomed to futility. Where Martiniano is finally able to understand his folly and arrange for his son to enter the kiva and so live in the harmony it had taken him so long to achieve, Rogier dies in psychological isolation, unable to release his passion into genuine human community.

For all that, however, the tragedy contains a triumph. March, Rogier's grandson, carries on a search encompassing many of Rogier's ideals. Of mixed race, March shows promise of reconciling the intuitive ways of his American Indian blood with the rational methods of his grandfather. Despite himself, Rogier has passed on to March a profound respect for depth and knowledge; one feels for him a deep sympathy, because for all his gruffness, even his selfishness, he has somehow managed to give March a profound respect for enduring value and the determination to search for it, for the enduring gold within the dense rock of material being.

The search for eternal value in the middle of flux is a final polarity. Tai Ling sought it in his meditation and Maria found it in her inseparability from natural cycles; even Martiniano found it by acquiescing to the Pueblo's ways. For Helen Chalmers, the search was for a way to integrate eternal value into the apparently mundane particulars of everyday living. Thus, even the discovery of eternal verities is not a final resting point. The eternal is continually juxtaposed to and interwoven with the mundane, and just as the action of the novels is given impetus by this polarity, so the movement of the world both rises from it and expresses it. As each new layer is peeled off, new polarities emerge.

Waters's writing reveals an attempt to penetrate and illuminate these symbolic and literal layers, and to find within movement the enduring values of human life. His characters seek these values within the temporal, within enduring change, the first cause and final truth. Thus, in Waters's novels, the Nahuatl hieroglyph "Ollin" comes to literary expression: that eternal movement comes from the tension between polarities. The reconciliation between polarities is found in the movement of tangible existence—in concrete substance, not abstract form; in the harmony within activity that expresses harmony with greater cycles, such as those of society, of one's locale, or of the earth. In this sense, the expression of the spirit of place is an expression of the unity of humankind, for all are subject to the same enduring, cyclic existence. In a wider sense, Waters's writing is rightly considered mystical, concerned with the oneness of people with others, with the earth, with all that exists.

Tim Lyons

OTHER MAJOR WORKS

NONFICTION: *Midas of the Rockies: The Story of Stratton and Cripple Creek*, 1937; *The Colorado*, 1946; *Masked Gods: Navaho and Pueblo Ceremonialism*, 1950; *The Earp Brothers of Tombstone: The Story of Mrs. Virgil Earp*, 1960; *Book of the Hopi*, 1963; *Leon Gaspard*, 1964 (revised 1981); *Pumpkin Seed Point: Being Within the Hopi*, 1969; *To Possess the Land: A Biography of Arthur Rockford Manby*, 1973; *Mexico Mystique: The Coming Sixth World of Consciousness*, 1975; *Mountain Dialogues*, 1981; *Brave Are My People: Indian Heroes Not Forgotten*, 1993; *Of Time and Change: A Memoir*, 1998; *Pure Waters: Frank Waters and the Quest for the Cosmic*, 2002 (Barbara Waters, editor).

MISCELLANEOUS: *A Frank Waters Reader: A Southwestern Life in Writing*, 2000 (Thomas J. Lyon, editor).

BIBLIOGRAPHY

Adams, Charles L., ed. *Studies in Frank Waters*. Las Vegas, Nev.: Frank Waters Society, 1978-1990. Contains a number of excellent critical essays on Waters.

Blackburn, Alexander. *A Sunrise Brighter Still: The Visionary Novels of Frank Waters*. Athens: Ohio University Press, 1991. Chapters on each of Waters's novels, with an introduction that surveys the writer's purposes and his career, and a conclusion arguing that Waters is a major American writer. Includes detailed notes and an extensive bibliography.

Deloria, Vine, Jr., ed. *Frank Waters: Man and Mystic*. Athens: Ohio University Press, 1993. Memoirs of Waters and commentaries on his novels, emphasizing his prophetic style and sense of the sacred. Also provides criticism and interpretation of Waters's work, looking specifically at his place in the history of Western literature and of mysticism in literature.

Dunaway, David King, and Sara L. Spurgeon, eds. *Writing the Southwest*. Rev. ed. Albuquerque: University of New Mexico Press, 2003. Collection of interviews, bibliographies, criticism, and excerpts from writers of the Southwest. This updated edition of the book is accompanied by a compact disc, featuring excerpts from the authors' interviews.

Lynch, Tom. "Toward a Symbiosis of Ecology and Justice: Water and Land Conflicts in Frank Waters, John Nichols, and Jimmy Santiago Baca." In *The Environmental Justice Reader: Politics, Poetics, and Pedagogy*, edited by Joni Adamson, Mei Mei Evans, and Rachel Stein. Tucson: University of Arizona Press, 2002. In this examination of the worldwide environmental justice movement Lynch compares the representation of water and land conflicts in the works of Waters and the two other authors.

Lyon, Thomas J. *Frank Waters*. New York: Twayne, 1973. Analyzes Waters's themes and artistic style. After sketching Waters's life, Lyon examines his major fiction and non-fiction, showing him to be a writer of ideas with a sacred theory of the earth and Hopi mythic values. Lyon also discusses his minor works, his book reviews, and his essays on writing. Includes a chronology, notes and references, an annotated bibliography, and an index.

Nizalowski, John. "Frank Waters: Prophet of the Sixth World Consciousness." In *Reading Under the Sign of Nature: New Essays in Ecocriticism*, edited by John Tallmadge and Henry Harrington. Salt Lake City: University of Utah Press, 2000. This analysis of Waters's work is included in a collection examining environmental themes in selected works of prose and poetry.

Waters, Barbara. *Celebrating the Coyote: A Memoir*. Denver, Colo.: Divina, 1999. A memoir by Waters's last wife. Barbara Waters discusses her grief at losing her husband but recalls that their life together was not without its difficulties.

LARRY WOIWODE

Born: Carrington, North Dakota; October 30, 1941
Also known as: Larry Alfred Woiwode

OTHER LITERARY FORMS

Larry Woiwode (WI-wood-ee) was once known primarily for his longer fiction, but as his career has evolved he has shown great diversity and variety. He has published short stories in such prominent literary periodicals as *The Atlantic Monthly* and *The New Yorker*, and several of his stories have been included in anthologies of the best stories published in given years. He has written book reviews and essays for many newspapers, including *The New York Times*. *The Neumiller Stories* (1989), a collection of thirteen previously uncollected stories, including three penned in the 1980's, expands the "family album" of narratives about the Neumiller clan that Woiwode began in his novels *Beyond the Bedroom Wall* and *Born Brothers*.

Woiwode has also published poetry, including the well-received collection *Even Tide* (1977). In 1993, he published another collection of short fiction titled *Silent Passengers: Stories*, and that same year he also published *Acts*, which contains his ruminations on the current state of Christianity and letters. His interest in frontier life and in the North Dakota frontier is explored in *Aristocrat of the West: The Story of Harold Schafer*, which was published by the North Dakota Institute for Regional Studies in 2000. Woiwode returned to narrative prose with *What I Think I Did: A Season of Survival in Two Acts* in 2000; this complex and poetic memoir describes his initiation into the writing life and his apprenticeship to *New Yorker* editor William Maxwell. His second memoir (of a projected trilogy), *A Step from Death*, was published in 2008; like *What I Think I Did*, *A Step from Death* eschews a straightforward, chronological organization, instead following thematic threads in different directions.

ACHIEVEMENTS

Larry Woiwode's first novel, *What I'm Going to Do, I Think*, won for him the prestigious William Faulkner Foundation Award for the "most notable first novel" of 1969 and the American Library Association Notable Book Award in 1970 and brought him immediate critical attention. The book was a best seller and was translated into several foreign languages. *What I'm Going to Do, I Think*, and the short fiction Woiwode was publishing, helped him earn a Guggenheim fellowship, awarded for literary excellence. His second novel, *Beyond the Bedroom Wall*, actually begun before *What I'm Going to Do, I Think*, was nominated for both the National Book Award and the National Book Critics Circle Award, and it won the American Library Association Notable Book Award in 1976. It became an even bigger commercial and critical success than his first novel. Woiwode received Bush Foundation fellowships in 1977 and 1978 for his work in fiction.

His third novel, *Poppa John*, was much less successful commercially and critically. The novel's premise and protagonist indeed represented a departure from the regional narrative Woiwode had successfully employed in his previous fiction, but it did earn the Cornerstone Best Book of the Year Award in 1982. In 1991, Woiwode was presented with the John Dos Passos Prize from Longwood University in recognition of the overall excellence of his body of work. His continued work in short fiction (with *The Neumiller Stories* and *Silent Passengers*) earned him the Nelson Algren Short Fiction Award in 1992 and the Association of Writing Programs Award for Short Fiction in 1999. Woiwode received the Lannan Foundation Fellowship for Literary Excellence in 2002 on the strength of his memoir *What I Think I Did*. Furthermore, although he has published only one book of poetry, he was named poet laureate for North Dakota in 1995 for his overall life in letters.

Poppa John notwithstanding, critics are quick to credit Woiwode's idiosyncratic, family-centered narratives with helping indirectly to rehabilitate the family chronicle, a genre long considered out of fashion. After a decade of relative publishing silence, Woiwode returned to this narrative genre in *Born Brothers* and *The Neumiller Stories*. Woiwode's evolving canon of Neumiller narratives depicts prodigal sons and daughters who, no matter where they tread, fulfill their destiny in rediscovering their roots and the family relationships that nurtured them early in their lives. Woiwode unabashedly admires the traditional nuclear family, and his fiction underscores the value of finding one's way by retracing one's steps. His narrative strength is thus seen in the fact that, even among readers accustomed to despondent, "lost" protagonists preoccupied with discovering the mysteries of life in the squalor of the city or some illicit relationship, Woiwode can make such old-fashioned premises seem startlingly fresh and appealing.

In the ebb and flow of many writers' careers, acclaimed first novels often permanently overshadow subsequent efforts, and the disappointment with—and apparent dearth of fresh ideas that followed after—the publication of *Poppa John* provoked many critics and readers to wonder if Woiwode had lost his narrative vision. Such concerns were answered with the publication of *Born Brothers* and *The Neumiller Stories*.

BIOGRAPHY

Larry Alfred Woiwode was born in Carrington, North Dakota, on October 30, 1941. He spent his early years in nearby Sykeston, a predominantly German settlement amid the rugged, often forbidding north-midwestern terrain. No doubt the beauty as well as the stark loneliness of this landscape heightened his appreciation for the effects of nature on individual character. At the age of ten, he moved with his family to Manito, Illinois, another evocatively midwestern environment capable of nurturing the descriptive powers of a budding fiction writer.

Woiwode attended the University of Illinois for five years but failed to complete a bachelor's degree, leaving the university in 1964 with an associate of arts degree in rhetoric. He met his future wife, Carol Ann Patterson, during this period and married her on May 21, 1965. With Carol he would eventually have four children. After leaving Illinois, Woiwode moved to New York City and supported his family with freelance writing, publishing in *The New Yorker* and other prestigious periodicals while working on two novels. He was a writer-in-residence at the University of Wisconsin, Madison, and had extended teaching posts at Wheaton College (Illinois) and at the State University of New York at Binghamton, where he served as a faculty member (intermittently) beginning in 1983. In 1977, he was awarded the doctor of letters degree from North Dakota State University.

Woiwode explains in his memoirs *What I Think I Did* and *A Step from Death* how his nascent Christian faith began to grow and gain strength in his life, and he is now known nationally as a Christian author (although his works are perhaps too complex to relegate him to the shelves dedicated to particularly religious writers).

He and his family returned to North Dakota in 1978 to maintain an organic farm. As detailed in his memoirs, Woiwode would continue to balance the farm life that spoke to him and nourished both his family life and writing with brief academic assignments at the University of North Dakota in Grand Forks and at Jamestown College.

ANALYSIS

To understand Larry Woiwode's craft and achievement, one must finally recognize the essentially religious character of his narratives and their thematic structure. He is an advocate for restoring a moral, even religious, voice to modern letters. While believing that the most important human questions are, in fact, religious ones, Woiwode rejects the notion that there can be legitimate, compelling "novels of ideas"; for him, such fiction connotes mere propagandizing. Woiwode handles such questions not by placing philosophical soliloquies in the mouths of sophisticated, worldly protagonists but by creating authentically ordinary characters and settling them comfortably into the concrete and utterly mundane world of daily life.

In achieving this effective depiction of what might be called heightened normality, Woiwode's prose is consistently active, alive, and unassuming, approaching at times the crisp clarity of Ernest Hemingway but touched with a finely tuned lyricism. While Woiwode has sometimes been criticized for lapsing too easily into didacticism or marring otherwise evocative scenes with excessive detail, his keen eye for the extraordinary ordinariness of life makes his narrative vision compelling and believable.

As a novelist, Woiwode stands apart from most of his contemporaries in refusing to drown his characters in the angst-ridden excesses that have become so conventional in the modern American novel. His characters are not helpless victims of their times but participants in them; they are accountable not so much for what has happened to them but for what they do in response to their circumstances. Their conflicts, from Chris Van Eenanam's enigmatic search for manhood in *What I'm Going to Do, I Think* to Poppa John's drive to recover his self-identity, are not merely contrived psychological dramas played out inside their own consciousnesses; rather, they are compelling confrontations with the very concrete world of everyday life. This is a world that registers as authentic to the reader precisely because of Woiwode's gift for realism.

Woiwode's characters eventually recognize that the answers to their dilemmas are only partly in themselves. In the reestablishment of personal trust in friendships and the nostalgia of forgotten familial relationships, they recover a sense of balance and worth in themselves. However obliquely, each major Woiwode character finds him- or herself in a quest for a transcendent moral order, a renewed trust in God and humanity that will provide a reference point for his or her life. This quest animates the character's rejection of narcissism and a search for a love and security that only marital and familial relationships can foster.

Woiwode's willingness to affirm that these relationships are central to self-fulfillment and to the stability of American culture makes him unique among a generation of writers whose thematic concerns tend to focus on their characters' dehumanization in society and alienation from family life and marital fidelity. Woiwode thus belongs in the company of self-consciously moralistic writers such as Walker Percy and Saul Bellow, who are more interested in the ways human beings survive and thrive in a fallen world than in the ways they capitulate to it. Like Percy, however, the importance of Woiwode's struggles with faith in his works (particularly in *Beyond the Bedroom Wall* and *Born Brothers*) takes on more significance as the author's later works follow a more spiritual bent.

When compared with other writers of his caliber, Woiwode cannot be considered a particularly prolific author. Two of his novels, however, have been critically acclaimed, national best sellers, and they are among the best American novels written after 1960. The publication in consecutive years of *Born Brothers* and *The Neumiller Stories* seems to have redeemed Woiwode from the ambivalent response to *Poppa John*, and his reputation as an important American writer in the second half of the twentieth century seems secure.

WHAT I'M GOING TO DO, I THINK

Woiwode's first novel, *What I'm Going to Do, I Think*, is an absorbing character study of two newlyweds, each of whom is originally drawn to the other as opposites proverbially attract. Chris Van Eenanam, the protagonist, is a listless mathematics graduate student, an unhappy agnostic unsure of his calling in life. The novel's title accentuates his self-doubt and indecision, echoing something Chris's father once said in observing his accident-prone son: "What I'm going to do, I think, is get a new kid." Ellen Strohe, his pregnant bride, is a tortured young woman, dominated by the overbearing grandparents who reared her after her parents' accidental death. Neither she nor Chris can abide their interference and meddling.

Despite the fact that little action takes place "live" before the reader, the psychological realism in Woiwode's use of compacted action and flashbacks and the patterned repetition of certain incidents carry the reader along as effortlessly as might a conventionally chronological narrative. The reader learns "what happens" primarily as events filter through the conversations and consciousness of Chris and Ellen Van Eenanam during their extended honeymoon at her grandparents' cabin near the northwestern shore of Lake Michigan. In this retreat from the decisions Chris elects not to face, the couple, now intimate, now isolated, confront a grim modern world that has lost its faith in a supreme being fully in control of his created universe. This loss is exemplified most dramatically in the lives of Chris and Ellen as they try to sort out the meaning of affection and fidelity in their new relationship as husband and wife and as potential parents. Ellen's pregnancy is at first a sign of a beneficent nature's approval of their union, but later, as each has a premonition of the unborn child's death, it becomes a symbol of an ambivalent world's indifference to their marriage and its apparent fruitlessness.

In the absence of a compensatory faith even in humankind itself, a secondary faith arguably derived from faith in God, Chris and Ellen come to realize that they have lost their ability to navigate a hostile world with lasting, meaningful relationships. Neither mathematics nor nature can fill the vacuum left by an impotent faith whose incessant call is to fidelity and perseverance without passion or understanding. In a suspenseful epilogue that closes the novel with an explanation of what has happened to them in the seven years following their marriage, Chris and Ellen return to their honeymoon cabin. Chris retrieves the rifle he has not touched in many years, and, as the action builds toward what will apparently be his suicide, he repeats to himself the beginning of a letter (suicide note?) that he could not complete: *"Dear El, my wife. You're the only person I've ever been able to talk to and this is something I can't say. . . ."*

As he makes his way to the lake, he fires a round of ammunition into a plastic bleach container half buried in the sand. In the novel's enigmatic final lines, Chris fires "the last round from his waist, sending the bullet out over the open lake." This curious ending seems intended by Woiwode to announce Chris's end of indecision—a recognition that his life can have transcendent meaning only through his embracing fully his marriage commitment to Ellen.

BEYOND THE BEDROOM WALL

The expansiveness and comic vitality of Woiwode's second novel, *Beyond the Bedroom Wall*, offer a marked contrast to *What I'm Going to Do, I Think*. In *Beyond the Bedroom Wall*, Woiwode parades sixty-three characters before the reader by the beginning of chapter 3. True to its subtitle, *A Family Album*, *Beyond the Bedroom Wall* is a sprawling, gangly work of loosely connected snapshots of the Neumiller family. An engaging homage to the seemingly evaporating family unit at the end of the twentieth century, the novel's "plot" is nearly impossible to paraphrase, consisting as it does of some narrative, some diary entries, and even its protagonist Martin Neumiller's job application for a teaching position. Given that Woiwode had previously published nearly a third of the forty-four chapters of *Beyond the Bedroom Wall* as self-contained short stories in *The New Yorker*, it is no surprise that the book reads as a discontinuous montage of events, images, and personalities.

The novel opens in part 1 with the funeral of Charles Neumiller, a German immigrant farmer who had brought his family to the United States before World War II, and it continues, to part 5, closing with stories of the third generation of Neumillers in 1970, bringing the Neumiller family full circle from birth to life to death. It is Martin Neumiller, Charles's son, a God-fearing, devoutly Catholic man and proud son of North Dakota, whose adventures and misadventures give the novel any unity it possesses. "My life is like a book," he says at one point. "There is one chapter, there is one story after another." The eccentric folks he encounters in and out of his extended family form a burlesque troupe of characters who boisterously sample both the joys and the sorrows of life on Earth.

In the Neumiller "family album," Woiwode lends concreteness to his notion that reality is a fragile construction, one that sometimes cannot bear scrutiny "beyond the bedroom wall"—that is, beyond the dreamy world of sleep, of its visions of what might be. Woiwode intimates that whatever hope there may be for fulfilling one's dreams, it is anchored in "walking by faith, and not by sight," by trusting in and actively nurturing family intimacy.

The rather sentimental, "old-fashioned" quality Woiwode achieves in this family chronicle, his evocation of once-embraced, now-lamented values, prompted critic and novelist John Gardner to place Woiwode in the company of literature's greatest epic novelists: "When self-doubt, alienation, and fashionable pessimism become a bore and, what's worse, a patent delusion, how does one get back to the big emotions, the large and fairly confident life affirmations of an Arnold Bennett, a Dickens, a Dostoevski? *Beyond the Bedroom Wall* is a brilliant solution."

Woiwode's eye for the rich details of daily life enables him to move through vast stretches of time and space in executing the episodic structure in this novel. His appreciation for the cadences of midwestern speech and his understanding of the distinctiveness of prairie life and landscape and its impact on the worldviews of its inhabitants recall other regional writers such as Rudy Wiebe and Garrison Keillor at their best.

POPPA JOHN

Poppa John is a shockingly short work when compared with the massive *Beyond the Bedroom Wall* and is more a novella than a novel. The book takes its title from the character Ned Daley played for many years on a popular television soap opera. His immense popularity beginning to overshadow the program itself, he is abruptly written out of the show in a dramatic "death." Ned thus finds himself suddenly unable to recover a sense of purpose, as he has lived for so long within the disguise of Poppa John, a fiery father figure who often quoted Scripture to his television family. Now close to seventy, outspoken and Falstaffian in appearance and behavior, he seeks his deeply lost identity. Ned to his wife but Poppa John to everyone else, he is lost in the malevolent nostalgia of growing old without self or self-respect.

The novel opens two days before Christmas, a few months after Poppa John's television death. Facing the Christmas season, broke, broken, and without prospects for the future, Ned and his wife, Celia, wander New York City, squandering their savings on gifts they had always wanted to buy for each other. Forced to "be himself," he finds he has leaned too heavily on the preacherlike Poppa John character, and his life begins to unravel. He is finally forced to face his own inconsistencies, his doubts, and even his sins, as Ned, an "elderly boy," is incapable of trusting in a life beyond the present. Speeding to a climax in its closing pages, the novel depicts Poppa John "coming to himself" on Christmas Day, realizing that he, after all these years, does believe in God, and therefore can come to believe in himself.

Poppa John perhaps deserved a better critical reception than it met on publication; as a more than interesting attempt to portray an elderly actor's disintegrating life, it contains some of Woiwode's most lyrical scenes. In the end, however, it remains an unsatisfying chronicle—in part because the complexity apparent in Poppa John's character is never fully realized, presented as it is in a very compressed time frame. While Poppa John emerges as a potentially authentic character in the early parts of the story, Woiwode gives the reader little insight into the motivations that prompt his sudden conversion experience at the climax.

BORN BROTHERS

In *Born Brothers*, Woiwode returns to the characters, setting, and moral center that brought him his greatest and most uniformly favorable critical attention. Woiwode begins what he calls not a sequel but a "companion volume" to *Beyond the Bedroom Wall* in the middle of the twentieth century, the narration filtered through the consciousness of Charles Neumiller, a lost soul searching his memories for a meaning to life and a purpose for living it. He finds both in exploring his relationship with his brother Jerome. Charles's fragmentary childhood memories in fact become the narrative building blocks for the often elliptical and multiperspective chronicle that unravels before the reader in an even more challenging sequence than that of *Beyond the Bedroom Wall*. *Born Brothers* contains less a plot than a chain of remembrances; as family members and their ahistorical interactions with Charles are paraded before the reader in a kind of visual patchwork, the reader is compelled to enter Charles's consciousness and see the world through his convoluted epistemology.

Despite his outward sophistication and sense of being, Charles is obsessed with suicide; he seems incapable of conceiving of a meaningful order outside the family structure
that had shaped his life and has now dissipated with the death of his mother and the col-
lapse of his marriage. In part, it is Woiwode's intent to explain American society's apparent moral disintegration—rampant promiscuity, unwanted pregnancy, and divorce—by
reference to the absence of strong family ties. Charles longs for the bond of brotherhood
he once shared, or thinks he shared, with elder brother Jerome. That idyllic childhood in
North Dakota, free from the cares and stresses of modern industrial life, impinges without
provocation upon Charles's consciousness. Charles's strange career as a "radio personality" who is both interviewer and interviewee is somehow emblematic of his need for conversion, for freedom from self. He needs an "outside," a reference point, which, Woiwode
hints, will come only from faith in the transcendent God whose eternal family Charles is
invited to join.

Woiwode makes few compromises for the reader unwilling to attend to—or, perhaps,
eavesdrop on—Charles Neumiller's open-ended musings. To refer to his ramblings as
stream-of-consciousness narration is to give them too precise a label, for not merely a consciousness is under consideration here but the history of a mind and a life as well. The
journey to and through that history is not one that the casual reader will be inclined to take,
which underscores the main criticism of Woiwode's prose shared even by critics sympathetic to his family chronicle: his apparent inattention to the toll his often exhaustive detail
takes on both his characters and his readers. Jonathan Yardley's judgment seems most apt:
"It's a pity to see a writer of Woiwode's talent and humanity stuck, at midcareer, in the
endless exploration and re-exploration of material that has yielded its last fresh insight if
not its last lovely sentence."

INDIAN AFFAIRS

With its broken sequence of scenes and lack of exposition or resolution of conflicts, *Indian Affairs* has elements of a postmodern novel. Woiwode uses this style to reflect the inner turmoil of Chris Van Eenanam, who appeared earlier as the main character of *What
I'm Going to Do, I Think*. Chris and his wife, Ellen, return to an isolated cabin in the Michigan woods so that Chris can write his Ph.D. dissertation on American poet Theodore
Roethke's natural philosophy and poetry. Mundane interruptions such as cutting firewood, installing a water pump, shopping, and tavern hopping distract him. A gang of
drunken Native American teenagers threatens him when he does not supply them with
beer, and a mysterious stalker forces him to keep a loaded gun handy. On a deeper level,
Chris undergoes an identity crisis—a need to affirm his masculinity, to cope with religious
and moral dilemmas, and to resolve the conflict of whether his roots are Caucasian or
American Indian.

Chris and Ellen's childless seven-year marriage has brought them no sense of permanence or hope for the future. Although they are thirty years old, Chris is still a graduate

student, and they are dependent on Ellen's wealthy grandparents for use of the cabin. Ellen's previous miscarriage and her ensuing barrenness symbolize the status of their marriage. Ellen resolves her unhappiness by recording her thoughts in a journal. Meanwhile, she joins a feminist discussion group, goes to a bar without an escort, and tries the hallucinogen peyote to ease her feelings of emptiness. Her conflicts disappear when she becomes pregnant again.

Chris spends much time with his bachelor friend Beau Nagoosa, a Chippewa Indian who has dropped out of white culture to build his own cabin. He supports himself as a woodcutter and justifies stealing wood on absentee landowners' property by telling himself it was once Native American land. Beau resents the invasion of white real estate promoters, who claim to represent Volunteers in Service to America (VISTA), yet he accommodates them and compromises his ideals.

Chris and Beau discuss humanity's role within the spiritual harmony of the natural world. For Chris, Roethke's claim that objects in nature are sentient is synonymous with Native American beliefs. Beau introduces Chris to peyote, which stimulates vivid sensory perceptions and fantasies but renders both Chris and Beau unable to cope with their real problems. Frustrated by chaotic events in his life and dissatisfied with the prospect of returning to academe in New York, Chris is overcome with depression. Feeling that nothing can guide him now except his own instincts, he decides to adhere to a line from one of Roethke's poems, "I'll be an Indian." Chris's future role as a teacher or leader is ambiguous.

As Chris begins to identify more strongly with his own Blackfoot Indian heritage and feel reverence for the natural world, conflicts escalate between the segregated white and Native American communities. The natural environment shrinks as urban development expands. Tribal leadership does not extend beyond exhibition dancing at powwows. American Indian families disintegrate, alcoholism and drug use destroy lives, and teenage youths engage in threat making and violence. Woiwode's realistic and tragic portrayal of Native American life offers no solution to the problems.

Readers of *Indian Affairs* will be able to appreciate the work most fully if they have read *What I'm Going to Do, I Think* and if they have more than a passing acquaintance with the philosophies and writings of Theodore Roethke and of the Native American cultural nationalist Vine Deloria. The underlying theme of the novel is that modern Native Americans lack effective leaders to guide them.

Bruce L. Edwards, Jr.; Martha E. Rhynes
Updated by Scott D. Yarbrough

OTHER MAJOR WORKS

SHORT FICTION: *The Neumiller Stories*, 1989; *Silent Passengers: Stories*, 1993.

POETRY: *Poetry North: Five North Dakota Poets*, 1970 (with Richard Lyons, Thomas McGrath, John R. Milton, and Antony Oldknow); *Even Tide*, 1977.

NONFICTION: *Acts*, 1993; *Aristocrat of the West: The Story of Harold Schafer*, 2000; *What I Think I Did: A Season of Survival in Two Acts*, 2000; *My Dinner with Auden*, 2006; *A Step from Death*, 2008.

BIBLIOGRAPHY

Cheaney, J. B. "Taming Memory: The Fiction of Larry Woiwode." *World and I* 17, no. 10 (October 1, 2002): 256-260. Presents a biographical sketch of Woiwode that particularly sheds insight on his spirituality and the autobiographical content of his fiction.

Freise, Kathy. "Home Again on the Prairie." *North Dakota Horizons* 23 (Summer, 1993): 19-23. Details Woiwode's connections with the state and its role in his books dealing with the Neumiller family.

Nelson, Shirley. "Stewards of the Imagination: Ron Hanson, Larry Woiwode, and Sue Miller." *Christian Century*, January 25, 1995, 82-86. Profile of the three novelists discusses their works and careers as well as the role of religion in their lives and writing.

Scheick, William J. "Memory in Larry Woiwode's Novels." *North Dakota Quarterly* 53, no. 3 (1985): 29-40. Discusses the importance of memory in *What I'm Going to Do, I Think*, *Beyond the Bedroom Wall*, and *Poppa John*. Identifies two types of memories in the works—those that make a character feel guilt and long for death and those that develop a sense of connection to family—and asserts that the ability to order these allows Woiwode's characters to achieve a balance between them.

Siconolfi, Michael T. Review of *The Neumiller Stories*, by Larry Woiwode. *America* 163 (December 1, 1990): 434-435. Discusses Woiwode's reworking of stories as they become parts of novels and then resurface as the short stories in this collection. Focuses on Woiwode's gift for depicting the "nurturing, eternal feminine" and on the novelist's acknowledgment of his grandmother's influence.

Woiwode, Larry. "Dylan to CNN." *Image: A Journal of the Arts and Religion* 28 (Fall, 2000): 95-101. Woiwode addresses the mass media's interactions with spirituality and religion. Provides some insight into the author's lack of patience with how Christians are sometimes portrayed.

_____. "An Interview with Larry Woiwode." *Christianity and Literature* 29 (Winter, 1979): 11-18. In a revealing early interview, Woiwode discusses the autobiographical nature of his work and the influences that shaped his narrative vision, the Jacob/Esau biblical framework of *Born Brothers*, his religious rebirth, and his future writing plans.

_____. "The Reforming of a Novelist." Interview by Timothy K. Jones. *Christianity Today*, October 26, 1992, 86-89. Woiwode discusses his conversion experience, the role of faith in his writing, and his view of the nonreligious, humanistic approach of the East Coast literary establishment.

_____. "Where the Buffalo Roam: An Interview with Larry Woiwode." Interview by Rick Watson. *North Dakota Quarterly* 63, no. 4 (Fall, 1996): 154-166. Woiwode discusses the influences on his work of the North Dakota landscape and the farming life.

BIBLIOGRAPHY

Every effort has been made to include studies published in 2000 and later. Most items in this bibliography contain a listing of secondary sources, making it easier to identify other critical commentary on novelists, movements, and themes.

THEORETICAL, THEMATIC, AND HISTORICAL STUDIES

Altman, Janet Gurkin. *Epistolarity: Approaches to a Form.* Columbus: Ohio State University Press, 1982. Examines the epistolary novel, explaining how novelists use the letter form to develop characterization, further their plots, and develop meaning.

Beaumont, Matthew, ed. *Adventures in Realism.* Malden, Mass.: Blackwell, 2007. Fifteen essays explore facets of realism, which was critical to the development of the novel. Provides a theoretical framework for understanding how novelists attempt to represent the real and the common in fiction.

Brink, André. *The Novel: Language and Narrative from Cervantes to Calvino.* New York: New York University Press, 1998. Uses contemporary theories of semiotics and narratology to establish a continuum between early novelists and those of the postmodern era in their conscious use of language to achieve certain effects. Ranges across national boundaries to illustrate the theory of the development of the novel since the seventeenth century.

Brownstein, Rachel. *Becoming a Heroine: Reading About Women in Novels.* New York: Viking Press, 1982. Feminist survey of novels from the eighteenth century through the latter half of the twentieth century. Examines how "becoming a heroine" defines for women a sense of value in their lives. Considers novels by both men and women, and discusses the importance of the traditional marriage plot.

Bruzelius, Margaret. *Romancing the Novel: Adventure from Scott to Sebald.* Lewisburg, Pa.: Bucknell University Press, 2007. Examines the development of the adventure novel, linking it with the medieval romance tradition and exploring readers' continuing fascination with the genre.

Cavallaro, Dani. *The Gothic Vision: Three Centuries of Horror, Terror, and Fear.* New York: Continuum, 2005. Study of the gothic novel from its earliest manifestations in the eighteenth century to the early twenty-first century. Through the lenses of contemporary cultural theories, examines readers' fascination with novels that invoke horror, terror, and fright.

Doody, Margaret Anne. *The True Story of the Novel.* New Brunswick, N.J.: Rutgers University Press, 1996. Traces the roots of the novel, traditionally thought to have been developed in the seventeenth century, to classical Greek and Latin texts that exhibit characteristics of modern fiction.

Hale, Dorothy J., ed. *The Novel: An Anthology of Criticism and Theory, 1900-2000.* Malden, Mass.: Blackwell, 2006. Collection of essays by theorists and novelists. Includes commentary on the novel form from the perspective of formalism, structuralism, poststructuralism, Marxism, and reader response theory. Essays also address the novel through the lenses of sociology, gender studies, and feminist theory.

_____. *Social Formalism: The Novel in Theory from Henry James to the Present*. Stanford, Calif.: Stanford University Press, 1998. Emphasizes the novel's special ability to define a social world for readers. Relies heavily on the works of contemporary literary and cultural theorists. Provides a summary of twentieth century efforts to identify a theory of fiction that encompasses novels of many kinds.

Hart, Stephen M., and Wen-chin Ouyang, eds. *A Companion to Magical Realism*. London: Tamesis, 2005. Essays outlining the development of Magical Realism, tracing its roots from Europe through Latin America to other regions of the world. Explores the political dimensions of the genre.

Hoffman, Michael J., and Patrick D. Murphy, eds. *Essentials of the Theory of Fiction*. 2d ed. Durham, N.C.: Duke University Press, 1996. Collection of essays by influential critics from the late nineteenth century through the twentieth century. Focuses on the essential elements of fiction and the novel's relationship to the world it depicts.

Lodge, David. *The Art of Fiction: Illustrated from Classic and Modern Texts*. New York: Viking Press, 1993. Short commentaries on the technical aspects of fiction. Examples from important and minor novelists illustrate literary principles and techniques such as point of view, suspense, character introduction, irony, motivation, and ending.

Lynch, Deirdre, and William B. Walker, eds. *Cultural Institutions of the Novel*. Durham, N.C.: Duke University Press, 1996. Fifteen essays examine aspects of long fiction produced around the world. Encourages a redefinition of the genre and argues for inclusion of texts not historically considered novels.

Moretti, Franco, ed. *The Novel*. 2 vols. Princeton, N.J.: Princeton University Press, 2006. Compendium exploring the novel from multiple perspectives, including as an anthropological, historical, and sociological document; a function of the national tradition from which it emerges; and a work of art subject to examination using various critical approaches.

Priestman, Martin, ed. *The Cambridge Companion to Crime Fiction*. New York: Cambridge University Press, 2003. Essays examine the nature and development of the genre, explore works by writers (including women and ethnic minorities) from several countries, and establish links between crime fiction and other literary genres. Includes a chronology.

Scaggs, John. *Crime Fiction*. New York: Routledge, 2005. Provides a history of crime fiction, explores key subgenres, and identifies recurring themes that suggest the wider social and historical context in which these works are written. Suggests critical approaches that open crime fiction to serious study.

Shiach, Morag, ed. *The Cambridge Companion to the Modernist Novel*. New York: Cambridge University Press, 2007. Essays explaining the concept of modernism and its influence on the novel. Detailed examination of works by writers from various countries, all influenced by the modernist movement. Includes a detailed chronology.

Vice, Sue. *Holocaust Fiction*. New York: Routledge, 2000. Examines controversies generated by novels about the Holocaust. Focuses on eight important works, but also offers observations on the polemics surrounding publication of books on this topic.

Zunshine, Lisa. *Why We Read Fiction: Theory of Mind and the Novel*. Columbus: Ohio State University Press, 2006. Applies theories of cognitive psychology to novel reading, explaining how experience and human nature lead readers to constrain their interpretations of a given text. Provides numerous examples from well-known novels to illustrate how and why readers find pleasure in fiction.

NATIVE AMERICAN LITERATURE

Cheyfitz, Eric, ed. *The Columbia Guide to American Indian Literatures of the United States Since 1945*. New York: Columbia University Press, 2006. Explores the emergence of fiction of Native Americans struggling against U.S. government oppression and sociocultural discrimination. Concentrates on works expressing resistance to oppressive actions and attitudes.

Laurence W. Mazzeno

Glossary of Literary Terms

absurdism: A philosophical attitude, pervading much of modern drama and fiction, that underlines the isolation and alienation that humans experience, having been thrown into what absurdists see as a godless universe devoid of religious, spiritual, or metaphysical meaning. Conspicuous in its lack of logic, consistency, coherence, intelligibility, and realism, the literature of the absurd depicts the anguish, forlornness, and despair inherent in the human condition. Counter to the rationalist assumptions of traditional humanism, absurdism denies the existence of universal truth or value.

allegory: A literary mode in which a second level of meaning, wherein characters, events, and settings represent abstractions, is encoded within the surface narrative. The allegorical mode may dominate an entire work, in which case the encoded message is the work's primary reason for being, or it may be an element in a work otherwise interesting and meaningful for its surface story alone. Elements of allegory may be found in Jonathan Swift's *Gulliver's Travels* (1726) and Thomas Mann's *Der Zauberberg* (1924; *The Magic Mountain*, 1927).

anatomy: Literally the term means the "cutting up" or "dissection" of a subject into its constituent parts for closer examination. Northrop Frye, in his *Anatomy of Criticism* (1957), uses the term to refer to a narrative that deals with mental attitudes rather than people. As opposed to the novel, the anatomy features stylized figures who are mouthpieces for the ideas they represent.

antagonist: The character in fiction who stands as a rival or opponent to the *protagonist.*

antihero: Defined by Seán O'Faoláin as a fictional figure who, deprived of social sanctions and definitions, is always trying to define himself and to establish his own codes. Ahab may be seen as the antihero of Herman Melville's *Moby Dick* (1851).

archetype: The term "archetype" entered literary criticism from the psychology of Carl Jung, who defined archetypes as "primordial images" from the "collective unconscious" of humankind. Jung believed that works of art derive much of their power from the unconscious appeal of these images to ancestral memories. In his extremely influential *Anatomy of Criticism* (1957), Northrop Frye gave another sense of the term wide currency, defining the archetype as "a symbol, usually an image, which recurs often enough in literature to be recognizable as an element of one's literary experience as a whole."

atmosphere: The general mood or tone of a work; atmosphere is often associated with setting but can also be established by action or dialogue. A classic example of atmosphere is the primitive, fatalistic tone created in the opening description of Egdon Heath in Thomas Hardy's *The Return of the Native* (1878).

bildungsroman: Sometimes called the "novel of education," the bildungsroman focuses on the growth of a young *protagonist* who is learning about the world and finding his or her place in life; typical examples are James Joyce's *A Portrait of the Artist as a*

Young Man (1914-1915, serial; 1916, book) and Thomas Wolfe's *Look Homeward, Angel* (1929).

biographical criticism: Criticism that attempts to determine how the events and experiences of an author's life influence his or her work.

bourgeois novel: A novel in which the values, preoccupations, and accoutrements of middle-class or bourgeois life are given particular prominence. The heyday of the bourgeois novel was the nineteenth century, when novelists as varied as Jane Austen, Honoré de Balzac, and Anthony Trollope both criticized and unreflectingly transmitted the assumptions of the rising middle class.

canon: An authorized or accepted list of books. In modern parlance, the literary canon comprehends the privileged texts, classics, or great books that are thought to belong permanently on university reading lists. Recent theory—especially feminist, Marxist, and poststructuralist—critically examines the process of canon formation and questions the hegemony of white male writers. Such theory sees canon formation as the ideological act of a dominant institution and seeks to undermine the notion of canonicity itself, thereby preventing the exclusion of works by women, minorities, and oppressed peoples.

character: Characters in fiction can be presented as if they were real people or as stylized functions of the plot. Usually characters are a combination of both factors.

classicism: A literary stance or value system consciously based on the example of classical Greek and Roman literature. While the term is applied to an enormous diversity of artists in many different periods and in many different national literatures, "classicism" generally denotes a cluster of values including formal discipline, restrained expression, reverence for tradition, and an objective rather than a subjective orientation. As a literary tendency, classicism is often opposed to *Romanticism*, although many writers combine classical and romantic elements.

climax/crisis: The term "climax" refers to the moment of the reader's highest emotional response, whereas "crisis" refers to a structural element of plot, a turning point at which a resolution must take place.

complication: The point in a novel when the *conflict* is developed or when the already existing conflict is further intensified.

conflict: The struggle that develops as a result of the opposition between the *protagonist* and another person, the natural world, society, or some force within the self.

contextualist criticism: A further extension of *formalist criticism*, which assumes that the language of art is constitutive. Rather than referring to preexistent values, the artwork creates values only inchoately realized before. The most important advocates of this position are Eliseo Vivas (*The Artistic Transaction*, 1963) and Murray Krieger (*The Play and Place of Criticism*, 1967).

conventions: All those devices of stylization, compression, and selection that constitute the necessary differences between art and life. According to the Russian Formalists, these conventions constitute the "literariness" of literature and are the only proper concern of the literary critic.

deconstruction: An extremely influential contemporary school of criticism based on the works of the French philosopher Jacques Derrida. Deconstruction treats literary works as unconscious reflections of the reigning myths of Western culture. The primary myth is that there is a meaningful world that language signifies or represents. The deconstructionist critic is most often concerned with showing how a literary text tacitly subverts the very assumptions or myths on which it ostensibly rests.

defamiliarization: Coined by Viktor Shklovsky in 1917, this term denotes a basic principle of Russian Formalism. Poetic language (by which the Formalists meant artful language, in prose as well as in poetry) defamiliarizes or "makes strange" familiar experiences. The technique of art, says Shklovsky, is to "make objects unfamiliar, to make forms difficult, to increase the difficulty and length of perception. . . . Art is a way of experiencing the artfulness of an object; the object is not important."

detective story: The so-called classic detective story (or mystery) is a highly formalized and logically structured mode of fiction in which the focus is on a crime solved by a detective through interpretation of evidence and ratiocination; the most famous detective in this mode is Arthur Conan Doyle's Sherlock Holmes. Many modern practitioners of the genre, however, such as Dashiell Hammett, Raymond Chandler, and Ross Macdonald, have de-emphasized the puzzlelike qualities of the detective story, stressing instead characterization, theme, and other elements of mainstream fiction.

determinism: The belief that an individual's actions are essentially determined by biological and environmental factors, with free will playing a negligible role. (See *naturalism*.)

dialogue: The similitude of conversation in fiction, dialogue serves to characterize, to further the *plot*, to establish *conflict*, and to express thematic ideas.

displacement: Popularized in criticism by Northrop Frye, this term refers to the author's attempt to make his or her story psychologically motivated and realistic, even as the latent structure of the mythical motivation moves relentlessly forward.

dominant: A term coined by Roman Jakobson to refer to that which "rules, determines, and transforms the remaining components in the work of a single artist, in a poetic canon, or in the work of an epoch." The shifting of the dominant in a *genre* accounts for the creation of new generic forms and new poetic epochs. For example, the rise of *realism* in the mid-nineteenth century indicates realistic conventions becoming dominant and *romance* or fantasy conventions becoming secondary.

doppelgänger: A double or counterpart of a person, sometimes endowed with ghostly qualities. A fictional character's doppelgänger often reflects a suppressed side of his or her personality. One of the classic examples of the doppelgänger motif is found in

Fyodor Dostoevski's novella *Dvoynik* (1846; *The Double*, 1917); Isaac Bashevis Singer and Jorge Luis Borges, among others, offer striking modern treatments of the doppelgänger.

epic: Although this term usually refers to a long narrative poem that presents the exploits of a central figure of high position, the term is also used to designate a long novel that has the style or structure usually associated with an epic. In this sense, for example, Herman Melville's *Moby Dick* (1851) and James Joyce's *Ulysses* (1922) may be called epics.

episodic narrative: A work that is held together primarily by a loose connection of self-sufficient episodes. *Picaresque novels* often have episodic structure.

epistolary novel: A novel made up of letters by one or more fictional characters. Samuel Richardson's *Pamela: Or, Virtue Rewarded* (1740-1741) is a well-known eighteenth century example. In the nineteenth century, Bram Stoker's *Dracula* (1897) is largely epistolary. The technique allows for several different points of view to be presented.

euphuism: A style of writing characterized by ornate language that is highly contrived, al-literative, and repetitious. Euphuism was developed by John Lyly in his *Euphues, the Anatomy of Wit* (1578) and was emulated frequently by writers of the Elizabethan Age.

existentialism: A philosophical, religious, and literary term, emerging from World War II, for a group of attitudes surrounding the pivotal notion that existence precedes essence. According to Jean-Paul Sartre, "Man is nothing else but what he makes himself." For-lornness arises from the death of God and the concomitant death of universal values, of any source of ultimate or a priori standards. Despair arises from the fact that an individual can reckon only with what depends on his or her will, and the sphere of that will is severely limited; the number of things on which he or she can have an impact is pathetically small. Existentialist literature is antideterministic in the extreme and rejects the idea that heredity and environment shape and determine human motivation and behavior.

exposition: The part or parts of a fiction that provide necessary background information. Exposition not only provides the time and place of the action but also introduces readers to the fictive world of the story, acquainting them with the ground rules of the work.

fantastic: In his study *The Fantastic* (1970), Tzvetan Todorov defines the fantastic as a *genre* that lies between the "uncanny" and the "marvelous." All three genres embody the familiar world but present an event that cannot be explained by the laws of the familiar world. Todorov says that the fantastic occupies a twilight zone between the uncanny (when the reader knows that the peculiar event is merely the result of an illusion) and the marvelous (when the reader understands that the event is supposed to take place in a realm controlled by laws unknown to humankind). The fantastic is thus essentially unsettling, provocative, even subversive.

feminist criticism: A criticism advocating equal rights for women in political, economic, social, psychological, personal, and aesthetic senses. On the thematic level, the feminist reader should identify with female characters and their concerns. The object is to provide a critique of phallocentric assumptions and an analysis of patriarchal ideologies inscribed in a literature that is male-centered and male-dominated. On the ideological level, feminist critics see gender, as well as the stereotypes that go along with it, as a cultural construct. They strive to define a particularly feminine content and to extend the *canon* so that it might include works by lesbians, feminists, and women writers in general.

flashback: A scene in a fiction that depicts an earlier event; it may be presented as a reminiscence by a character in the story or may simply be inserted into the narrative.

foreshadowing: A device to create suspense or dramatic irony in fiction by indicating through suggestion what will take place in the future.

formalist criticism: Two particularly influential formalist schools of criticism arose in the twentieth century: the Russian Formalists and the American New Critics. The Russian Formalists were concerned with the conventional devices used in literature to defamiliarize that which habit has made familiar. The New Critics believed that literary criticism is a description and evaluation of its object and that the primary concern of the critic is with the work's unity. Both schools of criticism, at their most extreme, treated literary works as artifacts or constructs divorced from their biographical and social contexts.

genre: In its most general sense, this term refers to a group of literary works defined by a common form, style, or purpose. In practice, the term is used in a wide variety of overlapping and, to a degree, contradictory senses. Tragedy and comedy are thus described as distinct genres; the novel (a form that includes both tragic and comic works) is a genre; and various subspecies of the novel, such as the *gothic* and the *picaresque*, are themselves frequently treated as distinct genres. Finally, the term "genre fiction" refers to forms of popular fiction in which the writer is bound by more or less rigid conventions. Indeed, all these diverse usages have in common an emphasis on the manner in which individual literary works are shaped by particular expectations and conventions; this is the subject of genre criticism.

genre fiction: Categories of popular fiction in which the writers are bound by more or less rigid conventions, such as in the *detective story*, the *romance*, and the *Western*. Although the term can be used in a neutral sense, it is often used dismissively.

gothic novel: A form of fiction developed in the eighteenth century that focuses on horror and the supernatural. In his preface to *The Castle of Otranto* (1765), the first gothic novel in English, Horace Walpole claimed that he was trying to combine two kinds of fiction, with events and story typical of the medieval romance and character delineation typical of the realistic novel. Other examples of the form are Matthew Gregory Lewis's *The Monk: A Romance* (1796; also known as *Ambrosio: Or, The Monk*) and

Mary Wollstonecraft Shelley's *Frankenstein: Or, The Modern Prometheus* (1818).

grotesque: According to Wolfgang Kayser (*The Grotesque in Art and Literature*, 1963), the grotesque is an embodiment in literature of the estranged world. Characterized by a breakup of the everyday world by mysterious forces, the form differs from fantasy in that the reader is not sure whether to react with humor or with horror and in that the exaggeration manifested exists in the familiar world rather than in a purely imaginative world.

Hebraic/Homeric styles: Terms coined by Erich Auerbach in *Mimesis: The Representation of Reality in Western Literature* (1953) to designate two basic fictional styles. The Hebraic style focuses only on the decisive points of narrative and leaves all else obscure, mysterious, and "fraught with background"; the Homeric style places the narrative in a definite time and place and externalizes everything in a perpetual foreground.

historical criticism: In contrast to *formalist criticism*, which treats literary works to a great extent as self-contained artifacts, historical criticism emphasizes the historical context of literature; the two approaches, however, need not be mutually exclusive. Ernst Robert Curtius's *European Literature and the Latin Middle Ages* (1940) is a prominent example of historical criticism.

historical novel: A novel that depicts past historical events, usually public in nature, and features real as well as fictional people. Sir Walter Scott's Waverley novels established the basic type, but the relationship between fiction and history in the form varies greatly depending on the practitioner.

implied author: According to Wayne Booth (*The Rhetoric of Fiction*, 1961), the novel often creates a kind of second self who tells the story—a self who is wiser, more sensitive, and more perceptive than any real person could be.

interior monologue: Defined by Édouard Dujardin as the speech of a character designed to introduce the reader directly to the character's internal life, the form differs from other kinds of monologue in that it attempts to reproduce thought before any logical organization is imposed on it. See, for example, Molly Bloom's long interior monologue at the conclusion of James Joyce's *Ulysses* (1922).

irrealism: A term often used to refer to modern or postmodern fiction that is presented self-consciously as a fiction or a fabulation rather than a mimesis of external reality. The best-known practitioners of irrealism are John Barth, Robert Coover, and Donald Barthelme.

local colorists: A loose movement of late nineteenth century American writers whose fiction emphasizes the distinctive folkways, landscapes, and dialects of various regions. Important local colorists include Bret Harte, Mark Twain, George Washington Cable, Kate Chopin, and Sarah Orne Jewett. (See *regional novel*.)

Marxist criticism: Based on the nineteenth century writings of Karl Marx and Friedrich Engels, Marxist criticism views literature as a product of ideological forces determined by the dominant class. However, many Marxists believe that literature operates according to its own autonomous standards of production and reception: It is both a product of ideology and able to determine ideology. As such, literature may overcome the dominant paradigms of its age and play a revolutionary role in society.

metafiction: This term refers to fiction that manifests a reflexive tendency, such as Vladimir Nabokov's *Pale Fire* (1962) and John Fowles's *The French Lieutenant's Woman* (1969). The emphasis is on the loosening of the work's illusion of reality to expose the reality of its illusion. Other terms used to refer to this type of fiction include "irrealism," "postmodernist fiction," "antifiction," and "surfiction."

modernism: An international movement in the arts that began in the early years of the twentieth century. Although the term is used to describe artists of widely varying persuasions, modernism in general was characterized by its international idiom, by its interest in cultures distant in space or time, by its emphasis on formal experimentation, and by its sense of dislocation and radical change.

motif: A conventional incident or situation in a fiction that may serve as the basis for the structure of the narrative itself. The Russian Formalist critic Boris Tomashevsky uses the term to refer to the smallest particle of thematic material in a work.

motivation: Although this term is usually used in reference to the convention of justifying the action of a character from his or her psychological makeup, the Russian Formalists use the term to refer to the network of devices that justify the introduction of individual *motifs* or groups of motifs in a work. For example, "compositional motivation" refers to the principle that every single property in a work contributes to its overall effect; "realistic motivation" refers to the realistic devices used to make a work plausible and lifelike.

multiculturalism: The tendency to recognize the perspectives of those traditionally excluded from the canon of Western art and literature. In order to promote multiculturalism, publishers and educators have revised textbooks and school curricula to incorporate material by and about women, members of minority groups, persons from non-Western cultures, and homosexuals.

myth: Anonymous traditional stories dealing with basic human concepts and antinomies. According to Claude Lévi-Strauss, myth is that part of language where the "formula *tradutore, traditore* reaches its lowest truth value. . . . Its substance does not lie in its style, its original music, or its syntax, but in the story which it tells."

myth criticism: Northrop Frye says that in myth "we see the structural principles of literature isolated." Myth criticism is concerned with these basic principles of literature; it is not to be confused with mythological criticism, which is primarily concerned with finding mythological parallels in the surface action of the *narrative*.

narrative: Robert Scholes and Robert Kellogg, in *The Nature of Narrative* (1966), say that by "narrative" they mean literary works that include both a story and a storyteller. The term "narrative" usually implies a contrast to "enacted" fiction such as drama.

narratology: The study of the form and functioning of *narratives*; it attempts to examine what all narratives have in common and what makes individual narratives different from one another.

narrator: The *character* who recounts the *narrative*, or story. Wayne Booth describes various dramatized narrators in *The Rhetoric of Fiction* (1961): unacknowledged centers of consciousness, observers, narrator-agents, and self-conscious narrators. Booth suggests that the important elements to consider in narration are the relationships among the narrator, the author, the characters, and the reader.

naturalism: As developed by Émile Zola in the late nineteenth century, naturalism is the application of the principles of scientific *determinism* to fiction. Although it usually refers more to the choice of subject matter than to technical conventions, those conventions associated with the movement center on the author's attempt to be precise and scientifically objective in description and detail, regardless of whether the events described are sordid or shocking.

New Criticism: See *formalist criticism.*

novel: Perhaps the most difficult of all fictional forms to define because of its multiplicity of modes. Edouard, in André Gide's *Les Faux-monnayeurs* (1925; *The Counterfeiters*, 1927), says the novel is the freest and most lawless of all *genres*; he wonders if fear of that liberty is the reason the novel has so timidly clung to reality. Most critics seem to agree that the novel's primary area of concern is the social world. Ian Watt (*The Rise of the Novel*, 2001) says that the novel can be distinguished from other fictional forms by the attention it pays to individual characterization and detailed presentation of the environment. Moreover, says Watt, the novel, more than any other fictional form, is interested in the "development of its characters in the course of time."

novel of manners: The classic examples of this form might be the novels of Jane Austen, wherein the customs and conventions of a social group of a particular time and place are realistically, and often satirically, portrayed.

novella, novelle, nouvelle, novelette, novela: Although these terms often refer to the short European tale, especially the Renaissance form employed by Giovanni Boccaccio, the terms often refer to that form of fiction that is said to be longer than a short story and shorter than a novel. "Novelette" is the term usually preferred by the British, whereas "novella" is the term usually used to refer to American works in this *genre*. Henry James claimed that the main merit of the form is the "effort to do the complicated thing with a strong brevity and lucidity."

phenomenological criticism: Although best known as a European school of criticism practiced by Georges Poulet and others, this so-called criticism of consciousness is also propounded in the United States by such critics as J. Hillis Miller. The focus is less on individual works and *genres* than it is on literature as an act; the work is not seen as an object but rather as part of a strand of latent impulses in the work of a single author or an epoch.

picaresque novel: A form of fiction that centers on a central rogue figure, or picaro, who usually tells his or her own story. The plot structure is normally *episodic*, and the episodes usually focus on how the picaro lives by his or her wits. Classic examples of the mode are Henry Fielding's *The History of Tom Jones, a Foundling* (1749; commonly known as *Tom Jones*) and Mark Twain's *Adventures of Huckleberry Finn* (1884).

plot/story: "Story" refers to the full *narrative* of *character* and action, whereas "plot" generally refers to action with little reference to character. A more precise and helpful distinction is made by the Russian Formalists, who suggest that "plot" refers to the events of a narrative as they have been artfully arranged in the literary work, subject to chronological displacement, ellipses, and other devices, while "story" refers to the sum of the same events arranged in simple, causal-chronological order. Thus story is the raw material for plot. By comparing the two in a given work, the reader is encouraged to see the narrative as an artifact.

point of view: The means by which the story is presented to the reader, or, as Percy Lubbock says in *The Craft of Fiction* (1921), "the relation in which the narrator stands to the story"—a relation that Lubbock claims governs the craft of fiction. Some of the questions the critical reader should ask concerning point of view are the following: Who talks to the reader? From what position does the narrator tell the story? At what distance does he or she place the reader from the story? What kind of person is he or she? How fully is he or she characterized? How reliable is he or she? For further discussion, see Wayne Booth, *The Rhetoric of Fiction* (1961).

postcolonialism: Postcolonial literature emerged in the mid-twentieth century when colonies in Asia, Africa, and the Caribbean began gaining their independence from the European nations that had long controlled them. Postcolonial authors, such as Salman Rushdie and V. S. Naipaul, tend to focus on both the freedom and the conflict inherent in living in a postcolonial state.

postmodernism: A ubiquitous but elusive term in contemporary criticism, "postmodernism" is loosely applied to the various artistic movements that followed the era of so-called high modernism, represented by such giants as James Joyce and Pablo Picasso. In critical discussions of contemporary fiction, the term "postmodernism" is frequently applied to the works of writers such as Thomas Pynchon, John Barth, and Donald Barthelme, who exhibit a self-conscious awareness of their modernist predecessors as well as a reflexive treatment of fictional form.

protagonist: The central *character* in a fiction, the character whose fortunes most concern the reader.

psychological criticism: While much modern literary criticism reflects to some degree the impacts of Sigmund Freud, Carl Jung, Jacques Lacan, and other psychological theorists, the term "psychological criticism" suggests a strong emphasis on a causal relation between the writer's psychological state, variously interpreted, and his or her works. A notable example of psychological criticism is Norman Fruman's *Coleridge, the Damaged Archangel* (1971).

psychological novel: A form of fiction in which *character*, especially the inner lives of characters, is the primary focus. This form, which has been of primary importance at least since Henry James, characterizes much of the work of James Joyce, Virginia Woolf, and William Faulkner. For a detailed discussion, see *The Modern Psychological Novel* (1955) by Leon Edel.

realism: A literary technique in which the primary convention is to render an illusion of fidelity to external reality. Realism is often identified as the primary method of the novel form: It focuses on surface details, maintains a fidelity to the everyday experiences of middle-class society, and strives for a one-to-one relationship between the fiction and the action imitated. The realist movement in the late nineteenth century coincides with the full development of the novel form.

reception aesthetics: The best-known American practitioner of reception aesthetics is Stanley Fish. For the reception critic, meaning is an event or process; rather than being embedded in the work, it is created through particular acts of reading. The best-known European practitioner of this criticism, Wolfgang Iser, argues that indeterminacy is the basic characteristic of literary texts; the reader must "normalize" the text either by projecting his or her standards into it or by revising his or her standards to "fit" the text.

regional novel: Any novel in which the character of a given geographical region plays a decisive role. Although regional differences persist across the United States, a considerable leveling in speech and customs has taken place, so that the sharp regional distinctions evident in nineteenth century American fiction have all but disappeared. Only in the South has a strong regional tradition persisted to the present. (See *local colorists*.)

rhetorical criticism: The rhetorical critic is concerned with the literary work as a means of communicating ideas and the means by which the work affects or controls the reader. Such criticism seems best suited to didactic works such as satire.

roman à clef: A fiction wherein actual people, often celebrities of some sort, are thinly disguised.

romance: The romance usually differs from the novel form in that the focus is on symbolic events and representational characters rather than on "as-if-real" characters and events. Richard Chase says that in the romance, character is depicted as highly stylized, a function of the plot rather than as someone complexly related to society. The romancer is more likely to be concerned with dreamworlds than with the familiar world, believing that reality cannot be grasped by the traditional novel.

Romanticism: A widespread cultural movement in the late eighteenth and early nineteenth centuries, the influence of which is still felt. As a general literary tendency, Romanticism is frequently contrasted with *classicism*. Although many varieties of Romanticism are indigenous to various national literatures, the term generally suggests an assertion of the preeminence of the imagination. Other values associated with various schools of Romanticism include primitivism, an interest in folklore, a reverence for nature, and a fascination with the demoniac and the macabre.

scene: The central element of *narration*; specific actions are narrated or depicted that make the reader feel he or she is participating directly in the action.

science fiction: Fiction in which certain givens (physical laws, psychological principles, social conditions—any one or all of these) form the basis of an imaginative projection into the future or, less commonly, an extrapolation in the present or even into the past.

semiotics: The science of signs and sign systems in communication. According to Roman Jakobson, semiotics deals with the principles that underlie the structure of signs, their use in language of all kinds, and the specific nature of various sign systems.

sentimental novel: A form of fiction popular in the eighteenth century in which emotionalism and optimism are the primary characteristics. The best-known examples are Samuel Richardson's *Pamela: Or, Virtue Rewarded* (1740-1741) and Oliver Goldsmith's *The Vicar of Wakefield* (1766).

setting: The circumstances and environment, both temporal and spatial, of a *narrative*.

spatial form: An author's attempt to make the reader apprehend a work spatially in a moment of time rather than sequentially. To achieve this effect, the author breaks up the *narrative* into interspersed fragments. Beginning with James Joyce, Marcel Proust, and Djuna Barnes, the movement toward spatial form is concomitant with the *modernist* effort to supplant historical time in fiction with mythic time. For the seminal discussion of this technique, see Joseph Frank, *The Widening Gyre* (1963).

stream of consciousness: The depiction of the thought processes of a *character*, insofar as this is possible, without any mediating structures. The metaphor of consciousness as a "stream" suggests a rush of thoughts and images governed by free association rather than by strictly rational development. The term "stream of consciousness" is often used loosely as a synonym for *interior monologue*. The most celebrated example of stream of consciousness in fiction is the monologue of Molly Bloom in James Joyce's *Ulysses* (1922); other notable practitioners of the stream-of-consciousness technique include Dorothy Richardson, Virginia Woolf, and William Faulkner.

structuralism: As a movement of thought, structuralism is based on the idea of intrinsic, self-sufficient structures that do not require reference to external elements. A structure is a system of transformations that involves the interplay of laws inherent in the system itself. The study of language is the primary model for contemporary structuralism. The structuralist literary critic attempts to define structural principles that operate intertextually throughout the whole of literature as well as principles that operate in *genres* and in individual works. One of the most accessible surveys of structuralism and literature available is Jonathan Culler's *Structuralist Poetics* (1975).

summary: Those parts of a fiction that do not need to be detailed. In *Tom Jones* (1749), Henry Fielding says, "If whole years should pass without producing anything worthy of . . . notice . . . we shall hasten on to matters of consequence."

thematics: According to Northrop Frye, when a work of fiction is written or interpreted thematically, it becomes an illustrative fable. Murray Krieger defines thematics as "the study of the experiential tensions which, dramatically entangled in the literary work, become an existential reflection of that work's aesthetic complexity."

tone: The dominant mood of a work of fiction. (See *atmosphere.*)

unreliable narrator: A narrator whose account of the events of the story cannot be trusted, obliging readers to reconstruct—if possible—the true state of affairs themselves. Once an innovative technique, the use of the unreliable narrator has become commonplace among contemporary writers who wish to suggest the impossibility of a truly "reliable" account of any event. Notable examples of the unreliable narrator can be found in Ford Madox Ford's *The Good Soldier* (1915) and Vladimir Nabokov's *Lolita* (1955).

Victorian novel: Although the Victorian period extended from 1837 to 1901, the term "Victorian novel" does not include the later decades of Queen Victoria's reign. The term loosely refers to the sprawling works of novelists such as Charles Dickens and William Makepeace Thackeray—works that frequently appeared first in serial form and are characterized by a broad social canvas.

vraisemblance/verisimilitude: Tzvetan Todorov defines vraisemblance as "the mask which conceals the text's own laws, but which we are supposed to take for a relation to reality." Verisimilitude refers to a work's attempts to make the reader believe that it conforms to reality rather than to its own laws.

Western novel: Like all varieties of *genre fiction*, the Western novel—generally known simply as the Western—is defined by a relatively predictable combination of *conventions*, *motifs*, and recurring themes. These predictable elements, familiar from many Western films and television series, differentiate the Western from *historical novels* and idiosyncratic works such as Thomas Berger's *Little Big Man* (1964) that are also set in the Old West. Conversely, some novels set in the contemporary West are regarded as Westerns because they deal with modern cowboys and with the land itself in the manner characteristic of the *genre*.

Charles E. May

GUIDE TO ONLINE RESOURCES

WEB SITES
The following sites were visited by the editors of Salem Press in 2009. Because URLs fre-quently change, the accuracy of these addresses cannot be guaranteed; however, long-standing sites, such as those of colleges and universities, national organizations, and gov-ernment agencies, generally maintain links when sites are moved or updated.

American Literature on the Web

http://www.nagasaki-gaigo.ac.jp/ishikawa/amlit

Among this site's features are several pages providing links to Web sites about specific genres and literary movements, southern and southwestern American literature, minority literature, literary theory, and women writers, as well as an extensive index of links to electronic text collections and archives. Users also can access information for five specific time periods: 1620-1820, 1820-1865, 1865-1914, 1914-1945, and since 1945. A range of information is available for each period, including alphabetical lists of authors that link to more specific information about each writer, time lines of historical and literary events, and links to related additional Web sites.

Books and Writers

http://www.kirjasto.sci.fi/indeksi.htm

This broad, comprehensive, and easy-to-use resource provides access to information about hundreds of authors throughout the world, extending from 70 B.C.E to the twenty-first century. Links take users from an alphabetical list of authors to pages featuring bio-graphical material, lists of works, and recommendations for further reading about individ-ual authors; each writer's page also includes links to related pages on the site. Although brief, the biographical essays provide solid overviews of the authors' careers, their contri-butions to literature, and their literary influences.

The Canadian Literature Archive

http://www.umanitoba.ca/canlit

Created and maintained by the English Department at the University of Manitoba, this site is a comprehensive collection of materials for and about Canadian writers. It includes an alphabetical listing of authors with links to additional Web-based information. Users also can retrieve electronic texts, announcements of literary events, and videocasts of au-thor interviews and readings.

A Celebration of Women Writers

http://digital.library.upenn.edu/women

This site presents an extensive compendium of information about the contributions of women writers throughout history. The "Local Editions by Authors" and "Local Editions by Category" pages include access to electronic texts of the works of numerous writers, including Louisa May Alcott, Djuna Barnes, Grazia Deledda, Edith Wharton, and Virginia Woolf. Users can also access biographical and bibliographical information by browsing lists arranged by writers' names, countries of origin, ethnicities, and the centuries in which they lived.

Contemporary Writers

http://www.contemporarywriters.com/authors

Created by the British Council, this site offers "up-to-date profiles of some of the U.K. and Commonwealth's most important living writers (plus writers from the Republic of Ireland that we've worked with)." The available information includes biographies, bibliographies, critical reviews, news about literary prizes, and photographs. Users can search the site by author, genre, nationality, gender, publisher, book title, date of publication, and prize name and date.

Internet Public Library: Native American Authors

http://www.ipl.org/div/natam

Internet Public Library, a Web-based collection of materials, includes this index to resources about writers of Native American heritage. An alphabetical list of authors enables users to link to biographies, lists of works, electronic texts, tribal Web sites, and other online resources. The majority of the writers covered are contemporary Indian authors, but some historical authors also are featured. Users also can retrieve information by browsing lists of titles and tribes. In addition, the site contains a bibliography of print and online materials about Native American literature.

LiteraryHistory.com

http://www.literaryhistory.com

This site is an excellent source of academic, scholarly, and critical literature about eighteenth, nineteenth, and twentieth century American and English writers. It provides numerous pages about specific eras and genres, including individual pages for eighteenth, nineteenth, and twentieth century literature and for African American and postcolonial literature. These pages contain alphabetical lists of authors that link to articles, reviews, overviews, excerpts of works, teaching guides, podcast interviews, and other materials. The eighteenth century literature page also provides access to information about the eighteenth century novel.

Literary Resources on the Net

http://andromeda.rutgers.edu/~jlynch/Lit

Jack Lynch of Rutgers University maintains this extensive collection of links to Internet sites that are useful to academics, including numerous Web sites about American and English literature. This collection is a good place to begin online research about the novel, as it links to hundreds of other sites with broad ranges of literary topics. The site is organized chronically, with separate pages for information about the Middle Ages, the Renaissance, the eighteenth century, the Romantic and Victorian eras, and twentieth century British and Irish literature. It also has separate pages providing links to Web sites about American literature and to women's literature and feminism.

LitWeb

http://litweb.net

LitWeb provides biographies of more than five hundred world authors throughout history that can be accessed through an alphabetical listing. The pages about each writer contain a list of his or her works, suggestions for further reading, and illustrations. The site also offers information about past and present winners of major literary prizes.

The Modern Word: Authors of the Libyrinth

http://www.themodernword.com/authors.html

The Modern Word site, although somewhat haphazard in its organization, provides a great deal of critical information about writers. The "Authors of the Libyrinth" page is very useful, linking author names to essays about them and other resources. The section of the page headed "The Scriptorium" presents "an index of pages featuring writers who have pushed the edges of their medium, combining literary talent with a sense of experimentation to produce some remarkable works of modern literature." The site also includes sections devoted to Samuel Beckett, Umberto Eco, Gabriel García Márquez, James Joyce, Franz Kafka, and Thomas Pynchon.

Novels

http://www.nvcc.edu/home/ataormina/novels/default.htm

This overview of American and English novels was prepared by Agatha Taormina, a professor at Northern Virginia Community College. It contains three sections: "History" provides a definition of the novel genre, a discussion of its origins in eighteenth century England, and separate pages with information about genres and authors of nineteenth century, twentieth century, and postmodern novels. "Approaches" suggests how to read a novel critically for greater appreciation, and "Resources" provides a list of books about the novel.

Outline of American Literature

http://www.america.gov/publications/books/outline-of-american-literature.html

This page of the America.gov site provides access to an electronic version of the ten-chapter volume *Outline of American Literature*, a historical overview of prose and poetry from colonial times to the present published by the U.S. Department of State. The work's author is Kathryn VanSpanckeren, professor of English at the University of Tampa. The site offers links to abbreviated versions of each chapter as well as access to the entire publication in PDF format.

Voice of the Shuttle

http://vos.ucsb.edu

One of the most complete and authoritative places for online information about literature, Voice of the Shuttle is maintained by professors and students in the English Department at the University of California, Santa Barbara. The site provides thousands of links to electronic books, academic journals, association Web sites, sites created by university professors, and many, many other resources about the humanities. Its "Literature in English" page provides links to separate pages about the literature of the Anglo-Saxon era, the Middle Ages, the Renaissance and seventeenth century, the Restoration and eighteenth century, the Romantic age, the Victorian age, and modern and contemporary periods in Britain and the United States, as well as a page focused on minority literature. Another page on the site, "Literatures Other than English," offers a gateway to information about the literature of numerous countries and world regions.

ELECTRONIC DATABASES

Electronic databases usually do not have their own URLs. Instead, public, college, and university libraries subscribe to these databases, provide links to them on their Web sites, and make them available to library card holders or other specified patrons. Readers can visit library Web sites or ask reference librarians to check on availability.

Canadian Literary Centre

Produced by EBSCO, the Canadian Literary Centre database contains full-text content from ECW Press, a Toronto-based publisher, including the titles in the publisher's Canadian fiction studies, Canadian biography, and Canadian writers and their works series, *ECW's Biographical Guide to Canadian Novelists*, and *George Woodcock's Introduction to Canadian Fiction*. Author biographies, essays and literary criticism, and book reviews are among the database's offerings.

Literary Reference Center

EBSCO's Literary Reference Center (LRC) is a comprehensive full-text database designed primarily to help high school and undergraduate students in English and the humanities with homework and research assignments about literature. The database contains massive amounts of information from reference works, books, literary journals, and other materials, including more than 31,000 plot summaries, synopses, and overviews of literary works; almost 100,000 essays and articles of literary criticism; about 140,000 author biographies; more than 605,000 book reviews; and more than 5,200 author interviews. It also contains the entire contents of Salem Press's MagillOnLiterature Plus. Users can retrieve information by browsing a list of authors' names or titles of literary works; they can also use an advanced search engine to access information by numerous categories, including author name, gender, cultural identity, national identity, and the years in which he or she lived, or by literary title, character, locale, genre, and publication date. The Literary Reference Center also features a literary-historical time line, an encyclopedia of literature, and a glossary of literary terms.

MagillOnLiterature Plus

MagillOnLiterature Plus is a comprehensive, integrated literature database produced by Salem Press and available on the EBSCO*host* platform. The database contains the full text of essays in Salem's many literature-related reference works, including *Masterplots, Cyclopedia of World Authors, Cyclopedia of Literary Characters, Cyclopedia of Literary Places, Critical Survey of Long Fiction, Critical Survey of Short Fiction, World Philosophers and Their Works, Magill's Literary Annual*, and *Magill's Book Reviews.* Among its contents are articles on more than 35,000 literary works and more than 8,500 writers, poets, dramatists, essayists, and philosophers, more than 1,000 images, and a glossary of more than 1,300 literary terms. The biographical essays include lists of authors' works and secondary bibliographies, and almost four hundred overview essays offer information about literary genres, time periods, and national literatures.

NoveList

NoveList is a readers' advisory service produced by EBSCO. The database provides access to 155,000 titles of both adult and juvenile fiction as well information about literary awards, book discussion guides, feature articles about a range of literary genres, and "recommended reads." Users can search by author name, book title, or series title or can describe the plot to retrieve the name of a book, information about the author, and book reviews; another search engine enables users to find titles similar to books they have enjoyed reading.

Rebecca Kuzins

CATEGORY INDEX

SUBJECT INDEX